Day Walker

32 Hikes in the
New York Metropolitan Area

Second Edition

New York-New Jersey Trail Conference
2002

Published by New York-New Jersey Trail Conference
156 Ramapo Valley Road
Mahwah, NJ 07430

First edition published in 1983

Library of Congress Cataloging-in-Publication Data
Day walker : 32 hikes in the New York Metropolitan Area / New York-New Jersey
Trail Conference.— 2nd ed.
   p. cm.
  Includes index.
  ISBN 1-880775-28-X (pbk.)
    1. Hiking—New York Metropolitan Area—Guidebooks. 2. New York
Metropolitan Area—Guidebooks.   I. New York-New Jersey Trail Conference.

GV199.42.N652 N483 2002
917.47—dc21

                                                           2002044835

Cartography by Liz Puhl
Cover Photography by George Garbeck
Cover, book design, layout, and typesetting by Margaret Trejo

Although the authors and publisher have tried to make the information as accurate
as possible, they accept no responsibility for any loss or inconvenience sustained by
any person using this book.

Acknowledgments

Many thanks to the volunteers who helped with this book, especially Jane Daniels, Tom Rupolo, Tor Meloe, and Palmer Langdon, who put a great deal of effort into starting the revisions. Mary Jo Robertiello coordinated the photographers' efforts, while Walt Daniels coordinated the cartography.

Others who contributed:

Dick Barrett

Daniel Chazin

Herb Chong

Brian Goodman

John Jurasek

George Petty

Charles Porter

Ruth Rosenthal

Contents

Introduction   *1*

NEW YORK CITY
Wetlands, Woodlands, and Wildlife   4

1   Alley Pond Park   8
    Queens, New York
    A collection of wetland and woodland walks, especially suited to
    children. 15 miles east of the George Washington Bridge.
    Convenient to public transportation.

2   Jamaica Bay
    Queens, New York   16
    A short walk through a world-famous bird sanctuary. 25 miles
    southeast of the George Washington Bridge. Convenient to public
    transportation.

3   Staten Island Greenbelt   22
    Staten Island, New York
    A short, easy set of trails, mainly in High Rock Park. Convenient to
    public transportation.

4   Riverside Park   30
    Manhattan, New York
    Open river views, leafy walks, spectacular cherry blossoms in spring,
    and Grant's Tomb, on an easy 3-mile walk. 5 miles south of the
    George Washington Bridge. Convenient to public transportation.

5   Van Cortlandt Park   40
    Bronx, New York
    An easy 3 miles through this scenic park, with optional explorations
    through Woodlawn Cemetery and the Van Cortlandt Mansion. Five
    miles north of the George Washington Bridge. Convenient to public
    transportation.

6   Pelham Bay Park   48
     Bronx, New York
     A 4-mile walk in New York City's largest park. Includes a rocky
     shoreline, a crescent beach, and wonderful seafood restaurants.
     10 miles north of the George Washington Bridge. Convenient to
     public transportation.

LONG ISLAND
For the Family   58
Easy walks for young and old, including notes on how to prepare novice
walkers for these walks.

7   Fire Island-Sunken Forest   62
     Sayville, New York
     A short, easy walk combining the sights and smells of forest and
     ocean. Includes a ferry ride. 55 miles east of the George Washington
     Bridge. Convenient to public transport.

8   Connetquot River State Park Preserve   70
     Oakdale, New York
     An easy walk in Long Island's largest park, including the Pine
     Barrens. 50 miles east of the George Washington Bridge. Convenient
     to public transportation.

9   Caumsett State Park   78
     Huntington, New York
     A bird sanctuary, meadows with daffodils in spring, and a cliff
     overlooking Long Island Sound on an easy 7-mile walk across an
     isolated peninsula. 45 miles east of the George Washington Bridge.
     Convenient to public transportation with walk to trailhead.

10   Muttontown Preserve   84
     Syosset, New York
     White pines and overgrown fields on an easy 1.5 mile walk in a
     preserve. 30 miles east of the George Washington Bridge. Convenient
     to public transportation.

WESTCHESTER COUNTY
The Works of Man

92

Walks for the rugged hiker and the casual walker on paths shaped by
man-made railroads, aqueducts, and highways.

11 Bronx River Pathway

96

Valhalla, New York

Two walks in the Bronx River Reservation, suitable for young
children. Convenient to public transportation. 20 miles northeast of
the George Washington Bridge.

12 Old Croton Aqueduct

104

Tarrytown, New York

A favorite stroll for generations, this easy but long (11-mile) walk has
views of the Hudson and Palisades, history, architecture, and wild
areas. It can be shortened or lengthened to taste. 20 miles north of
the George Washington Bridge. Convenient to public transportation.

13 Mianus River Gorge

120

Bedford, New York

An easy 6 miles along a deep hemlock-shaded gorge. 35 miles
northeast of the George Washington Bridge. No public transportation.

14 Ward Pound Ridge Reservation

126

Pound Ridge, New York

A 3.7-mile moderate walk from tall pines along a river to a lovely
picnic area. 40 miles northeast of the George Washington Bridge.
Public transportation and a taxi ride.

15 Rockefeller State Park Preserve

134

Sleepy Hollow, New York

A moderate 6-mile walk with vistas of the Hudson River in a
preserve. 20 miles north of the George Washington Bridge, with
many miles of trails, wetlands, woodlands, meadows, and a lake.
Convenient to public transportation with a walk to trailhead.

16 Blue Mountain Reservation

142

Peekskill, New York

A swimming beach and picnic area, with a 4.5 mile walk that winds
to a mountain top overlooking the Hudson River. 35 miles north of
the George Washington Bridge. Convenient to public transport with
a walk to trailhead.

17 Teatown Lake Reservation   148
    Ossining, New York
    An easy 3-mile walk in an area of forests, wetlands, hills, and
    meadows surrounding a beautiful lake. 25 miles north of the George
    Washington Bridge. No public transportation.

ROCKLAND COUNTY
The High Hills Call   154
The most mountainous terrain of the metropolitan area, with complex
geology and natural history.

18 Hook Mountain   158
    Nyack, New York
    A demanding 5.3-mile walk to a spectacular view of the Tappan Zee,
    past ruins of a forgotten industry, then along a level path on the
    banks of the Hudson River. 20 miles north of the George Washington
    Bridge. Convenient to public transportation.

19 Pine Meadow Lake   168
    Sloatsburg, New York
    A popular climb along a rocky stream through hills and past a
    cascade to a mountain lake. 30 miles northwest of the George
    Washington Bridge. Convenient to public transportation.

20 Claudius Smith Den   176
    Tuxedo Park, New York
    Eight moderately difficult miles up the mountain to the hideout of a
    notorious bandit gang of the Revolutionary War era. 30 miles
    northwest of the George Washington Bridge. Convenient to public
    transportation.

21 Bear Mountain   184
    Bear Mountain, New York
    Nine strenuous miles for the very fit. 40 miles from the George
    Washington Bridge. This hike includes a gorge walk along a stream,
    a steep climb to and from the top of the mountain, and superb views.
    Convenient to public transportation.

HUDSON HIGHLANDS
Nature's Landscape
192

An area of rugged mountains and beautiful river views.

22 Camp Smith Trail
Manitou, New York
Six moderately strenuous miles accessed from the eastern side of the
Bear Mountain Bridge. 40 miles from the George Washington
Bridge. Public transportation with a walk to trailhead.
196

23 Canada Hill
Manitou, New York
Seven moderate miles, partly upward on the Appalachian Trail and
descending on carriage roads. 40 miles from the George Washington
Bridge. Public transportation with a walk to trailhead.
204

24 Bull Hill and Cold Spring
Cold Spring, New York
A strenuous, 5.5-mile hike to a summit providing breathtaking views
over the Hudson River. Can include sightseeing in Cold Spring.
50 miles from the George Washington Bridge. Convenient to public
transportation with a walk to the trailhead.
210

25 Breakneck Ridge
Breakneck Station, New York
A very steep and strenuous 5.7 miles with a 1,200-foot vertical
climb. Wonderful views of the Hudson River and West Point.
50 miles from the George Washington Bridge. Convenient to public
transportation.
218

26 Crows Nest and Storm King
Cornwall, New York
A strenuous 7-mile hike in an area of wild ravines, mountain
streams, and rich foliage. 50 miles from the George Washington
Bridge. No public transportation.
224

NORTHERN NEW JERSEY
Native American Paths   230
An area originally inhabited by Native Americans, who were replaced by
settlers who farmed, mined iron and copper, and produced charcoal.

27 The Palisades   234
    Alpine, New Jersey
    Spectacular cliffs and wooded ravines on a challenging 4-mile walk
    along the Hudson. 7 miles north of the George Washington Bridge.
    Convenient to public transportation.

28 Ramapo Mountain State Forest   244
    Pompton Lakes, New Jersey
    A moderate 7- to 8-mile walk in a mountainous forest. 25 miles west
    of the George Washington Bridge. Convenient to public
    transportation.

29 Paterson/Garrett Mountain   252
    Paterson, New Jersey
    A tour of a renovated nineteenth century industrial district with side
    trips to a thundering waterfall, a castle-like home turned into a
    museum, and a mountain park overlooking the city. 15 miles from
    the George Washington Bridge. Convenient to public transportation.

30 Watchung Reservation   262
    Mountainside, New Jersey
    A meadow with wildflowers, a silent hemlock glen, and a deserted
    village on a moderately strenuous, 7.5-mile hike. 30 miles west of the
    George Washington Bridge. Convenient to public transportation.

CENTRAL NEW JERSEY
The View From Here   270
A relatively flat area ranging from ocean marshes to farming country
farther inland. History abounds.

31 Cheesequake State Park   272
    Matawan, New Jersey
    Salt- and fresh-water marshes, a cedar swamp, and a gentle upland
    woods on an easy 3-mile walk. 40 miles south of the George
    Washington Bridge. Public transportation and a taxi ride.

Contents

32 Delaware and Raritan Canal   282
   Kingston, New Jersey
   *A 5-mile stroll along the towpath of a historic canal, now popular
   for canoeing and fishing, with a side trip through the campus of
   Princeton University. 55 miles southwest of the George Washington
   Bridge. Convenient to public transportation.*

Park and Transportation Information   290

Index   293

Membership Information   303

An Introduction
Walking in the Greater New York Metropolitan Area

When the first edition of *Day Walker* was published in 1983, its stated purpose was "to encourage young and old alike to enjoy walking as a hobby and to introduce the many nearby green areas that walkers can visit." Implicit was a secondary goal: to enable walkers to reach varied terrain and scenery *by public transportation*. Almost 20 years later, the same purposes motivate this second edition.

The metropolitan area includes the five boroughs of New York City and the counties of Nassau, Suffolk, Westchester, Rockland, Passaic, Bergen, Union, Morris, Essex, and Middlesex. This book presents a sample of walks, all open to the public, all within 60 miles from the George Washington Bridge, and most accessible by public transportation.

In difficulty, these walks vary from easy to very strenuous; in length, they vary from less than a mile to nine miles or more, although the longer walks and hikes can be shortened by alternative paths included in the descriptions. The areas through which the walks pass are as varied as the walks themselves: mountains, glacial moraines, salt marshes, ponds, lakes, rivers, meadows, and man-made surroundings such as woods roads, aqueducts, and a canal.

The walk descriptions also include information on geology, history, flora and fauna, birding, and Native American lore. Many include side excursions to mansions, museums, towns, and cities, of interest to many.

This second edition of *Day Walker* updates the first in several ways. First, some new walks have been added, mainly in the Hudson Highlands, that feature scenes of incredible beauty but also are quite strenuous. The description of each walk now begins with a table listing distance, hiking time, and rating (of difficulty). This information is accurate to the best of our ability; novice hikers, especially, should take careful note.

Second, some walks have been removed; sometimes the lands traversed by the walks have reverted to private ownership, or they have changed so much that the walks are no longer feasible.

Third, the walks have been checked and revised for accuracy of the descriptions, but detailed instructions can easily become outdated. We ask your help in keeping this and the companion books of the New York-New Jersey Trail Conference (especially the *New York Walk Book* and the *New Jersey Walk Book*) up to date.

Since the first edition in 1983, e-mail, the Internet, and the cell phone have arrived. These tools enable the walker to find and communicate information in ways never imagined 20 years ago. For example, a walker can use the Internet to confirm which train goes to a destination and its schedule. A new page at the back of this book, Park and Transportation Information, lists phone numbers and web sites where you can obtain information on most of the areas covered in our walks as well as phone numbers for bus and rail companies. A cell phone can be used to call for a return taxi ride to the station. Note that carrying a cell phone on any walk or hike is a good idea, in case of accident or getting lost.

If you discover changes to any of the information in this book as you walk or travel to a destination, please communicate the changes to the New York-New Jersey Trail Conference e-mail address or web site.

Walking is one of the simplest pastimes known, and, we are told, one of the healthiest. Any number of people, of any age, can participate, in any season. For most of the walks in this book, a good pair of walking shoes and a backpack containing water and food are all you will need. Enjoy!

— Joyce Barrett, *Editor*

Hints on Following a Trail

Trails are generally marked with *blazes*, small rectangles or other shapes of different colors, either painted on or attached to trees or rocks at approximately eye level. These blazes communicate various messages. Trails begin with a triangle of three blazes, with a single blaze at the top, and end with a triangle with the single blaze at the bottom. Two blazes indicate a change in direction, with the top blaze indicating the direction of the turn. Where a blaze is not practical, watch for a pile of stones, called a cairn, or an arrow on rocks. Some parks use signs at trail junctions.

Always watch for the next blaze in front of you. If you cannot see one, turn around and see if you can spot one going the other way; it may indicate where the next blaze in front of you should be. Remember that trails can change; check for blazed trees knocked down by storms. Check your map and, if necessary, retrace your steps until you find a blaze.

Both the *New York Walk Book* and the *New Jersey Walk Book* contain a detailed section called "Suggestions for Hikers," including information on appropriate clothing, trail safety, equipment to carry along, how to follow a trail, and what to do if you are lost.

New York City

IN MEMORIAM

NEW YORK CITY
Wetlands, Woodlands, and Wildlife

One's first reaction to the statement that New York City has wetlands, woodlands, and wildlife is that you must be joking. Yet 13% of the city's landmass, or 26,000 acres, is city-owned parkland. Over 8,000 acres, or 30%, is open space: forests, meadows, dunes, fields, and water. These figures for open space do not include the state and federal parklands within the city, ranging in size from 9-acre Empire-Fulton Ferry State Park along the East River to the 9,100-acre Jamaica Bay Wildlife Refuge, managed as part of Gateway National Recreation Area. These open areas provide a respite for city dwellers and habitats for birds and animals.

Present day New York City was at one time about 50% wetlands, which were thought to be little more than breeding grounds for pests. As the demand for space increased, the salt marshes along the shores were filled in and developed until, by the late 1990s, there remained about 5,000 acres of salt marsh.

Our ancestors were right about wetlands being a breeding ground. However, wetlands are more than an nursery for pests. Saltwater wetlands provide nourishment for invertebrates and fish who are part of the aquatic food chain for birds migrating along the Atlantic Coast Flyway, one of the world's three major bird migration routes. The edges of salt marshes are home to black grass, spike grass, and sea lavender, while farther from the water one finds marsh elder and the groundsel tree. Stands of phragmites are indicative of disturbed soil. They have limited food value, but serve as nesting sites for marsh wrens and red-winged blackbirds.

The demand for land in New York City has also meant that freshwater creeks and ponds have been paved over, filled in, and diverted into culverts or sewers. About 2,000 acres of freshwater ponds, marshes, bogs, and swamps remain in the city. Visitors to freshwater wetlands will find marsh and sensitive ferns, skunk cabbage, and jewelweed. Like their "salty" cousins, freshwater wetlands are nurseries. Depending on the depth of water, they providing breeding grounds for frogs, turtles, fish, and birds.

About 6,000 years ago, New York's regional climate reached its present state. Deciduous forests evolved with oaks, hickories, and American chestnuts dominating and white pines and eastern hemlocks establishing themselves in poorer soils. Whereas Native Americans lived in harmony with their environment, making little or no impact, the European settlers, in their attempt to tame the wilderness, cleared forests to establish pastures and farmlands. Virgin forests were gone by the American Revolution.

For the person taking the time to look, there is a variety of wildlife in New York City. In addition to creatures and plants in the wetlands and open space areas described above, one can find wildlife that has adapted to city life. Peregrine falcons live on skyscrapers and bridges, feasting on a ready supply of pigeons. Raccoons and possums have changed their lifestyle, often making use of dumpsters and garbage cans. Coyotes have been sighted in Woodlawn Cemetery, near Van Cortlandt Park.

The choice of walks in New York City includes one from each borough, with opportunities to explore geology, history, architecture, birds, and water. Surrounded by busy highways, Alley Pond Park has a split personality. In the north, meadows and salt marsh rim a creek-fed flat area. In the southern section, forests surround kettle ponds. Alley Pond Park's outdoor education center explains the role of wetlands.

Internationally known, the Jamaica Bay Wildlife Refuge is a prime birding spot where thousands of water, land, and shore birds stop each year during migration. The trail system allows visitors to explore the diverse habitats of the refuge in the 250 (of 9,100) acres that are accessible.

Riverside Park in Manhattan was built on land that is fill and has views of the river along portions of its route. This urban oasis has 27 species of breeding birds. Van Cortlandt Park in the Bronx is accessible from two subway lines. Its meadows link low-lying wetlands with the rolling hills of the forest. The hike through the park passes by fresh-water wetlands and is in woodlands. Pelham Bay has fertile mud flats, saltwater marshes, and woodlands. Both these city parks offer opportunities for birding.

Finally, the hiker on Staten Island Greenbelt goes over hills, by ponds, and through the woods and can stop at the visitors center in High Rock Park to learn more about the natural environment.

Photo by Tom Rupolo

1

Alley Pond Park

Distance	0.25 to 1.8 miles
Hiking time	An hour or less
Rating	Easy

Alley Pond Park in Queens is located in what once was a marsh teeming with wildlife. Matinecock Native Americans lived in the nearby woods and came down to the shore of Little Neck Bay for fish and shellfish. Even in the 1930s, a colonial gristmill still stood on the banks of Alley Pond. Then came the highways. The pond was filled in and the marsh sliced up by the Long Island Expressway and the Cross Island Parkway. The Long Island Expressway divided the park into two major areas, the wetlands in the north and the woodlands in the south.

The remains of the marsh became a dumping place for refuse and rusting automotive bodies. Two local residents, Joan and Hy Rosner, were concerned about the destruction of the wetlands and began to discuss the problem with neighbors. Soon a small nature center was established in the park. City officials and school administrators became convinced of the need to preserve what was left and to create a demonstration project on the role of wetlands. The small nature center was superseded in 1976 by the Alley Pond Environmental Center (APEC), which runs projects and workshops on birding, photography, orienteering (a map and compass exercise), and nature study. A new building for the environmental center was dedicated in 1991. The center offers guided trail walks and hosts various programs and activities for both children and adults. For further information, call the center at (718) 229-4000, or write to APEC, 228-06 Northern Boulevard, Douglaston, NY 11363.

APEC is particularly well set up for children. The walks are short, and the center also conducts nature-craft demonstrations. The center is home to several types of animals that the children can watch and sometimes touch and hold. Teachers with classes should contact the center for further details; a typical program will consist of an indoor orientation, a discovery walk on the trails, hands-on activities, and time in the natural science area.

One unusual display at the center is the recreated Douglaston Estate Windmill, located just to the rear of APEC. In 1986, concerned citizens of Douglaston banded together to save a historic windmill that had been built about 1870 and was slated for demolition. They managed to have

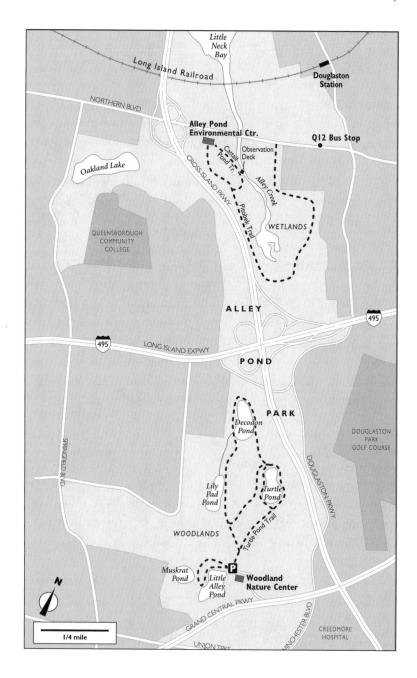

it moved two miles down Northern Boulevard to APEC. As they were completing its restoration and preparing to open it to the public, an arsonist destroyed the structure. Once again, the community rallied together and in short order a new windmill was constructed on the site, using the original restoration design plans. This working example of history is now open for the public to enjoy.

The basic topography of the Alley Pond area is glacial. During the last ice age, a huge ice sheet pushed ahead of it the dirt and boulders that were to create Long Island. The first plants after the glacial retreat were subarctic species and evergreens. As the climate warmed, these were replaced in gradual stages by the present flora and fauna. The heritage of the glacial age persists in the form of the land. The uplands to the west and south of the center are the dirt and rocks pushed by the glacier, a feature called a moraine.

APEC has set up a network of trails in the wetlands around the center and in a woodlands a short distance away, to the west of the Cross Island Parkway. Maps may be obtained at the center. (Be sure to call the number listed above for open hours.) Fires, unleashed pets, and alcoholic beverages are prohibited.

If you particularly enjoy APEC, you may want to volunteer to work there. Volunteers are the backbone of the center, and they are supported by several staff members. Volunteer application forms are available at APEC. Whether or not you end up volunteering, the Alley Pond Environmental Center has many things to offer the nature student, environmental activist, birder, parent, child, or the person who simply wants to be outdoors and walk.

Directions Alley Pond Park and APEC in the wetlands area are located on the south side of Northern Boulevard in Little Neck, Queens, about 15 miles east of the George Washington Bridge. By subway, take the 7 train to Main Street-Flushing, the last stop. Cross the street to board the

Q12 bus from the stop in front of the department store on Main Street and Roosevelt Avenue. The bus goes east on Northern Boulevard; leave it at the first stop after the Cross Island overpass. APEC is just a few feet from the stop.

You may also take the Long Island Rail Road. Take the train to the Douglaston station, then walk south along Douglaston Parkway 0.3 mile to Northern Boulevard. Cross Northern Boulevard, then turn right (west) on the sidewalk and follow Northern Boulevard for less than 0.5 mile to the APEC entrance.

By car, leave the Cross Island Parkway at Northern Boulevard, heading east. The center is a few hundred yards east of the intersection on Northern Boulevard. You will pass the APEC center and make an immediate right into the entrance to the parking lot.

Directions to the woodlands area of the park are a little different. To get to there by public transportation from most parts of the city, take the E or F train to Union Turnpike-Queens Boulevard. Take the Q46 bus on Union Turnpike going east. Get off at Winchester Boulevard. Walk north (uphill) on Winchester Boulevard past the tennis court parking area and under the Grand Central Parkway overpass, then turn left up the car ramp to the parking lot.

By car, go west on Northern Boulevard to Springfield Boulevard, make a left and continue to Union Turnpike. Another left onto Union Turnpike will bring you to Winchester Boulevard (immediately before Creedmore Hospital). Turn left again onto Winchester Boulevard to the underpass of the Grand Central Parkway. Directly beneath the underpass, a final left takes you uphill to the park's upper parking lot.

Wetland Walks   The wetland trails near APEC are often muddy; hiking boots or rubber boots are suggested. The marsh area has very little shade or shelter, so a hat is advisable. You may want to use insect repellent regardless of the time of year.

The simplest trail in the wetland area is the Cattail Pond Trail, 0.25 mile long. Follow the sign to the trailhead next to the parking lot. This short walk leads south to a platform overlooking Cattail Pond, a marsh that becomes a pond in the wet season. From here, a side trail leads east to a view over Alley Creek. There are many boardwalks over the muddier sections of the main trail. Soon after, the Cattail Pond Trail comes to a sitting area, just before it returns to the center.

A longer trail, Pitobek Trail (also called the Meadow Trail), runs from APEC south to the bridge that takes the Long Island Expressway over Alley Creek. From the trailhead on the west side of the APEC parking lot, it is 1.8 miles long and takes about an hour to walk. The beginning of the path is well defined by a covering of cedar chips. The route follows the edge of the marsh, passing through tall reeds and under archways formed by the many varieties of trees that flourish in this wet environment. You will pass occasional side trails that head deeper into the marsh or end abruptly within a few feet. From the trail's end at the bridge, you can then either retrace your steps or return following the path on the east side of the marsh, which ends at the Northern Boulevard overpass spanning the pond, approximately 0.25 mile east of APEC.

If you remain quiet and very still on these trails, you will likely encounter a number of types of wildlife. The park is on the Atlantic flyway, and the marshes are popular stopping places for migrating ducks and geese. At least 52 species of birds have been sighted here. Opossums, raccoons, rabbits, turtles, and even an occasional fox have been spotted. Bring binoculars, if you have a pair.

This park is nestled between areas of very intense land development, and urban life invades nature's solitude at times. Parts of the Pitobek Trail are just a few feet from the Cross Island Parkway, so expect sections of the walk to be accompanied by some traffic noise. Still, the minor intrusions are overshadowed by the pleasant walk through the remote open fields further along the trail.

Photo by Tom Rupolo

Woodland Walks The woodland area of Alley Pond Park lies to the south of the wetlands and, from APEC, on the other side of both the Long Island Expressway and the Cross Island Expressway. It's a fast and easy drive from the center. (See directions above.) However, in 2001 this area is under construction, and the entrance from the Grand Central Parkway is closed.

The Turtle Pond Trail in the woodland area is a short walk (about 0.5 mile) around a pond that is shaped like a turtle's head and body. Proceed north from the parking lot to a blacktop path (it is slightly to your right); continue north on this path. (Do not take the paved path that is to the left of the parking lot.) You will come very shortly to two wooden posts on either side of the road. In a few hundred feet, where the blacktop path turns sharply to the left, continue straight ahead on a dirt path that leads into the woods. There will now be green markers on the trees and wood chips on the trail. Turn right at the next fork and follow the trail around Turtle Pond. You can walk up to the pond's edge, which may be slippery because of mud and wet leaves.

At Turtle Pond you may encounter a blue heron or a red-winged blackbird. In autumn, the foliage provides a colorful frame for migrating birds. The surface of the pond is covered with tiny floating duckweed. Toads, frogs, and turtles live here. Nearby is an area burned over by an arsonist's fire in 1977. Note the succession of plants; the area is now overgrown with colonizing plants. To appreciate animal activity here, return at dawn or dusk. At the last few stations on the guided walk, you may hear the rumble of frogs, birdsong, or the scratching of crickets.

There are three more ponds in this area to which you can walk on other trails in the park. They are well worth visiting and, like the trail around Turtle Pond, are easy to walk and short in distance.

2

Jamaica Bay

Distance	5 miles
Hiking time	2-3 hours
Rating	Easy

*H*iking in the New York area is very much like living in the New York area: diverse backgrounds and traditions persevere and survive next door to one another, each adding to the unique cosmopolitan brew. It's not surprising, then, that Jamaica Bay Wildlife Refuge is flanked by John F. Kennedy International Airport and served by a subway line. Like most New York neighbors, they have learned to get along most of the time.

Approximately 100,000 people a year visit this district of the Gateway National Recreation Area, a federal park that straddles three New York City boroughs and New Jersey. Encompassing over 9,100 acres, Jamaica Bay offers diverse habitats: salt marsh, upland fields and woods, fresh and brackish water ponds, and open expanses of bay and islands. Serious birders come to the refuge to spot some of the 330 species sighted to date, but the majority of visitors are here to learn about nature and spend a couple of hours outdoors on the trails leading from the visitors center.

First-time visitors to the refuge will need a permit. Obtainable free at the visitors center, it lists refuge regulations and should be signed and dated. Holders of these passes are requested to use them on subsequent visits. Administered by the National Park Service rangers, the visitors center offers trail guides, bird/species lists, and Gateway brochures. The visitors center and parking lot are open daily, except federal holidays, from 8:30am to 5:00pm. The trails, however, are open from sunrise to sunset. Hours may change, and it is suggested that you call the refuge at (718) 318-4340 in advance of your visit. Pets are not allowed in the refuge; picnicking is allowed only in a small area near the visitors center.

No extensive preparations are necessary for a hike in the refuge. The trail around West Pond is circular, level, and clear, with no possibility of getting lost. Sturdy shoes are advisable because of the gravel underfoot. Along the way are many benches, which are perfect for sitting quietly and observing the abundant wildlife. Although the hike is short, walkers can extend their visit by taking advantage of these rest areas. Should you choose to explore the eastern side of the refuge, which is less developed, put on hiking boots or high rubber boots, as the trails may be muddy and

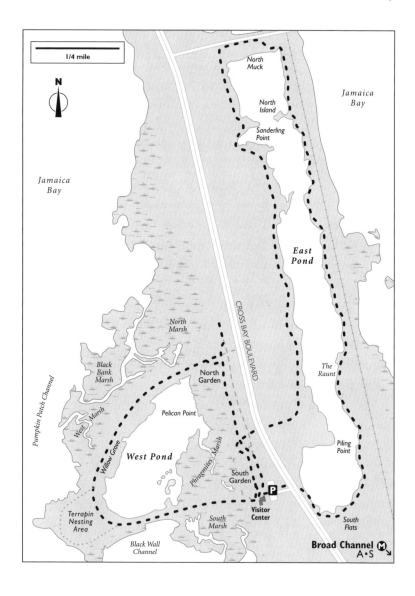

1/4 mile

N

North
Muck

North
Island

*Jamaica
Bay*

Sanderling
Point

*East
Pond*

*Jamaica
Bay*

North
Marsh

The
Raunt

Black
Bank
Marsh

North
Garden

CROSS BAY BOULEVARD

Pumpkin Patch Channel

West Marsh

Pelican Point

West Grove

West Pond

Piling
Point

Phragmites Marsh

South
Garden

P

South
Flats

Terrapin
Nesting
Area

South
Marsh

Visitor
Center

Black Wall
Channel

Broad Channel Ⓜ
A·S

wet. Insect repellent is advisable. The tall phragmites reeds harbor insects that enthusiastically welcome the visitor.

Fall is the best time to visit Jamaica Bay. Both the foliage and the wildlife put on their brightest show. Autumn olive brings forth pink berries, and the pokeweeds turn deep purple. Migrating birds descend on the refuge in great numbers as they make their way south on a time-less path. Jamaica Bay sits on the Atlantic flyway, one of the major migration routes for waterfowl and shore birds. Ducks such as baldpate, scaup, and pintail stop off during their migration. Canada and snow geese frequent the refuge as well. Shore birds such as herons, herring gulls, piping plovers, terns, and even phalaropes nest within the refuge. Binoculars are necessary for effective birding.

Jamaica Bay Wildlife Refuge was created by a process of reverse urban development. In 1938, the lands that were to become the refuge were a contested property. The New York City sanitation commissioner saw the area as a future dumping site for the city's burgeoning waste load. The city's parks commissioner, Robert Moses, had other ideas. He envisioned the area as a recreation site with sparkling white beaches and green-shaded waterfront parks. Moses took his dream to the public in a brochure that juxtaposed two possibilities: a steaming garbage heap or sailing craft skimming blue waters.

Moses' campaign succeeded. State legislation transferred Jamaica Bay to his New York City Parks Department. But the waters of Jamaica Bay proved to be too polluted for swimming. Plans were shelved while work to clean up the bay began. Matters rested until a happy accident on a local rail line intervened and led, eventually, to the creation of the wildlife refuge.

The rail line traversing Jamaica Bay was built in 1877 as a branch of the Long Island Rail Road. A severe fire destroyed a long section of trestle over the bay in 1950, and the railroad decided to abandon the line. New York City bought the fire-ravaged passage, planning to dredge and replace the trestle with an embankment. At this point Commissioner Moses reentered the picture. In return for dredging rights, Moses obligated the city to create two freshwater ponds within the yet undeveloped recreation area. These two ponds, West Pond and East Pond, soon began to attract waterfowl and shore birds, and they are the heart of today's refuge. These projects completed the basic construction of the refuge, and in 1953 it became the Jamaica Bay Wildlife Refuge.

If it took Robert Moses to establish the refuge through municipal manipulation, it took another man to create the current landscape: Herbert Johnson, a horticulturist with the New York City Parks Department. Appointed resident superintendent and given a free hand by Commissioner Moses, Johnson gathered cuttings from other locations. He introduced shrubs such as autumn olive, *Rosa rugosa*, *Rosa multiflora*, pokeweed, and bayberry, which produce fruit attractive to birds and other wildlife. Seedlings of Japanese black pine were brought from nearby Jacob Riis Park. To stabilize the shifting sands, beach grasses and grains were planted. Johnson hoped to attract and feed shore birds and migrating waterfowl through planned habitat development.

And attract birds he did. Species not seen around the metropolitan area for many years were soon to be found at Jamaica Bay. Glossy ibises hadn't been reported in the New York area for almost a century, but they breed at the refuge today. The snowy egret was pronounced extirpated in 1923, a victim of the demand for its feathers. With heavy jet airplane traffic in the sky above, thousands of people walking nearby annually, and millions living and working almost within sight of its nests, the snowy egret is once again a resident in the neighborhood.

Directions   Jamaica Bay Wildlife Refuge straddles Cross Bay Boulevard in Broad Channel, Queens. It is accessible by car, mass transit, and bicycle.

If using mass transit, take the eastbound A train whose destination is marked Far Rockaway or Rockaway Park, **not** Lefferts Blvd. Get off at Broad Channel Station, walk west to Cross Bay Boulevard, then turn right (north) and proceed for about 0.5 mile to the refuge. Coming from Brooklyn, at the terminus of the number 2 IRT subway take the Q35 bus to its last stop and transfer to the Green Line, Q21, which passes the refuge.

To drive to the refuge, take the Belt Parkway east to Cross Bay Boulevard, turn south, cross the North Channel Bridge, and watch for the refuge entrance 1.5 miles on the right. From the Long Island Expressway, take Woodhaven Boulevard (which becomes Cross Bay Boulevard) south to the refuge. Note that driving to Jamaica Bay in summer can be difficult; the boulevard is a major access road to the Rockaways, so weekend beach crowds often jam the route.

The Walks   The area of the refuge on the west side of the Cross Bay Boulevard—West Pond—is presently more developed and will, therefore, be of greater interest to most walkers. Here, a 1.7-mile gravel trail from the visitors center circles the 45-acre West Pond.

On the opposite side of Cross Bay Boulevard is the section of the refuge sometimes known as the "wild area," or East Pond, which is more than twice the size (117 acres) of West Pond. Use the pedestrian crossing at the stoplight and follow a short trail to the pondside. In early June the refuge staff begins lowering the water level to expose mudflats, which later in the summer will become foraging and resting places for migratory shore birds. The trail has a short extension leading to the small, secluded Big John's Pond, with a blind for viewing wildlife: water fowl, wading birds, painted and snapping turtles, an occasional muskrat.

Photo by Don Burmeister ©2000

3
Staten Island Greenbelt

Distance	2.5 miles
Hiking time	1.5 hours
Rating	Easy

*M*uch of this walk over hills, through forests, and around ponds and wetlands was once intended by highway planners to be a six-lane concrete path down the backbone of Staten Island. The highway would have destroyed four natural ponds gouged out by glacial action, twenty thousand trees, and most of the area now comprising the Staten Island Greenbelt. Saved through a long and cooperative effort by many conservation groups, including the New York-New Jersey Trail Conference, the land now harbors a variety of small animals and many plants, as well as abundant wildflowers and butterflies. Located within the city limits, the area allows hikers to get away from the automobile.

The Greenbelt consists of a network of trails that winds for about 30 miles, usually out of sight of houses and roads. Some of these trails end at bus stops for easy access to public transportation. Each of the four main trails is blazed a different color—blue, white, red, or yellow—marked by two-by-three-inch paint blazes on trees, rocks, and poles. High Rock Park, which forms one corner of the Greenbelt, contains additional trails in lavender, green, and white on red (the Paw Trail).

This leisurely 1.5-hour ramble takes place mostly in High Rock Park, in areas surrounding the High Rock Park Environmental Education Center. In addition, the Richmondtown Restoration, described in detail at the end of this section, is worth a visit in its own right.

Directions   The Staten Island Greenbelt is about 30 miles south of the George Washington Bridge. Using public transportation is recommended so you can experience the sights and sounds of New York Harbor. The Staten Island Ferry runs from South Ferry, Manhattan, to St. George Terminal, Staten Island. The ride, with a view of the Statue of Liberty and the Verrazano Bridge is approximately 25 minutes. From the St. George Ferry Terminal (you may want to pick up a bus map here), take the S74 bus toward Tottenville. You will need a Metrocard or exact change for the bus ride. Ask the bus driver to let you off at Richmond Road, near Rockland Avenue. From the bus stop, walk ahead on Richmond Road to the corner of Richmond Road and Rockland Avenue.

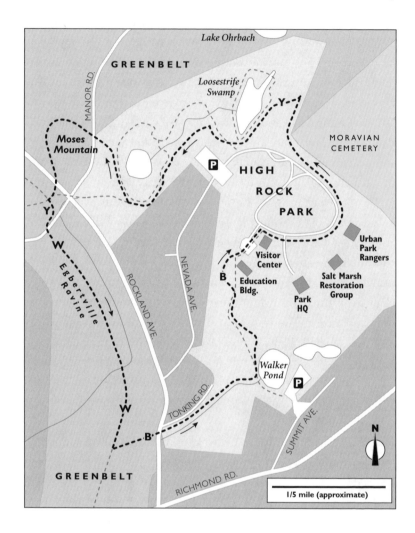

Turn right onto Rockland Avenue. Approximately 0.25 mile up Rockland Avenue, turn right onto Tonking Road, which is marked with blue blazes.

Alternatively, you can also take Staten Island Rapid Transit (SIRT) from the ferry. From the St. George Ferry Terminal, take the SIRT train to New Dorp Station. This system is similar to the New York City bus and subway system in that you need a token or Metrocard to ride. From New Dorp Station, take the S57 bus heading toward Port Richmond and get off at the bus stop on Rockland Avenue, near Tonking Road. From the bus stop, walk about 0.25 mile on Rockland Avenue to the corner with Tonking Road. Turn right onto Tonking Road.

To drive to the Greenbelt, you will need to take the Staten Island Expressway (I-278), either via the Verrazano Bridge from Brooklyn, or via the Goethals Bridge if you are coming from New Jersey. Once on Staten Island, exit the expressway onto Richmond Road, which is located on the eastern side of Staten Island near the Verrazano Bridge. Do not take the Richmond Avenue exit, which is closer to the Goethals Bridge. Once on Richmond Road, follow it south to Rockland Avenue (a distance of about 4 miles) and turn right onto Rockland Avenue. Approximately 0.25 mile up Rockland Avenue, make a right onto Tonking Road. Drive up Tonking Road until the dead end, where there is a small parking area.

The Staten Island Ferry ride is a favorite trip for sight-seers. As you leave the Manhattan Terminal, directly ahead is Governor's Island. This prime piece of real estate was a federal military installation and, until recently, a Coast Guard station. Although its future use has not been determined, access to the island is very limited. The white building on shore to the left is a ventilating shaft for the Brooklyn-Battery Tunnel. Soon, to your right, you will see the Statue of Liberty rising 302 feet above the water to the tip of her torch. Beyond is New Jersey.

Notice that Staten Island is much closer to New Jersey than to New York. Legend has it that Staten Island became part of New York when, in a contest, a New Yorker was the first to sail around it in one day. It was

discovered by Verrazano in 1524 and named Staaten Eylandt by Henry
Hudson less than 100 years later in honor of the States General of the
Netherlands. Its official name, given to it by the British, is Richmond.

The Walk   At the dead end of Tonking Road, the blue trail enters the
woods (you will need to go around the left side of a locked gate). The
trail is very flat and easy to walk along and the entire loop is approximately 1.5 miles.

As you continue on the trail, you will see Walker Pond on the right.
The blue trail winds around and gradually goes uphill to the headquarters of High Rock Park. At the top of the hill there is a women's rest
room on the left and an environmental education center on the right,
where maps of the Greenbelt trails are available. Continuing up, on the
right side of the blue trail is the visitors center (maps are also available
here), behind which is the men's rest room. From here, the blue trail
begins to follow a paved road, through a parking lot. Soon you will pass
a small native plant garden with several benches. Follow the road past
the ranger station and downhill. Stay on this road until you are in sight
of a swampy area and small pond, with picnic benches nearby. (Do not
follow the blue blazes into the woods to the right, but stay on the road
instead. On a tree near the benches, you will see a yellow blaze, marking a yellow trail that goes in both directions. Follow the yellow trail to
the left. (You will know you have followed the trail in the wrong direction if you soon walk along a fence-line marking the boundary of the
Moravian Cemetery. Turn back and head in the other direction.)

Following the yellow trail, cross a brook on a small man-made bridge
and make an immediate left. Cross another small bridge, take an immediate right, and continue following the yellow trail. The yellow trail is
joined by a green trail, and both turn to the right. Make this right turn,
following the yellow trail across a boardwalk and several bridges. The

trail crosses a road (Manor Road); follow it straight ahead as it circles three sides of the base of "Moses Mountain," made of rock removed from a hill during the construction of the Staten Island Expressway. The "mountain" is now covered with trees and bushes.

The yellow trail leaves the woods at Rockland Avenue. Make a left on Rockland Avenue to the intersection with Manor-Meisner Road. Cross diagonally at the intersection to the Egbertville Ravine, a protected area. Looking up the ravine, its left side is adjacent to Manor Road and its right side is adjacent the entrance road to the Eger Home, a health care and rehabilitation center. Follow this entrance road a few yards until you see the white trail going along the side of the ravine. Follow the white trail down into Egbertville Ravine. Go over a bridge, staying on the white trail as it veers to the right. You will come out at Eleanor Street, which is now marked as a blue trail. Make a left on Eleanor Street and follow it to Rockland Avenue. Cross Rockland Avenue, turn right and then immediately left onto Tonking Road.

The bus stop is down the hill and across Richmond Road opposite where you got off. Two buses use this stop. The S74 goes directly back to the ferry terminal. The S54 goes to the New Dorp Rapid Transit Station, a more comfortable ride than the bus.

Historic Richmondtown is an authentic village and museum complex interpreting three centuries of daily life and culture on Staten Island. It is open Wednesday through Sunday from 1–5pm. The plan of the Staten Island Historical Society is to establish and maintain a slice of the past for us to visit. The ambitious program envisions a collection of more than thirty houses and structures dating from colonial times to the turn of the twentieth century.

Richmondtown began as a landing for Indian traders coming in on the Fresh Kills. It was originally called Cocklestown because of the mounds of shells left by the Native Americans. Richmondtown was the hub of the island and the scene of Revolutionary-era skirmishes. For some years, it was the county seat. When St. George (the part of the island where the ferry docks) outgrew and surpassed it, Richmondtown declined.

The oldest building, Voorlezer's House, dates from before 1696. Built by the Dutch congregation, it is the oldest schoolhouse still standing in the United States and is a National Historic Landmark. Other buildings of various dates are the settings for demonstrations of a variety of early crafts and trades. The historical museum occupies an 1848 brick building. Inside are archaeological relics, costumes, farm utensils, etc. A gift shop in the form of an old-fashioned store stocks real penny candy.

The Church of Saint Andrew, although in the restoration area, did not have to be moved to its present site. It is an historical building in its own right. Originally built in 1708, it was reconstructed in 1872 following a fire. The church was chartered by Queen Anne of Great Britain, who donated a silver chalice and other gifts to the church. The graveyard surrounding the church is the resting-place of several Revolutionary War soldiers. The father and grandfather of Mother Elizabeth Seton are also buried here.

Photo by Tom Rupolo

4
Riverside Park

Distance	3 miles
Hiking time	1.5 hours
Rating	Easy

This unique urban landmark, 316 acres hugging the Hudson River from 59th to 152nd Streets, has historic character, great inherent beauty, and diverse environments.

The original Riverside Park was designed by Frederick Law Olmsted, famed designer of Central and Prospect Parks, in the 1870s. At that time, the park (including Riverside Drive) extended only from hillside to the bottom of the slope. Below the slope were open railroad tracks, and beyond were the banks of the Hudson, with dumps, decaying barges, squatters' hovels, and junkyards. The smell of cattle cars and the noise of endless switching infuriated local residents, but funds were lacking to complete the park. Finally, in the 1930s, money was allocated; a major reconstruction began. Everything in the park from the base of the slope to the bulkhead at the river's edge was created as part of New York City Parks Commissioner Robert Moses' West Side Improvement project.

Riverside is an urban park: during peak weather, it is busy with families, dog walkers, joggers, and cyclists and offers little quiet or serenity. However, many changes and enhancements to its natural aspects are under way. The Riverside Park Fund, a non-profit support organization formed in 1986, has changed the face of the park. Working in partnership with New York City Parks and Recreation, the fund augments municipal budget, contributes to the Master Plan for restoration, and coordinates local citizen involvement in developing horticultural and other park amenities.

This is pleasing to the many New Yorkers who use the park for diverse activities. Though well used, Riverside Park and even Mother Nature somehow bear up; in the midst of everything, leeks, burdock, and garlic still grow wild here and there, attracting West Side cooks who may sneak to favorite spots to collect such edibles.

A walk in this park, Manhattan's longest, should be savored, not hurried. There are tennis, softball, basketball, and soccer games to watch, Hudson River traffic to review, and urban folk doing their thing: jogging, cycling, and dog walking as well as less strenuous reading, sunning, people watching, and fishing. The way is level and mostly paved. Much of

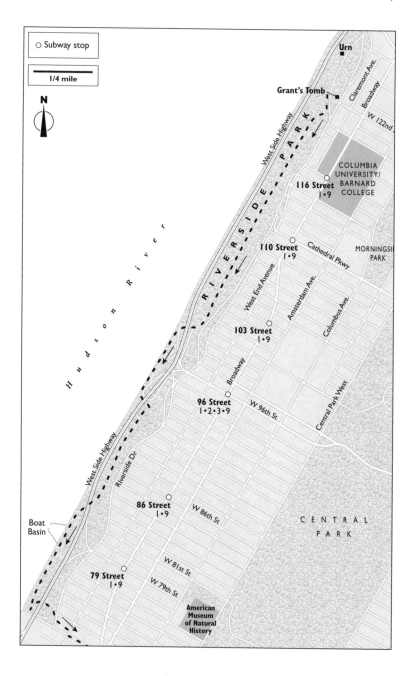

Subway stop

1/4 mile

N

Urn

Grant's Tomb

Claremont Ave.

Broadway

West Side Highway

W 122nd

RIVERSIDE PARK

COLUMBIA
UNIVERSITY/
BARNARD
COLLEGE

116 Street
1•9

Hudson River

110 Street
1•9

Cathedral Pkwy

MORNINGSI
PARK

West End Avenue

Amsterdam Ave.

103 Street
1•9

Columbus Ave.

Broadway

96 Street
1•2•3•9

W 96th St

Central Park West

West Side Highway

Riverside Dr

86 Street
1•9

W 86th St

C E N T R A L

P A R K

Boat
Basin

79 Street
1•9

W 81st St

W 79th St

American
Museum
of Natural
History

the parkland runs along the very edge of the Hudson. Since the park parallels nearby subway and bus lines, a walk can be as long or as short as one would like.

One can start at either the north or south end of the park or anywhere along the way. Until recently, the park's southernmost point was at West 72nd Street where Riverside Drive begins. However, a new section developed in 2000 extends to 59th Street. By 2005, the present route is expected to be part of the Hudson River Valley Greenway, originating at Battery Park and providing a continuous route for pedestrians and bicycles past Albany, almost 160 miles.

Walkers in the park may use two or sometimes three levels. The upper level is usually sidewalk along Riverside Drive—tree lined, with benches, occasional statuary, and children's play areas on the way. The middle, bench-lined level connects upper and riverfront levels and winds through wooded areas, gardens, promenades, playing fields, and play areas. The lowest, waterfront level, though not continuous, proceeds most of the way. There are a number of short tunnels under the overhead parkway, and many interconnecting paths access the upper levels. Although the routes and levels may seem complicated, there is no possibility of losing one's way; the Hudson River is Riverside Park's western boundary, Riverside Drive its eastern border.

The route is mostly paved. However, throughout the park there are smaller paths, many unpaved. Directly underground is a tunnel containing rail tracks; ventilation gratings are found at various places, and the sound of trains rushing through the tunnel beneath one's feet is a surprise. Formerly a freight line of the New York Central Railroad, these tracks now lead to Penn Station at 34th Street, currently used by Amtrak for passenger trains to Albany and beyond.

The second newest section of Riverside Park is the "Cherry Walk." Located directly on the river, half the path is designated for bicycles, the other for pedestrians. It extends from 125th Street to just above the

96th Street public tennis courts, with no access between these points. Thereafter there is a tunnel underpass under the highway with a way to the uphill part of the park and Riverside Drive itself. Above are Grant's Tomb, Riverside Church, and the Columbia University complex.

Before beginning the walk through Riverside Park, you may want to visit the surrounding area, which is rich in history and cultural institutions. Columbia University, established in 1754, and then known as King's College, is located here, bounded by West 114th and 120th Streets, Amsterdam Avenue, and Broadway. An acropolis of neoclassical buildings, the campus is a creation of McKim, Mead, and White, whose architecture is found throughout New York City. Sculptures by Rodin, French, Moore, Lipschitz, and others can be found on the campus. St. Paul's Chapel, a 1907 Byzantine/Renaissance building, is not to be missed. (Campus tours originating at the Low Library are available.)

South of the university are many bookstores and eateries. Close by, on Amsterdam Avenue at 112th Street, is the Cathedral of St. John the Divine, begun in 1892 and still under construction. French Gothic in style, the facade, with portals, pinnacles, and rose window, is most imposing. When St. John's is completed, it will be the world's largest cathedral. Its spectacular interior hosts concerts, exhibitions, performances and community events.

120th Street is lined with apartment and university buildings. This area was a battlefield during the American Revolution. After a headlong retreat up Manhattan, Washington's troops made a stand along what is now 120th Street. A block south were the British; the two lines fired at each other until the British finally broke. This brief battle was one of the first successes of the colonial amateurs against trained European soldiers.

Across from the park on Riverside Drive is Riverside Church, funded by John D. Rockefeller, Jr., and built in 1930. In part modeled after Chartres Cathedral, it houses the world's largest carillon. The tower and observation deck offers spectacular views and on Sundays, carillon concerts. Inside are 16th-century stained glass windows and neo-Gothic carved choir stalls. Guided tours are available (212-870-6769).

Just north of the church is the General Grant Memorial, the largest mausoleum in the United States. Grant's Tomb, as it is commonly known, is the final resting place of the 18th president of the United States, Ulysses S. Grant, and his wife, Julia. Its size reflects public admiration for this Union general credited with winning the Civil War. Riverside Park existed before the tomb and terminated at this point. When the tomb was completed in 1898 (at a site once proposed by George Washington for the U.S. Capitol), the park's architect warned it would be extremely unfortunate if the remains of the dead were to be brought into such close association with the gaiety of the Promenade. His fears were unfounded: currently children play baseball on the steps of the tomb, which is surrounded by colorful free-form benches covered with ceramic mosaic patterns that contrast strikingly with the Tomb's severity.

Just north of Grant's Tomb directly is the brow of Claremont Hill, some 140 feet above the Hudson River. If you walk west of the hill and across Riverside Drive West and head south on the sidewalk, you will come to a quaint and affecting little monument about 100 yards northwest of the tomb. Just off Riverside Drive, a marble urn sits enclosed by a fence at the edge of a steep drop-off. The urn is inscribed, "Erected to the Memory of an Amiable Child." In 1797, a five-year-old boy who lived nearby was killed in a fall from these rocks. His father erected the urn.

Later, forced by business reverses to leave the area, he asked that the monument be preserved. His request has been honored to this day by succeeding generations of builders, developers, and urban planners, who have otherwise utterly transformed these heights.

Directions   Local trains 1 and 9 run north-south on Broadway, two blocks east of Riverside Drive. These stop at stations along Broadway: 72nd, 79th, 86th, 96th, 103rd, 110th, 116th, and 125th streets. Riverside Park may be accessed from just about any street along the route. Several north/south bus routes are within walking distance of Riverside Park: M5 runs on Riverside Drive itself, M104 on Broadway, M7 and M11 buses on Amsterdam Avenue, and the M10 on Central Park West. All connect with east/west lines as well. If you are traveling by car, the West Side Highway runs along the Hudson River with exits at 158th, 125th, 96th, 79th and 57th Streets. Park anywhere near Broadway/Riverside Drive, either on the street or in parking garages.

The Walk (Southbound)   Enter the main part of Riverside Park via the path opposite 120th Street and follow the paved path down the stairway, past side paths that diverge left along the slope. There are public tennis courts to the north.

Walk south along the path from the tennis courts. Here the path is through woodland, in spring filled with birdsong. In fact, this area around 116th Street is designated a bird sanctuary, where bird walks are offered during fall and spring migrations. Shortly thereafter is the first of several mock battlements overlooking the Hudson. At the second, smaller one, the area below opens up enough to accommodate a variety of playing fields, which stretch southward for nearly a mile. Not long thereafter, the path opens unobtrusively into a mall. You can follow the path that forks left or walk straight ahead through the long promenade (which runs nearly to 96th Street) under the double row of trees. In summer, the mall is busy with picnickers, bicyclists, joggers, and volley-ball players. In winter, after a snowfall, it is quiet and majestic; cross-country skiers may appear in periods of heavy snow. At 105th Street, down steps from this promenade, is an outdoor café, open during warm seasons on weekdays after 3pm and on weekends after 10am.

As the mall ends, the path curves a little to the right, then forks, with the left fork running along a playground and then to Riverside Drive. The right fork dips down to an underpass beneath the highway. Follow the right fork under the overpass. Here is another point where one may choose one of two levels along which to proceed: either down to the river's edge or higher up through more wooded sections.

As one passes under the arch, the view of the Hudson opens up. Far to the north is the George Washington Bridge and "Cherry Walk" heading north to 125th Street. The view directly across the Hudson offers the Palisades, with residential and commercial development on the high bluffs and at the water's edge. Farther south is the 79th Street Boat Basin, followed by the city's piers; some are preserved in decrepit condition as a reminder of New York's former days as a bustling harbor. Others still function for cruise ships and naval vessels. Barges, tankers, tugs, sailboats, and cruisers move on the river, accompanied by the ever-present Circle Line ships. Overhead pass helicopters and jets.

Proceeding south, all the land around 96th Street at the river was created by fill from Moses' West Side Improvement. Where there was once a small bay, metal railings run along the top of the breakwater. Adults and small boys fish at intervals along this river edge. Narrow as the area is between the highway and the river, there is room for 10 clay tennis courts and two parking lots for sightseers. (At one time this area was known as Strikers Bay. In 1776, on the day before the Battle of Harlem Heights, three British ships anchored here in an attempt to impede the colonial retreat.)

Continue to walk south, past a grove of locusts and sweet gums. Shortly beyond the tennis courts, the path forks again. One branch accompanies an access road under the parkway; the other leads straight ahead, becoming merely a 5-foot-wide dirt path squeezed between the highway and the river. Places so close to the Hudson are rare, so you may be tempted to take this path down toward the 79th Street Boat Basin, where the river-edge promenade resumes.

However, continuing on the upper promenade will also eventually lead to the boat basin, back under the highway. You will pass some interestingly shaped cherry trees and walk through an opening in a low wall onto double paths of the long esplanade between 94th and 82nd Streets.

This esplanade curves around the foot of the slope from Riverside Drive. At its north end are a large, tree-shaded playground and elaborate community flower gardens. Plan to visit this area during spring or summer when the glorious English gardens are in bloom. Above the playground, completely hidden from this spot in summer, is an open slope that in winter snow offers great sledding, perhaps the best in Manhattan. Just above the slope on Riverside Drive at 89th Street is the circular Soldiers' and Sailors' Monument. Completed in 1902 to commemorate New York City's Civil War dead, it is modeled after the Monument of Lysicrates in Athens.

From the esplanade the view to the west is across the Hudson to New Jersey; it is more open in seasons when trees are leafless. Toward the end of the esplanade, a path drops down to the river on the right. It leads back down to the river's edge and then to the 79th Street Boat Basin. If you remain on the esplanade a short distance, you will find a memorial to the Warsaw Ghetto, completed in 2001 and surrounded by flower gardens. Immediately beyond the stone wall to the right, stone steps wind down to the lowest level and the river's edge. Before taking the steps, stop to look around. The rocky knoll ahead, almost hidden from this angle by the trees, is unofficially called Mt. Tom. Just before and to the right of the knoll is a playground with restrooms.

The stairs lead to a small clearing below the esplanade, where the curious can peer through the grilled door to see the enormous railroad tunnel that runs beneath the park. Take the underpass beneath the highway, which opens up on the other side to another grand vista. Ornamental cherry trees line the path along the river's edge past the boat basin. Try to walk this section in the spring, when the blossoms are spectacular.

The 79th Street Boat Basin is home to various craft and about 85 year-round houseboat inhabitants. (Compared to private marinas, city marinas are rather spartan, but this one offers parking in an underground 200-car garage as part of the rent.) The many-tiered structure to your left houses the parking lot and railroad tracks. A café is set here among vaulted arches designed by Guastavino, at the site of a fountain used as a performance space during summer months.

South of the café and marina, this lower part of the park widens to include ballfields, a playground, and a stadium popular with local joggers. Benches line the walk. (To leave the park here, circle around the track and take the staircase up to the landing. Look back for a long view over the river. Walk through the tunnel under the highway to the other side and the upper level of the park. Continue straight ahead to Riverside Drive; walk two blocks eastward along West 72nd Street to the 72nd Street subway stop.)

To continue, walk along the river on the newly completed South Waterfront, 72nd–59th Street, with its public pier extending into the river. This is (July 2001) the southern end of the park.

5
Van Cortlandt Park

Distance	3.6 miles
Hiking time	3-4 hours
Rating	Easy

Van Cortlandt Park is one of the largest and most varied of New York City's parks. Located in the northwest corner of the Bronx at the border with Yonkers, it has many miles of trails, bridle paths, and paved paths. Van Cortlandt Park is suitable for short or long strolls. The varied terrain offers plenty of room for a full day's walk. On sunny weekend days, the picnic areas will be crowded, and the Parade Ground fields will be filled with soccer, football, rugby, and cricket (Van Cortlandt Park is one of the few New York City sites where cricket is played). However, an urbanite can get in touch with history and nature and find peace and quiet in the surrounding woods. Bicycles are not allowed on any unpaved park roads.

The Van Cortlandt House Museum and the Urban Forest Ecology Center are open to the public and worth visiting. The Museum [(718) 543-3344] is open Tuesday through Friday 10am to 3pm, Saturday and Sunday 11am to 4pm. Open hours for the Ecology Center (run by Urban Park Rangers) are erratic; call for information at (718) 548-0912 or (718) 430-1832. Stop in the Urban Forest Ecology Center to pick up a free map of the trails, useful if you plan to explore trails not described here. There are rest rooms between the two buildings.

The Van Cortlandt House Museum is the oldest building in the Bronx. In 1639, Wiechquaeskeck Native Americans sold much of what is now parkland to the Dutch West India Company, which sold it in 1646 to Adriaen van der Donck, a prominent New Netherlands lawyer. Frederick Philipse, a British merchant, described as New York's wealthiest man, bought the property from Van der Donck's widow in 1693. In 1694, he sold a tract of land that is now part of the park to Jacobus Van Cortlandt, a future mayor of New York. In 1698 Van Cortlandt married Eva Philipse and in 1699 bought 76 acres encompassing the site where the house stands. During the 1690s, Tibbetts Brook was dammed to power grist- and sawmills, creating Van Cortlandt Lake. Built in 1748 by Jacobus' son Frederick, the Van Cortlandt Mansion (now known as the Van Cortlandt House Museum), remained the colonial plantation house of the Van Cortlandt family, who farmed through the 1870s. The

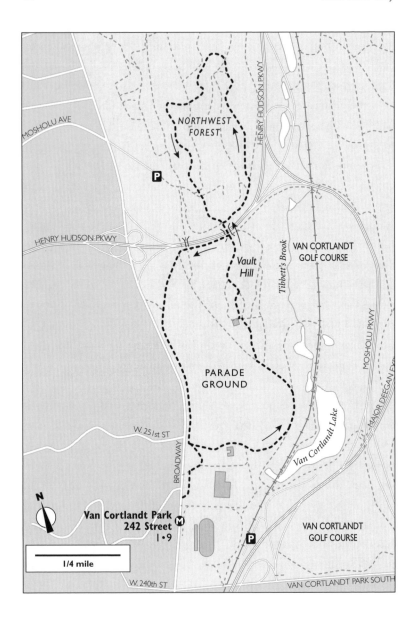

Georgian style three-story house was occupied by the Van Cortlandt family until 1888, when it became the property of New York City and the park was established. Listed on the National Registry of Historic Places, both the interior and exterior of the Van Cortlandt House Museum are designated New York City Landmarks.

Early in the Revolutionary War, the British General, Sir William Howe, moved his army onto the Van Cortlandt estate. Thus during most of the war, the mansion was behind British lines. George Washington occupied it at different three times. The first was in 1776 during an early campaign that ended in the Battle of White Plains. Later, in 1781, Washington met with the French commander Rochambeau to plan military strategy while 5,000 of their troops waited on the Parade Ground and Vault Hill. Washington's final stay was in 1783, before marching triumphantly into a Manhattan newly surrendered by the British.

The Van Cortlandt Mansion is now restored to its former elegance. The rooms give an idea of the life of a well-to-do Dutch-English family in the late 18th century and are furnished with 17th- and 18th-century American, Dutch, and English pieces. The basic construction material of the house is rubblestone accented by brick trim around the windows. One unusual touch is the figures placed above the windows. These show the Dutch heritage of the builder, for although rare in America such architectural elements were common in Holland.

On the grounds of the mansion are an herb garden and an outdoor exhibit consisting of a section of a brick window frame with iron bars. This was originally part of an infamous British prison for American soldiers in lower Manhattan and was moved to its present site in the early 1900s.

If you have time, walk over to nearby Woodlawn Cemetery, one of the most lavish cemeteries in the world. The entrance is at the intersection of Jerome Avenue and East 233rd Street, abutting the east side of Van Cortlandt Park. The cemetery, where the rich and famous have been buried in tombs that rival the mansions they lived in, opened in 1865. A Belmont rests in a replica of St. Hubert Chapel. Jay Gould has a Greek temple. Woolworth lies in Egyptian splendor. Others buried in the cemetery include Herman Melville, Joseph Pulitzer, Bat Masterson, Fiorello LaGuardia, Barbara Hutton, Irving Berlin, and George Cohan. The cemetery is a tranquil place—a world of trees, shrubs, and flowers. A map of the cemetery and its grave sites is available at the main office near the entrance gate.

Directions   The park is easily reached by car or public transportation. The northern terminus of the Broadway number 1 and 9 trains at West 242nd Street and Broadway is at the southwest corner of the park. From that station, number 9 buses run along Broadway north to Yonkers and beyond. Westchester Beeline buses 1, 2, 3 and the Manhattan Express Bus BxM3 all provide access to the Northwest Forest area as well. The Northeast Forest section is a short walk from the last stop of the number 4 train on Jerome Avenue at Woodlawn Cemetery. The Bx16, Bx34, Westchester Beeline 4, 20, and 21, and the Manhattan Express Bus BxM4B provide service to the east side and the Northeast Woods.

The Henry Hudson, Sawmill, and Mosholu Parkways meet in the park. Just west of this intersection, the Henry Hudson Parkway crosses Broadway. If arriving by car, take the Broadway exit (Exit 23) from the Henry Hudson Parkway and continue north or south on Broadway until you find a parking space. Within the park are two parking areas. One at the stables (a turn off the east side of Broadway opposite Mosholu Avenue and a number 9 bus stop, just north of the Henry Hudson exit) puts you at the trailhead leading into the Northwestern Forest. Another can be found at the VC Golf House.

An alternative route would be the Major Deegan Expressway to the Van Cortlandt Park South exit. Off the northbound exit ramp, make a sharp left turn at the yield sign and head through the underpass following signs to the Van Cortlandt Golf House. Off the southbound exit ramp, make a left turn onto Van Cortlandt Park South and the next left at the traffic light. Bear to the left and drive through the underpass to the Golf House. The free parking lot is the first one on the left after the underpass.

The Walk   The suggested walk of three or six miles follows the Cross Country Running Course into the Northwest Forest. The course is marked by metal arrows easily identified by the silhouettes of a tortoise and a hare. (On fall weekends, the course is very busy during race times. Hikers need to be alert and respectful of the runners.) The trail surface varies between pavement and gravel, and the route is simple to follow. It begins on the Parade Ground, winds through Vault Hill, and forms a loop through the Northwest Forest.

Enter the park at West 242nd Street on the right (east) side of Broadway and walk north to West 246th, passing the park stadium, swimming pool, and Van Cortlandt Museum grounds, the last surrounded by a tall wrought-iron fence. (Save a visit to the house and grounds for after your walk.)

Continue past the house to a wide path that circles the Parade Ground and playing fields. You are now on the Cross Country Running Course. The paved path continues straight ahead north toward Vault Hill, the rocky ridge on the left. Initially, the path runs parallel to the golf course. Farther ahead is the rail bed of a spur of the Putnam Division of the New York Central Railroad. This short commuter route ran between Highbridge in the Bronx through the Van Cortlandt Station (situated where the Golf House is now) to Getty Square, Yonkers, between 1888 and 1943.

Turn left at the next intersection and ascend a terraced path. The path levels off shortly and you will come to a post. To the left, toward the rocky outcrop jutting up from the playing field, is the Van Cortlandt family burial plot, surrounded by a stone wall and a wrought-iron fence.

In 1776 this vault was the hiding place for the records of New York City under British rule; the city's recording clerk was Augustus Van Cortlandt. No markers remain above ground; only a square patch of grass covers the vault below. It is worth continuing ahead along either of the unmarked trails to see the view from the peak of the rocky outcrop. Below, teams compete on the vast field of the Parade Ground, and straight ahead, to the south is the New York skyline.

Return to the main path and across an iron bridge over the Henry Hudson Parkway; a second bridge can be seen to the west. You are now in a more heavily wooded part of the park called the Northwest Forest. The first red building you come to is a restroom, open during warmer months. The very large red building beyond that is the stable of the Riverdale Equestrian Center. Farther on this road is a compost demonstration site that is fenced in and locked at times. The trail ends at an open area, Howell Grove; its center is a hexagonal flowerbed dedicated to the memory of Alfred H. Howell, nature lover, community supporter, and great friend of Van Cortlandt Park.

The gravel path to the right is a continuation of the Cross Country Running Course, a 0.75-mile loop that parallels the parkway then heads west and returns to the bridge. Large oak trees, offering a hint of the age of this park, border the path. Just beyond, a side trail veers to the right and the old bridle path, a 1.6-mile loop. The left path leads to the Cass Gallagher Nature Trail, another circular path, winding 1.25 miles through this quadrant of the park Cass Gallagher was a longtime Bronx environmentalist, especially devoted to Van Cortlandt Park.

Finishing the loops, one may recross the bridge to the trailhead of the John Muir Nature Trail, which transects the 2-mile width of the park in an east-west direction. This well-blazed trail leaves the park at East 238th Street.

If returning to the starting point, pass the John Muir trailhead, turn left and head down the hill, once again paralleling the Henry Hudson

Parkway on your right. The trail passes under a bridge and swings south, parallel to Broadway, on the west side of the Parade Ground. It passes Aesop's Bench (a large bronze bench/statue of hare and tortoise with the inscription "slow and steady wins the race") and ends where it began near the Van Cortlandt House Museum.

Additional Walks Both the Croton Aqueduct Trail and the old Putnam Railroad Trail (the latter formerly running north from Highbridge in the Bronx to Brewster in Putnam County) can be found at the south end of Van Cortlandt Park. They are separate initially but come together in the park's extreme northern edges, making a circular hike possible. Starting in Van Cortlandt Park, the Croton Aqueduct Trail can be followed north for more than 25 miles, with the exception of an interruption in Yonkers.

Photo by Tom Rupolo

Photo by Tom Rupolo

6
Pelham Bay Park

Distance	4-6 miles
Hiking time	2 hours
Rating	Easy

*P*elham Bay Park is New York City's largest park. Located in the northeast corner of the Bronx, its more than 2,700 acres offer miles of footpaths through dense woods and along the rocky coastline of Long Island Sound. There are wetlands, woodlands, and the mile-long Orchard Beach. Since the beach is very crowded during the summer, the best time to visit is during other seasons. Even on the clearest days of spring or fall, the area will be nearly deserted. In winter, you may encounter a few birders and cross-country skiers. The paths are generally flat.

Pelham Bay Park was originally a collection of small islands, beachy peninsulas, and extensive salt marshes. Orchard Beach did not exist until the 1930s when Robert Moses created the facility; Twin and Hunter islands were actually separate islands, and Pelham Bay was not buried under a vast parking lot. The Native American inhabitants were the Siwanoy, who shared a common language and lifestyle with the Wiechquaeskeck of the Van Cortlandt area. The rich aquatic life of the coast supported the Siwanoy, who settled along the inlets and shorelines of the bay and sound. Two major villages were situated near Turtle Cove and the area of the later Bartow-Pell Mansion, adjacent to interior woods and fields.

In 1654, Thomas Pell, an English doctor from Connecticut, bought 9,000 acres from the Siwanoy chieftains. The treaty for the purchase was signed at the famous Treaty Oak, destroyed by fire in 1906; an iron fence and an American elm mark the site. This vast area of land, which included much of the East Bronx and lower Westchester, became the Manor of Pelham, created by King's Charter in 1661. Shortly after, a manor house was built on the property; it was destroyed during the American Revolution. In 1730, the boundary between New York and Connecticut was settled with the Native Americans on the Pell's front lawn. In 1842, Robert Bartow, a descendant of Pell, built the mansion, now known as the Bartow-Pell Mansion, and settled into it. The mansion and its carriage house are listed on the National Register of Historic Places, and designated as Landmarks by the City of New York Landmarks Preservation Commission.

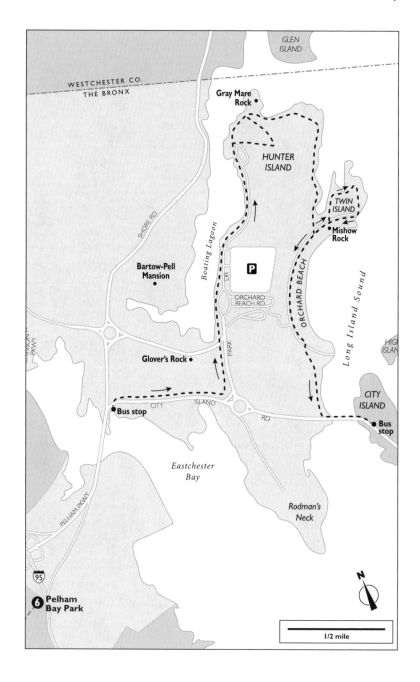

In October of 1776, when Washington and the Continental Army evacuated New York City after the battle of Harlem Heights, the British landed forces of thousands of well-drilled, well-armed men and cannon on Rodman's Neck (part of what is today Pelham Bay Park). The plan of British General Sir William Howe was to cut across Westchester and intercept Washington's underarmed, underfed, dispirited army retreating along the Bronx River to White Plains. Colonel John Glover and some eight hundred Massachusetts patriots confronted the redcoats. The only barrier between the British and the American Army, Glover's men, although enormously outnumbered and outgunned, intercepted and inflicted great casualties on the British force. Washington and his weak, vulnerable army were able to proceed safely through Westchester to White Plains. Glover's success is commemorated on Orchard Beach Road, where an historical marker is affixed to Glover's Rock.

Directions   Pelham Bay Park is 10 miles from the George Washington Bridge and can easily be reached by car or public transportation. By car, take the Hutchinson River Parkway or New England Thruway (I-95) to the Orchard Beach exit. Follow the road through a traffic circle to the other side and continue ahead to the first road on your left. Turn onto this road and you will shortly see the enormous parking lot.

By public transportation, you can ride the number 6 subway to the last stop, Pelham Bay Park. Take Bx29 City Island bus to the park. From Memorial Day to Labor Day you can also take the Bx5 or the Bx12 to Orchard Beach. All the buses stop at various points in the park and are scheduled to arrive every 20 or 30 minutes, depending on the day of the week and the time of day. (Bus maps are available free at all NYC subway stations.) When returning from the park, you can access other subway lines from the westbound Bx12 bus, which runs along Fordham Road straight across the Bronx and into Manhattan. It connects with all north-south subway lines: 5, 2, D, 4, 1, 9, A.

Leaving the terminus of the number 6 train, the bus crosses I-95 and the Hutchinson River Parkway, entering the park on Pelham Parkway. The bus will cross Pelham Bridge over the Hutchinson River. As soon as it passes the large war memorial to your right, notify the driver that you want to get off at the next stop, City Island Road. Cross the road and turn right on the paved path, following it on a low hill, paralleling City Island Road. The path narrows and soon passes "Turtle Cove," a minia-ture golf course, driving range, and snack bar. Just beyond, the path turns left (north), following the shore of the pond. Don't cross the road when the path ends; remain on the grassy edge along the west side. You will soon be at the Hutchinson River Parkway's access to the beach (it comes in from the left). Here is a traffic island; at its center is a large sign for Orchard Beach, made entirely of stones. Detour to walk fifty feet west of this intersection and stop at Glover's Rock.

Cross the access road and continue straight ahead, with the lagoon to the left (west). The modern multilevel structure just in sight is a tower erected for viewing the 1964 United States Olympic Rowing Trials held on the lagoon. Continue along the grass to the parking lot. Car drivers join the hike here.

The Walk   Begin at the northwest corner of the parking lot (a gravel path leads from this corner through the phragmites) toward the kayak and canoe launching area. Walk along the northern side of the parking lot, ignoring small trails that lead off to the left. Near the center of the lot, beyond the picnic tables, follow a path that heads north into the woods. It becomes wider and more defined as you proceed north through this area, still known as Hunter Island though an island no longer.

Hunter Island takes its name from John Hunter, who bought this land in the early 19th century when it was still an island. Between 1804 and 1811, he erected a mansion on top of the hill. The mansion is gone, and the northern end of the onetime island is covered with dense woods and crossed by a network of footpaths and old roads. Trails cut through waist-high masses of goldenrod, jewelweed, and reeds. This area is especially beautiful in May when wild geraniums sport thousands of purple blooms. Some of the lesser-used trails become so overgrown at the height of summer that they can't be followed. Near the middle of the island are the remains of John Hunter's home. All that is left are the overgrown remnants of his landscaping.

Walk on the main trail, which stays close to the lagoon for a distance. There are some footpaths coming into the trail from the right. Ignore them. You will find much damage along this part of the trail. It can be muddy and wet much of the time. Here the woods shelter rabbits, raccoons, chipmunks, and sometimes deer.

Birds are present in good variety and number. The best time to see them is from October through May when mosquitoes are few and the park is quiet. Raptors are a specialty: red tailed hawks, kestrels, and sometimes rough-legged hawks frequent the abandoned landfill near the entrance to the park. Offshore are greater scaup ducks, horned grebes, buffleheads, other waterfowl, and perhaps an occasional red throated loon. There are always the common herring gulls, some black-backed gulls and cormorants. In addition to the waterfowl, Pelham Bay Park is known for its great horned owls, year-round residents that breed in several areas of the park. Long-eared owls and saw-whet owls are winter resident species. Barn owls occasionally nest in the park as well.

Here at the northwest end of Hunter Island, a point of land juts out. The trail leads toward an enormous gray boulder on this point. It is a glacial erratic, a rock carried to this spot and left behind when the ice sheet receded. The Siwanoys named this rock Gray Mare; it and

Mishow, another erratic located near the north end of Orchard Beach, were sacred to the Native Americans. Leave the rock and detour a bit by walking along the shoreline. The shoreline here along Long Island Sound is much rockier than it was along the marshy island shore. This is the southernmost point of rocky shoreline on the eastern coast of North America. The bedrock has a complex geological history and dates back about a half a billion years, much older than the Sound itself, which was a river valley until the post-glacier rising waters flooded it.

A walk on the rocks reveals the gradients of shore life. In the top zone, the area covered only intermittently by water, barnacles adhere to the rock. Seaweed, brown algae, blue mussels, and green sea lettuce are found at the next lower zone. Lower still one finds red algae. Finally, the muddy shallows between Hunter Island and Twin islands form the habitat of mussels and large clams.

Return to the main trail and head south. You will soon arrive at a wide path leading left, heading to the remnants of a footbridge that once spanned the inlet. The bridge to the Twin Islands has been removed for safety, and access to the island is now from the northern edge of Orchard Beach only. The main trail continues south and ends when you are within sight of the Orchard Beach boardwalk. A large sign designates the trail as the Kazimiroff Nature Trail. Dr. Theodore Kazimiroff was instrumental in leading the efforts to limit the city's attempts to expand the landfill you passed on the way to the park. (It was part of a huge Department of Sanitation operation within the park that was to have included all 375 acres of the marshland, which New York State legislation finally designated as the Thomas Pell Wildlife Refuge in 1967).

When you reach the boardwalk along Orchard Beach, turn left and head toward the red brick structure, a small environmental center open only during July and August. During those months you will be able to pick up trail maps and brochures.

Photo by Tom Rupolo

To explore Twin Islands, walk along the esplanade to a sign, "Twin Islands Preserve," and take the gravel path to the top, passing several smaller trails that lead off to the shore. The trail ends at the marshy tip of the island. Ahead lies Two Trees Island, reachable at low tide by hopping across the rocks. Returning, you can create a loop walk by following the woods path along the western shore of Twin Islands.

Continue south along the esplanade that overlooks Orchard Beach. The beach sweeps before you, a crescent of fine sand a mile long and 200 yards wide. On a hot weekend the crowd will be enormous; on a relatively cool day when school is in session there will be few distractions from the breathtaking vista. Just offshore are Hart and City islands, the latter with its picturesque houses and boat builders' workshops jutting out over the water.

The Bartow-Pell Mansion Museum and Gardens, an historic site on Shore Road a short distance north of the Bartow Circle, offers a view of wealthy country living in the 19th century. With carriage house and grounds, the City of New York bought it in 1888 as part of the future Pelham Bay Park. In the 1920s, after years of neglect, the International Garden Club assumed responsibility for restoring the mansion's richly ornamented interior and developing its collections and gardens. In 1946, the building was opened to the public as a New York City museum exhibiting furniture, decorative arts, and paintings from the first half of the 19th century. Recently the Bartow-Pell Landmark Fund has begun restoring the carriage house. The city maintains the mansion's exterior and surrounding nine acres. Hours are Wednesday, Saturday, and Sunday, noon–4pm. For information call (718) 885-1461.

All of this beach area is man-made. Until the 1930s, Hunter Island was an island in fact as well as in name. Swimming facilities had been developed in the park earlier in the century, including a granite boathouse and a sea wall so poorly located that except at low tide there was no beach below it at all. In 1934, Robert Moses built another of his great beaches. He removed all the old construction and dumped tons of sanitary landfill into the shallows between Rodman's Neck and the mainland. The parking lot was built on the fill. Barge loads of fine-grained sand were floated up from the Rockaways and Sandy Hook, New Jersey. New bathhouses were built, Egyptian in style, much the vogue during that time period. The project was a favorite of Moses.

Continue along the esplanade. Bus riders should follow the boardwalk to the main pavilion; the bus depot is at its south end (but remember that these number 12 buses run only from Memorial Day to Labor Day). Those who arrived by car can return to the parking lot on

Orchard Beach Drive, then drive via Park Drive to City Island Circle and on to City Island. Or they can continue as walkers, following the boardwalk. Take the first path at the south end of the pavilion, then the first paved path to the left. This path heads south along the shoreline and picnic grounds, becomes a dirt footpath, and continues to the City Island Bridge.

Eventually, a scramble up an embankment at the end of the footpath puts the walker onto the bridge that links City Island to the Bronx mainland.

Along City Island Road are stops for the Bx29 bus to head back (west) to the Pelham Bay Park subway station and the terminus of the westbound Bx12 bus with access to other subways. Car drivers retrace their route of travel.

City Island was settled by the Dutch in 1685 and originally called Minnewits Island. Reminiscent of a New England fishing town, it is incongruously located within New York City limits. To this day it retains its maritime roots as a prominent shipbuilding and yachting center. Boat yards, marinas, and sailing schools are numerous. Rowboats can be rented at the first road on the left past the bridge. The island's one public school was erected on the grounds of the former Nevin Boat Yard, builder of a number of America's Cup contenders. On City Island, visitors may want to linger and explore the narrow streets, taking in the atmosphere of this unique community, visiting one of the several crafts studios, antiques shops and art galleries, perhaps dining at one of the island's famous seafood restaurants. To learn more about the history of this seafaring community, dubbed "The Seaport of the Bronx," call the City Island Chamber of Commerce at (718) 885-9100.

Long
Island

LONG ISLAND
For the Family

When the bud bursts green on the twig and the drone of the power mower fills the air, families start to think about a walk in the outdoors. Preparing for family walks is a skill, and Long Island is a good place to begin for the family with young and inexperienced walkers. The areas are small and the woods tend to be level, reducing the possibility of getting lost. Trails are sandy, with few rocks to catch young toes or cut stumbling bodies. The only problem of note is the possibility of acquiring a tick, so children should be warned to stay out of the brush and they should be inspected after a walk.

Equipment and preparation can be held to a minimum: a few snacks and a canteen. A more elaborate kit might include a bird- or plant-identification book and binoculars.

The simplicity of walking on Long Island does not mean that parents have to avoid the more rugged areas. It does mean that preparation and experience are required. Even very young children can be taken into any area within range of the day walker, if the adults have first scouted the trail and they respect the capabilities of their children.

Infants and toddlers can go almost anywhere in a carrier. A walk to them is just another outing, like a shopping trip. Remember that walkers are generating heat by their exercise but an infant in a carrier is not and therefore may require warmer clothes. Otherwise the preparations are the same as those for any outing: a diaper, a towel, and perhaps some formula in the pouch under the seat of the child carrier. On longer outings a belt-style fanny pack is useful for carrying and getting at the necessary paraphernalia. Parents using rugged strollers rather than carriers can also use trails, provided they head for the smooth paths of Caumsett State Park.

The two-to-four age group is more difficult to handle on an outing than are infants. Kids in this age group still have to be carried at least part of the way, but they're heavier. Their preferences are more pronounced and often more difficult to satisfy. Here are one mother's suggestions for coping with two-to-four-year-olds:

1. Candy (M & Ms, sour balls, lollipops, anything with sugar that won't melt), to be used as a reward for distance covered, the completion of quiet time, etc.
2. Rest only on "resting rocks"—these are rocks of particular sizes and shapes, and definitely at least a quarter or half mile apart.
3. Look for the baby elephant (who's always just behind any two-year-old!).
4. Talk them up—ask them to be on the lookout for trail markers, tell them about the flowers and trees by the trail, ask them what they want for birthdays or holidays.

The four-to-seven age group can also be challenging. Some of these children can walk as far as their parents. But, like the younger ones, they can be fickle and unpredictable. Coaxing, stops, and games may be required. Be prepared to declare a walk finished when it looks as if the kids have had it for the day—but be prepared for the miraculous recovery that may follow a stop for candy or for dangling tired feet in a stream.

From age seven on up through the teens, young people become increasingly stronger as walkers. Often they can walk faster than their parents, particularly after the first half hour or so. This group can handle greater responsibility. They should have their own packs and gear. They should be able to invite friends along, and they can have a voice in the prewalk planning. Once they know enough to stop and wait at trail intersections, they should be able to set their own pace.

Walking with several children has its own techniques. One child is always faster than the others, and the slower ones get mad. This problem may be solved by letting them take turns. If your children squabble, letting each invite a friend may help to reduce conflicts.

Walks with children have their special requirements, but also their own benefits. For the children, walking gives training in self-reliance and group responsibility. Families can be active together, at a cost any family can afford. For parents, there's the opportunity to know their children better, from that magic time when young eyes and tiny hands begin to discover the world.

The best times to hike Long Island are spring and fall, when the large summer crowds at major resorts along the shoreline have retired to their urban habitats. During these periods, there are beautiful sunsets, the moorlands of the South Fork are more inviting in their solitude, and the weather is temperate to cool. If you do hike in the summer, it is best to start early and finish by noon.

7
Fire Island-Sunken Forest

Distance	1.5 miles
Hiking time	1 hour
Rating	Easy

The Sunken Forest is a unique and fascinating natural area: a 250-year-old American holly forest located within the Fire Island National Seashore. It is a cool, moist, and fragrant environment—an enchanting contrast to the sun, sand, and salt water of the nearby beach. From the ferry landing at Sailors Haven, one walks on boardwalks through juniper, oak, pine, sour gum, red maple, and sassafras. The dunes are covered with bearberry and American beach grass; small areas of marshland are tucked in among the thickets. Along the way, there are breathtaking views of the ocean and Great South Bay. For information, call the Fire Island National Seashore Park Headquarters at (631) 289-4810 or the visitors center in Sailors Haven (May to October) at (631) 597-6183.

Sunken Forest offers an easy walk that should be taken quietly and unhurriedly, so that the sights, sounds, and smells of the forest and ocean can be enjoyed. Spring and late summer through early fall are good times to go: these seasons are quieter, less frantic, with fewer boats and people. Migrating waterfowl spotted on land and sea these times of year provide another incentive. You may find that you will return to this sanctuary often, to refresh the spirit and enjoy the beach in all its seasons, moods, and colors.

The entire walk takes about an hour; afterward, there's sunning and swimming on Fire Island's uncrowded beaches of wonderful fine white sand.

When you return to the mainland, you may want to visit Sayville, one village in this part of Long Island where the downtown shopping area has not been made obsolete by nearby shopping centers. There are places to eat, antique and craft shops, clothing stores, florists, and a superb bookstore. Most of the shops are on or near Main Street (Montauk Highway).

The Sayville area was once occupied by the Secatogues. In 1697, the land was given to William Nicholls by King William III of England. The first tenant of what is now Sayville village was John Edwards, who built a house here in 1761. The oldest house still standing was built in 1785 and is now a museum and the home of the Sayville Historical Society.

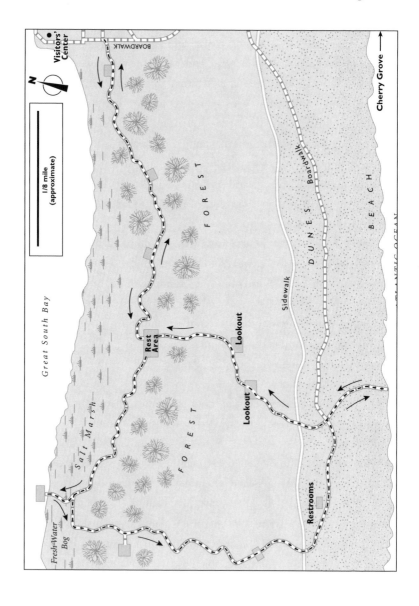

Located at the corner of Edwards and Collins Streets, you will pass it on your way to or from the ferry. During the summer, the museum is open on Thursday afternoons; it is open on the first and third Sunday of each month during the rest of the year.

Directions   Fire Island and Sunken Forest are easy to reach by public transport. From New York City and western Long Island, take the Long Island Rail Road to Sayville, then a taxi to the ferry terminal on River Road, from which the ferry goes to Sailors Haven. The trip from Penn Station takes approximately an hour and a half.

If you have time and feel ambitious, you can walk the mile from the station through the old village of Sayville to the ferry. Walk south from the station on Lakeland Avenue (also called Railroad Avenue). Cross Main Street (Montauk Highway) and continue south on the same street you were on, which is now called Gillette Avenue. When this street ends at the T, turn left on Edwards Street to Foster Avenue, where you turn right. At the intersection of Foster Avenue with Terry Street there is a Fire Island Ferry sign. Follow the sign directing you left on Terry Street to River Road. Turn right here. The ferry terminal is on the left and the parking lot is on the right, across the street.

By car, the distance from the George Washington Bridge to Sayville is 55 miles. Take Exit 59 south on the Long Island Expressway. Go south on Ocean Avenue, bear left on Lakeland Avenue (Route 93), crossing Veterans Highway, Sunrise Highway, and the Long Island Rail Road tracks. From there, the directions are the same as those above for walkers. (There is a fee for both the ferry and for parking.)

The 30-minute ferry ride from Sayville to Sailors Haven on Fire Island runs on a frequent summer schedule, less frequently from May through October. For current ferry information, telephone (631) 589-8980. When you purchase your ticket, make sure you get a schedule so that you can plan your return trip.

As the ferry approaches Fire Island, this barrier beach stretches east and west before you. Well over a dozen communities dot its 32-mile length. Most of them can be reached by ferry from Bay Shore, Sayville, or Patchogue. The National Seashore has acquired nearly 20 miles of oceanfront. Three have been developed: Smith Point West, Watch Hill, and Sailors Haven. In addition, there are county parks, including Smith Point County Park at the eastern end of the island and a state park, Robert Moses State Park, at the western end of the island.

Fire Island is a barrier island, the terminal moraine of the last ice sheet to cover the east 10,000 years ago. Its beaches boast fine white sand, mostly quartz, but also containing bits of garnet, tourmaline, and magnetite. A row of primary dunes faces the sea side of the island, with an inland set of secondary dunes of varying height. At one point, these secondary dunes are quite high and thus afford vegetation greater protection from the salt spray, or "aerosol," that otherwise limits the vertical height of native flora. This is the area known as Sunken Forest. (The salt "aerosol" is blown from the Atlantic across the island by the predominant winds—typically from the southwest—more so during the seasons of growth. In a sense, the phenomenon can be considered "salt spray pruning.") The 250-year-old forest is predominantly American holly, service berry, pitch pine, red maple, and tupelo (sour gum), with an understory of cat briar and herbaceous plants that vary with the seasons. Highbush blueberry is common on the edges of the forest.

Currents and waves formed sand bars, which eventually joined to create a continuous stretch of sand. This constantly shifting environment is where land accumulation and erosion occur simultaneously. When storms tear at the island, dunes are eroded and sand is blown and washed away. Some years, entire houses are lost to the sea. In winter the beach is narrow, as the sand washes offshore to form a bar. In summer the beaches widen again as sand returns. The width of Fire Island varies with these changes, ranging from a quarter of a mile to a few hundred feet.

At Sailors Haven, there is a boat marina, with docks and boardwalks. At a snack bar/small store one may purchase food, souvenirs, tanning lotions, Fire Island guides, and newspapers. The visitors center and small museum is open only from July 4th to Labor Day. Stop here to obtain *Exploring the Sunken Forest*, which describes a self-guided nature walk of the Sunken Forest. Markers along the trail correspond to numbered descriptions in the booklet.

The Walk   As you leave the visitors center, the entrance to the nature trail is in front of you. To protect yourself and the environment, stay on the boardwalk. Poison ivy (with its three shiny leaves that are red in autumn, green in spring and summer) grows everywhere. Along the first portion of the trail you will be introduced to many of the plants of the area. Consult the free booklet for explanations. By the time you have learned to recognize them, you will have reached the loop portion of the trail, where the interrelationships between the environment and its life forms are presented.

The forest in many places seems impenetrable, although some erosion is visible. Much of this erosion was caused by foot traffic before the boardwalk was built. Although you may not see them, many animals live in the forest. During the warm season the air is alive with the call of birds, including catbirds, warblers, towhees, and brown thrashers.

Migrating waterfowl are an added attraction during the spring and fall migration peaks: mergansers, scoters, buffleheads, northern gannets, ruddy ducks, coots, etc., are to be found in the Great South Bay as well as on the Atlantic. Overhead, seasonal hawks can be frequently spotted as well. White tailed deer abound in the forest, and occasional weasel, opossum, rabbits, red fox, and mice can be sighted. Many varieties of butterflies are found during the summer months. The black racer snake, two turtle species (the eastern box turtle and the spotted turtle), and Fowler's toads are also in evidence for the quiet observer.

Holly trees of great age and size grow here. Notice how the trunks and limbs of many of the trees are twisted and contorted, mute testimony to the harshness of the natural environment. Near the boardwalk also grow sassafras trees, with their deeply ridged reddish-brown bark and leaves with one, two, or three lobes.

Benches are found in many places along the boardwalk. When you come to a large rest area, turn right and take the exit leading toward the bay. Do not take the path immediately ahead on your left that leads to the beach. You will be returning on this path later. The boardwalk passes through a salt marsh, where tall phragmites reeds grow. Go straight ahead to the platform on the Great South Bay. If it isn't foggy, you can see Long Island from here. Continue along the boardwalk as it turns left. The boardwalk now passes over a fresh-water bog, where cattails

Photo by Don Burmeister ©1999

rustle dryly in the breeze. Then it reenters the forest, passing another rest area on the right.

Follow the boardwalk straight ahead. Shortly it leaves the forest and enters the beach area. Take the cement walk (note the restrooms at the 90-degree bend here) until you reach a boardwalk that stretches from forest to ocean. Turn right to go over the dunes and head to the beach. When ready, return on the boardwalk and continue straight ahead past the cement walk to the forest. Go up the stairs and stop at the lookouts over the sand dunes to observe the line of dunes that protects the forest from the harsh salty wind and makes its existence possible. Notice the low, thick patches of bearberry growing on the dunes. Bearberry, an evergreen, has white flowers in the spring, red berries in the fall. Salt in the air kills nearly everything that attempts to grow higher. One exception is the red cedar, a species highly resistant to the salt concentration.

Standing here, with the sea breeze, the intricate and delicate forest flowing away from the dunes, and the vast ocean beyond, is sufficient to make the trip worthwhile.

Continue on the boardwalk and you will soon return to the rest area, at which you took the exit to go to the bay. Here there is a large stand of old holly trees, one of which was found to be 190 years old. Cross the rest area and take the path on your right. You will now be retracing your steps to return to the beginning of the hike.

(A short walk to the right (west) along the beach would bring you to Point O' Woods. This is an old and dignified community of uniformly brown-shingled homes, where signs of wealth are evident. It is a contrast to Cherry Grove, to the east of Sailors Haven, which has its own unique liberated flavor.)

The ferry back to Sayville leaves from the visitors center where you arrived. You may want to relax, beachcomb, swim, and wade. If you swim, stay between the flags, where lifeguards are stationed during the season.

8

Connetquot River State Park Preserve

Distance	4.5 miles
Hiking time	3 hours
Rating	Easy

Connetquot River State Park Preserve is an oasis hemmed in on all sides by some of Long Island's major highways. It is a preserve, meaning that there are no ball fields, playgrounds, or picnic tables. It covers almost 3,700 acres of land, making it the largest park on the island. The intent is to leave the land as it was and limit its use to walking, horseback riding, and fishing. It is a haven for trout fishermen, as the state maintains a hatchery on the property, from which it feeds fish into the preserve's many ponds and streams.

In the mid-18th century, the land in this vicinity was part of William Nicholls' Islip Grange. His 51,000-acre tract was the largest manor on Long Island. Nicholls purchased his first land from Chief Winnequaheagh of the Connetquots in 1683. Near the park entrance on the right is a gristmill that dates from the mid-1700s. The narrow road running past the mill is the original South Country Road. It was laid out in 1733 and for many years was the only east-west road on the south shore. An important stagecoach route, it was traveled by George Washington on his historic tour of Long Island in 1790.

The main building of this complex was originally an inn, built in 1820 by Eliphalet Snedicor. The area was renowned for its hunting and fishing, and in 1866 a group of wealthy men purchased the inn and surrounding acreage and formed the South Side Sportsmen's Club. Many members, including W.K. Vanderbilt, Commodore F.G. Bourne, and W. Bayard Cutting, built opulent estates along the Great South Bay. The club used, maintained, and protected the land for over 100 years. Then the state purchased it and in 1973 opened the Connetquot River State Park Preserve to the public.

The preserve includes part of Long Island's famous pine barrens. The terrain is flat and sandy, and mostly filled with low- and highbush huckleberry and blueberry; tiny wintergreen grows under stands of pitch pine and oak. The pitch pine is especially suited to this dry, sandy terrain. Forest fires are common in the pine barrens. Oaks and most other trees are usually killed by fire, but most pitch pines survive because of their

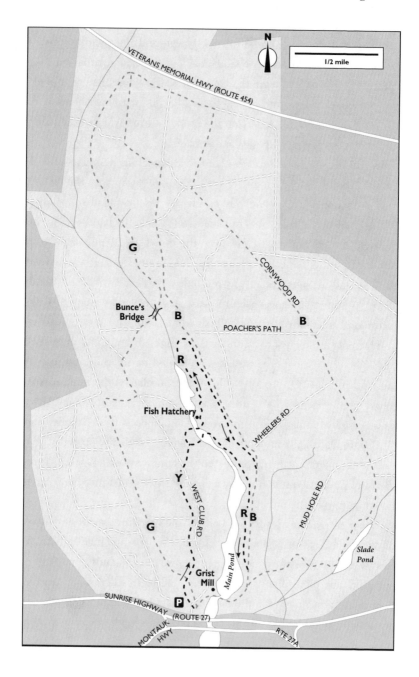

thick bark. In fact, fire is the only thing that will open some pitch pine cones and allow them to release their seeds.

It is interesting to think of the people who lived in these woods centuries ago. Long Island Native Americans stayed along rivers like the Connetquot during the cold winter months and moved to the shore to fish and clam during the summer. The tribes of Long Island were renowned for their wampum, money carved from the abundant clam and whelk shells of the south shore. One translation of Paumanouk, a Native American name for Long Island, is "Isle of Tribute." Whenever fierce tribes from the mainland threatened war, the peace-loving Native Americans of Long Island were able to buy them off with payments of their beautiful wampum.

Access to the preserve is by permit and reservation, which means that a day before the hike you simply call (516) 581-1005 and give your name and the number of people in the party. [There is a modest entrance fee.] When crowded, entrance to the park may be limited to the people who have made advance reservations. At other times, it appears that no list is consulted and visitors are admitted after paying the fee. The preserve is open year-round, Wednesdays through Sundays, 8am to 4:30pm; it is also open on Tuesdays from April 1 through September 15. The trails are open until sunset, but the administrative buildings close at 4:30pm. On occasion the preserve has been shut for extended periods because of tick and other insect invasions, so call ahead for current information. Pick up the free map of the trails at the entrance booth.

Directions   The preserve is easily reached from anywhere on Long Island and New York City. It is 50 miles east of the George Washington Bridge, a drive of about an hour via the Southern State Parkway. Get off at Exit 44 of the Southern State and continue east on Sunrise Highway (Route 27). Take the Pond Road exit, continue to the overpass, cross

over to the westbound lanes and find the park entrance after a short
distance on the right. Be alert for the big sign to the entrance of the preserve. There is a large parking lot next to the tollbooth.

Most of those coming from points west using public transportation
will be taking the Long Island Rail Road to the Great River station on
the Montauk Line. From the station, walk north on Connetquot Avenue,
cross over Route 27 on the bridge, turn right, and walk along Route 27
to the entrance to the park. The distance from the station is about
1.5 miles.

The Walk   There are several trails starting to the left and right of the
gristmill. This hike will proceed on the yellow trail north to the hatchery and then onto a dirt path along a pond to Bunces Bridge; the return
will be along the red and blue trails.

Pick up the yellow trail by turning left on a paved road as you go
north from the parking lot. Go past the historical buildings to the end of
the road, where the stables are. Watch for deer, which seem quite un-
afraid of quiet walkers. There are also chipmunks, wild turkeys, ospreys,
great blue herons, egrets, and a variety of hawks. Even bald eagles have
been spotted in the park, as have winter wrens, brown creepers, wood
ducks, and nesting bluebirds.

At the end of the road, the yellow trail goes north, to the right. A
green trail heads off to the left. Proceed on the yellow trail, which soon
leaves the paved road to become a path full of wood chips. A paved road
(West Club Road) will appear on the right and parallel the yellow trail
for a distance. You will see many white blazes in all parts of the preserve.
These blazes indicate a through trail that does not appear on the maps
given out at the tollbooth, and day hikers should not go on this trail.
(There is, however, one short segment of this walk where you are asked
to use the white-blazed trail.) You will also see signs to bird sanctuaries,

which you are warned not to enter. You will sometimes cross open fields or fire lanes that are cut across the preserve to contain fires that may break out.

About a half-hour into the hike, cross the road to your right and continue on the yellow-blazed trail to the fish hatchery. There are rest rooms here next to a parking lot. The hatcheries are off to the right. Watch for the trout that thrive in this clean, cool river. Fish are hatched and grown here, and then released to the Connetquot and Nissequogue Rivers for the enjoyment of those, both human and avian, who fish. With luck, you should be able to spot ospreys or herons fishing nearby. The foliage in this vicinity becomes more diverse because of its proximity to the Connetquot River. It is especially beautiful in late September and October, when cinnamon ferns, swamp maples, and blueberry and huckleberry bushes turn to gorgeous shades of red and gold.

The yellow trail ends at the hatchery. Now take the white-blazed path going north that closely parallels the pond but does not abut it. There is a small path along the brook and wooden platforms from which people who are fishing can cast their lines. Continue on the white-blazed trail until you come to a large grassy area crossed by a green-blazed trail. This is the same green trail you encountered at the start of the hike. Turn right onto the green trail and continue to Bunces Bridge, named for the man who built the original bridge. Cross the bridge over the Connetquot River. This river is almost entirely spring-fed groundwater and is well protected by the surrounding parkland. It is considered by many to be the cleanest river along the eastern seaboard.

From Bunces Bridge, the green trail goes to your left and a blue trail heads to the right. Beyond the bridge, these trails do not offer much of interest. The green trail, which is really a bridle path all the way, goes toward the northern part of the preserve and ends at the fence alongside Veterans Memorial Highway. It is difficult to walk on because

Photo by L. Cuomo

the sand has been unsettled by the trod of horses. The entire blue trail (here, Brook Road) makes a complete, 8.4-mile loop of the preserve, going up to the Veterans Memorial Highway and returning to the parking lot; the better half of it is south of Bunces Bridge. Often the blazing is intermittent and confusing. Consult the map and stay alert.

Turn right at Bunces Bridge onto the blue trail and follow it south. You will soon come to an intersection with the red trail, which, at this point, forms a U turn. Turn right onto the red trail; follow it along the east side of the brook to the fish hatchery and the parking lot. If you are visiting the preserve in late April, you may to fortunate to see a profusion of wood anemones and marsh marigolds. (If you stay on the blue trail, which the red trail will join after the U turn, you will also return to the parking lot.) The main pond will be off to your right, and as you walk around the southern part of it, you will pass the gristmill on your left. The parking lot will now be in sight.

9
Caumsett State Park

Distance	7 miles
Hiking time	4 hours
Rating	Moderate

I solated on the Lloyd Neck peninsula, Caumsett State Park encompasses the 1,500-acre former estate of Marshall Field III. Here one can observe shore birds at the salt marsh, enjoy a grand view of Long Island Sound from the mansion, or ramble along miles of trails through pastoral scenery or along the beach. The walk described here is about seven miles long and covers the circumference of the park; shorter walks are easily fashioned from the many trails that wind through the center of the park. Cross-country skiers use the park's trails during the winter. The park also offers, by advance registration, a variety of special guided programs. The majority of the trails are level and smooth; the main loop from the parking area to the mansion is paved.

The park is open from 8am to 4:30pm daily. A limited number of fishing permits are available by advance registration; applications may be secured at any state park. Dogs are not permitted. For further information, call (516) 423-1770. When you arrive at the entrance booth for the parking area, ask for the free map of the park.

Not far from Caumsett are several other points of interest. Consider exploring the nearby Target Rock National Refuge. Target Rock, which like Caumsett occupies a former estate, lies two miles east on Lloyd Harbor Road. The name is derived from a 14-foot boulder that rests on the beach. The rock reportedly served as a target for British gunnery practice during the Revolutionary War. Admission is free, but a permit must be obtained from the Refuge Manager at Target Rock Road, Lloyd Neck, Huntington, NY 11743, or phone (516) 271-2409.

In terms of wildlife, plant life, terrain, and walking trails, Target Rock Refuge is a smaller version of Caumsett. The best times to visit are the spring, when the formal azalea gardens are in bloom, and the winter, when rafts of waterfowl wait on Huntington Bay for warmer weather, sometimes in such great numbers that the floating ducks appear to form a solid black cover. Harbor seals have been sighted occasionally in the area.

For those interested in early American history and architecture, a visit to two nearby pre-Revolutionary homes of the Lloyd family might be worthwhile. The Henry Lloyd Manor House, known as the Salt Box and

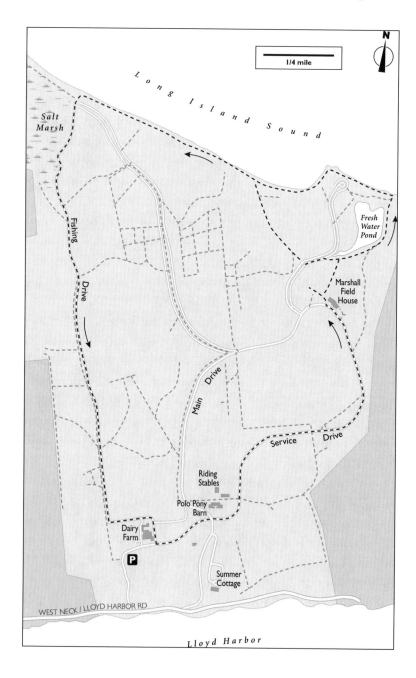

built in 1711, was restored by the Lloyd Harbor Historical Society in 1978. The house is open during the summer. The Joseph Lloyd Manor, built in 1766, is owned and operated by the Society for the Preservation of Long Island Antiquities. The home, overlooking the harbor, was also owned by Jupiter Hammon, the first published black poet in America. The home is open from 1 to 5pm, Saturdays and Sundays between Memorial Day and Columbus Day. A modest fee is charged for admission.

Directions   If you are using public transportation, take the Long Island Rail Road from Penn Station to Huntington. At the station, taxis are available for the long (eight miles) and expensive trip to the park. Don't forget to arrange for the return trip with the driver. A public telephone is available at the dairy complex adjacent to the parking area.

If you are coming by car, the park is 45 miles from the George Washington Bridge. Take the Long Island Expressway to Exit 49N. Continue north for several miles on Route 110, across Route 25, to Huntington. Turn left on Main Street (Route 25A), go three blocks, and turn right on West Neck Road. Follow West Neck Road onto Lloyd Harbor Road to the park entrance. A fee is charged for entrance and parking from Memorial to Labor Day. Street parking is not allowed on the roads outside the park.

The Walk   The walk begins on the paved driveway that leads to the mansion (east initially). Notice the large gray buildings on your left; rest rooms and a public telephone are available on the far side of the complex. These buildings housed the dairy operations on the estate during Mr. Field's residence. In addition to providing for its own dairy needs, the estate supplied its own meat, vegetables, water, and electricity.

In 0.33 mile from the entrance booth, the paved road crosses another paved road. Continue straight ahead toward the grassy meadows. The large brick building on your left, with a fountain near the junction, is the polo pony barn; it is often mistaken for the mansion itself.

In the summer, the meadows behind the barn are alive with the aerial acrobatics of barn swallows as they catch insects just above the ground. The flat, expansive terrain lacks any hint of proximity to a major city. The air is clean; except for the park's pickup trucks, an exquisite silence prevails. Soon the road nears a wooded area, which in spring is carpeted with daffodils. Rhododendrons signal the approach to the mansion.

Stay on the paved road until you reach the mansion, about 1.5 miles from the entrance booth. Ignore the few side dirt paths coming in from the right. The mansion was built around 1925 and is in excellent condition. It has been leased to the Queens College Center for Environmental Teaching and Research. Visitors are not allowed in any of its 65 rooms, but they may enjoy its gardens.

Step around to the rear of the buildings and enjoy a view, spectacular if the weather is clear, of Long Island Sound and the Connecticut shoreline eight miles away. The lawn slopes gently from a stone balustrade toward a freshwater pond below; this is a fine spot to stop for a few minutes. You may want to see what remains of a once beautiful formal garden west of the building. Walk across the grass on the left side of the mansion as you face it. Go up to the large iron gates, turn right to a small foot path around the gates. Look down at the garden. It must have been beautiful at one time, but is now overgrown with weeds.

As you walk back from the garden ruins toward the mansion, look for a path that starts just to the left of the end of the stone balustrade. This is the entrance to a rustic rock garden. The stone steps here lead down past masses of yew and laurel to the freshwater pond.

At the pond you may see turtles basking in the sun. The trail circles around the east side of the pond and comes quite suddenly to the beach. One moment you are in a deciduous forest with woodland birds; the next, you are standing on a sandy beach listening to gulls and waves lapping at the shore. Here on the north shore the contrast is more dramatic than it is on the south shore, where one gets a sense of the ocean for miles before actually arriving at the beach.

As you turn west (left) along the beach, you will pass boulders that were carried here by glaciers from areas far away. The variety of their colors and textures invites speculation as to their exact origin.

Continue west 0.5 mile to the cliffs, which border the beach. They rise higher toward the west and are easily the most spectacular natural feature of the park. They are easily eroded and climbing them is not advised. The cliffs tower a hundred feet above the beach and are white to red in color. Water oozes out in places, washing wet clay down and across the beach in intricate patterns. Scoop up some wet clay and feel its fine texture. Let the water run out of it until it is malleable, then shape it with your fingers. With a little imagination, you can see how clay has provided creative inspiration to artisans through the ages.

To the west, beyond the cliffs, is a salt marsh. The area is a bird sanctuary for snowy egrets and an occasional great blue heron. A sandspit stretches into Long Island Sound on the other side of the sanctuary. If you wish to go out and explore it, a boardwalk bridges the softer areas of the marsh. Prickly-pear cactus can be seen here.

The return road to the parking lot can be found at the northeast corner of the marsh, at a small parking lot reserved for people with fishing permits. Two roads lead back to the park entrance from here; the road perpendicular to the beach is the most direct.

The woods along the road are rich in bird life. Among the species you are likely to see are the rufous-sided towhee, brown thrasher, brown creeper, chipping sparrow, and several varieties of woodpecker. A great gray owl, a rare bird normally found in northern Canada, has made ornithological history by appearing in Caumsett Park and its environs. The red fox also inhabits this area. By walking quietly, you will greatly increase your chances of seeing wildlife. Continue south until the dairy complex appears on your left. The parking lot lies just beyond the complex.

10

Muttontown Preserve

Distance	1.5 miles
Hiking time	1 hour
Rating	Easy

*T*he Muttontown Preserve contains 550 acres of fields and woodlands and 10 miles of walking trails. These trails are marked with color-coded posts set in the ground. The general public may enter without permit or fee to ramble these trails from 9:30am to 4:30pm daily. Some of the trails are also used by horseback riders. The preserve is a facility of the Nassau County Department of Recreation and Parks; the phone number of the preserve office is (516) 571-8500.

The land of the preserve, including a large section south of Muttontown Road that is closed to walkers, was purchased by the county from the estate of Landsell Christie, with smaller parcels coming from the Hammond and McKay families. The 50-acre parcel containing the nature walk was a donation of Mrs. Alexandra McKay, whose chateau and elegantly landscaped estate are visible behind the fence from the green trail. The Nassau Department of Recreation and Parks opened this section to the public in March 1970.

After you've taken the circuit of marked trails, you may want to explore further. The section south of the fence consists of fields, with rolling hills to the south. Originally the area was farmed, as nearby land still is. The open fields and the water pipes, troughs, and farm implements still in evidence bear testimony to the land's former use. A dairy farm was active here in the early 1920s. Before then, sheep were raised; local people say that Muttontown got its name from the sheep that farmers herded from here to Syosset.

This southern section of the preserve also contains the vandalized ruins of the house once owned by the exiled king of Albania, Ahmed Bey Zogu, who ruled as King Zog from 1928 to 1946. He was driven from his country by Mussolini in 1939 and died in Cannes, France, in 1961. He never lived on the property, and Nassau County purchased it in 1968. Some ruins overgrown with vegetation are the only remains.

In the northeastern corner of the preserve is a short, steep climb up High Point. High Point is a glacial kame, or mound, some 50 feet above

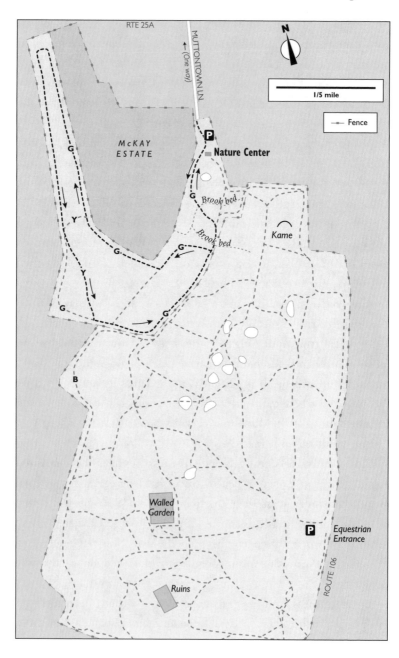

RTE 25A

N

MUTTONTOWN LN

↑ (One way)

1/5 mile

●—● Fence

P

McKAY
ESTATE

■ **Nature Center**

G

G

Y

G   G

Brook bed

Brook bed

Kame

G   G

Y

G   G

B

Walled
Garden

P

Equestrian
Entrance

ROUTE 106

Ruins

the surrounding fields. Unfortunately, its significance is geologic rather than scenic; the view from the top is blocked by heavy foliage. Nearby, a kettle pond is the site of the only persimmon trees in the preserve. The woodlands generally are dominated by oak, black birch, and Norway spruce, with thickets of blueberry, maple-leaf viburnum, brier, and mountain laurel. Hawks, owls, woodpeckers, raccoons, opossums, rabbits, and foxes reside here throughout the year. This section of the park is particularly rewarding for the nondirected walker. Rather than setting up a strict itinerary of sights and stops, the visitor can stroll, ready to change course should a tempting goal present itself. It is possible to wander off course in the preserve but difficult to get truly lost, since walking in any direction brings one before long to the wire fence on the perimeter.

The preserve is uncrowded at all seasons, except when school children on organized outings visit the nature center on weekdays, or when Boy Scout troops are camping in the fields. Parking can sometimes be difficult, but spaces usually open up before too long. Littering, picnicking, and flora gathering are prohibited. Picnickers are allowed to use the lawn behind the nature center, where there are toilet and waste-disposal facilities.

The preserve hosts other activities besides walking. In winter, cross-country skiing has been permitted. The Nassau Hiking and Outdoor Club schedules events here in orienteering, a form of cross-country time trial that tests endurance and map and compass skills.

Year-round activities at Muttontown include star-gazing; birding; and guided foliage, geology, and night walks. The most popular activity is birding. The quiet here attracts a variety of species—over 150 species annually. Past sightings are listed inside the nature center.

One can enjoy a scenic circuit hike in the northwestern part of the preserve, which is mainly level and wooded. After heavy rains, though, some trails may become rutted and muddy. The nature center offers a self-guiding map to the trails, which have lettered stations for nature observation. The recommended walk will be on the self-guided green trail and will take about an hour. **Note:** The preserve's map does not show the full length of the green trail.

Directions   Public transportation is available via the Long Island Rail Road to Syosset station. From the station, the experienced walker can walk (1.75 miles) and the less ambitious can complete the trip by taxi. The Syosset Taxi Company can be reached at (516) 624-8075. Arrange with the cab driver for the return trip; or phone from the preserve office, if open, or from the nearby International House of Pancakes on Route 25A north of the preserve (opposite Muttontown Lane).

If walking from the station to the preserve, go north on Jackson Avenue to Muttontown Road and then head west on the road past Route 106 to the preserve. Enter at the first equestrian gate past the intersection, 1.75 miles from the Syosset depot, on the north side of Muttontown Road. From here, using a compass, head north toward the nature center and the start of the walk. Note that Muttontown Road, on the south side of the preserve, is not the same as Muttontown Lane, the short street between the preserve and Route 25A.

By car, the preserve is 30 miles from the George Washington Bridge. Use Exit 41N from the Long Island Expressway or Exit 35N from the Northern State Parkway. Here, Route 106 (Jericho-Oyster Bay Road) goes north 4.3 miles to Route 25A (North Hempstead Turnpike). Be sure to stay right at the fork on Route 106 at 0.8 mile past the expressway. Soon the undeveloped expanse of the preserve will be seen on the left. Look for Walnut Avenue just past the north end of the preserve and turn left (west) onto it. A block later, turn left (south) onto Muttontown Lane to the preserve. The turn onto Walnut Avenue comes up just two blocks before Route 25A. Anyone reaching Route 25A should turn around and then turn right onto Walnut Avenue (or Vernon Avenue or Locust Avenue). A small and sometimes crowded parking lot is located within the grounds of the preserve.

The Walk   From the nature center, walk south on the green trail, a broad path marked by posts, past a shallow man-made pond that sometimes dries up during droughts. Frogs and turtles can be seen here, and the preserve staff claims to have seen red-backed salamanders. In less than 0.25 mile, the path approaches the iron fence that runs through the preserve. Turn here to the right, still on the green trail. You are now walking southwest.

Past a brook bed, the green trail skirts an overgrown field on the right and reaches an intersection 0.25 mile from the starting point. Turn right and for 500 feet follow the green trail as it meanders along the west side of the field. The trail makes an abrupt turn to the right and goes down a short slope and up to another fence. It shortly veers away from the fence and into a thicket. But the path parallels the fence, with the Chelsea estate on the other side. The Chelsea estate is now the property of Nassau County.

Soon the fence and then the trail turn north. Here the trail enters the cool and quiet stand of eastern white pine and larch. At the fallen tree trunk polished by time and resting walkers, a post indicates a yellow trail leading west. This trail rejoins the green trail as it returns from its most northern point. This is the path that the nature center's staff recommends using to return to the center. For the full walk, stay on the green trail [(not shown on the map)] and continue north. Avoid the shiny leaves of poison ivy and enjoy a soft, fragrant passage on a floor of pine

Photo by L. Cuomo

needles. Watch for chickadees and grosbeaks, here to feed on the cone seeds.

In 0.75 mile from the starting point, the trail nears Route 25A. It curves west and uphill to overlook the road, then continues around to the south. In 0.25 mile it passes a yellow-blazed post, the other end of the loop cutoff that began near the polished tree trunk. Watch now for a second yellow-marked post a few feet farther down the green trail. Follow the yellow trail here along a heavily wooded short-cut. When you meet the green trail again, follow it along the boundary fence, where bobwhites and their chicks have been seen.

You are now in a section of the preserve that horseback riders like to use, so be ready to step aside. Soon there is an opening in the preserve fence. This leads to many interesting but mostly unmarked trails in the larger part of the preserve to the south of the fence.

Continue on the green trail, going east about 200 feet to a left turn in the green trail. Listen for the croak of pheasants in the fields and look for warblers feeding on berries in shrubs and saplings. Before long you pass a familiar brook bed and can turn left on the final as well as the first leg of the circuit, past the man-made pond to the nature center for a round trip of a little more than 1.5 miles.

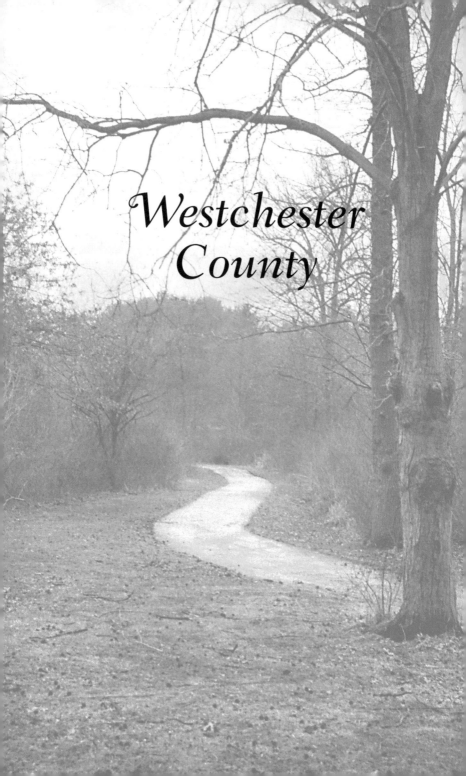

Westchester
County

WESTCHESTER COUNTY
The Works of Man

For the walker, Westchester County is a better place to live than to visit. The southern part of the county, roughly the area below the Cross Westchester Expressway, has ample public transportation, but the northern section has the large parks. The county nearest to New York City and metropolitan New Jersey has no large natural area as good for walking as Van Cortlandt Park. Worse, such areas as do exist often require that the visitor pay a much higher entrance fee than the local resident. Perhaps the most attractive park in the county, Ward Pound Ridge Reservation, has no access via public transit and is farther from the metropolitan area than Harriman State Park.

This frustrating state of affairs is partly a result of the political tension between the city and the county. By keeping parks small and restricting their usage, county officials can keep out the masses from the city. But in justice to Westchester politics, the main factor at work is geography.

It is geography that has shaped the works of man here. Unlike Rockland and Putnam Counties, with their rugged mountains and twisting valleys, Westchester's terrain is lower, with long ridges and straight valleys that lead directly to New York City. These valleys required only technology and economic demand to become high-volume transportation corridors.

Technology arrived in the 1840s; the railroads quickly and permanently shaped the land and the patterns of its use. When New York City finally reached its present boundaries by 1900, the railroads were ready to open Westchester up to new thousands. The automobile not only strengthened ongoing development, but also further inhibited the establishment of parks. In the 1890s, the great incentive for the establishment of such parks as Van Cortlandt and Pelham Bay was the fact that large recreational preserves had to be created where people lived. With the advent of the automobile, the citizen could hop in his car and head for Harriman or the distant Catskills for walking and recreational pleasure.

As the suburbs spread out along the river valleys, golf courses took over most of the remaining natural areas of the ridges. Thus ended any lingering dream of a large park to preserve the deep woods and clear streams that Henry Hudson found.

But if the works of man have altered much in Westchester, much remains to offer enjoyment and challenges to both the rugged hiker and the casual walker. Many of the preserves and parks make for fine "hit-and-run" family walking: drive up, visit a favorite antique or specialty shop, walk for an hour or two, drop by a farm stand, and head back home. Not for the hiking purist, perhaps, but a very workable approach to recreation.

In recent years more exciting walking opportunities have been developed in the county. The Rockefeller State Park Preserve—donated by the family to the state in 1983—is the jewel in the county crown. Its trails offer something for everybody and it is well laid out, with a scenic lake in its midst. In 1995 the new Camp Smith Trail in the northern part of the county was inaugurated by the New York-New Jersey Trail Conference (see hike description in the Hudson Highlands chapter). The Mianus River Gorge Preserve, which continues to expand, may be a pocket-size park, but it packs a wallop. It is unsurpassed in the concentration of its beauty.

If the works of man have taken away natural environments in Westchester, they also have given in return. The Old Croton Aqueduct and the Bronx River Parkway are both created environments, each as artificial as Riverside Park. Just the same, each offers an enjoyable walking experience. As a hiker once wrote, "There are only a few places in this or any metropolitan area where a person can go out and walk. Just walk, not worrying about roots and rocks and climbs, but building something physical until the sweat breaks through and the muscles fall into a natural rhythm that leaves the miles behind." The parkway walk is prettier, but the aqueduct is quieter—without the rush of traffic. While much of the parkway trail is little used, the aqueduct is a social experience, with joggers and bicyclists, gardeners, and dog walkers sharing the trailway.

II

Bronx River
Pathway

Distance	5 miles or 3.6 miles
Hiking time	2.5 hours or 2 hours
Rating	Easy

The Bronx River Pathway is located within the Bronx River Reservation, an 800-acre linear park created as an adjunct to the Bronx River Parkway that was opened in 1925. The reservation extends 13.2 miles into Westchester along a narrow strip of land from New York City to the Kensico Dam Plaza in Valhalla.

As presently developed, the pathway consists of three distinct segments: a 1-mile "loop" in Mount Vernon, a 3.6-mile section between Bronxville and Scarsdale, and a 5-mile section from Hartsdale to the Kensico Dam Plaza in Valhalla. A map of these routes can be obtained by writing to the Department of Parks, Recreation and Conservation, 25 Moore Avenue, Mount Kisco, NY 10549, or by calling (914) 242-PARK. During warm weather months, a portion of the Bronx River Parkway, from Scarsdale Road to the County Center, is closed to vehicular traffic and open only to cyclists from 10am–2pm on Sundays. These "noiseless" Sunday periods are good times to walk the adjacent pathway.

Hikes on the Bronx River Pathway can be of varying lengths since the trail runs alongside the Harlem Division of the Metro-North Railroad, with stations every few miles. The trail is generally flat from beginning to end and poses no difficulties beyond endurance. The pathway is best savored by taking it in small bites. There are no blazes but signs are posted.

Valhalla to Hartsdale   This hike will cover the northern part of the pathway, starting at Valhalla and walking south to Hartsdale. The walk does not offer a wilderness experience, but it is an ideal choice for those who want a pleasant, relatively level walk convenient to public transportation. It also works well for those carrying, wheeling, or walking with very young children.

Directions   The train ride to Valhalla from Grand Central Station takes about 45 minutes. From the Valhalla station, walk south to the old station (abandoned in the early 1980s and redeveloped as a restaurant, with an ancient wooden railroad car and a caboose attached). Cross over

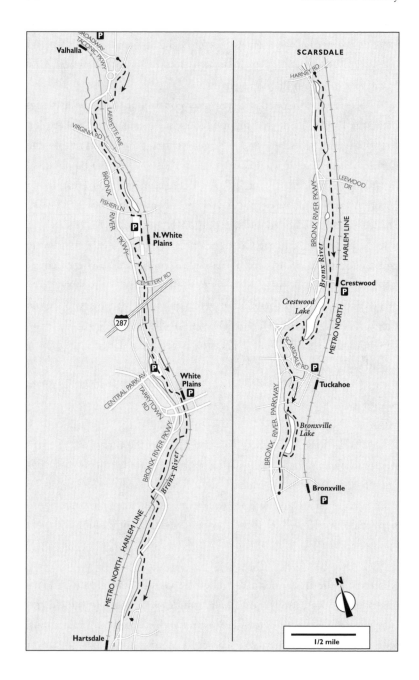

Valhalla

Broadway
Taconic Pkwy

Lafayette Ave

Virginia Rd

Bronx River Pkwy

Fisher Ln

N. White
Plains

Cemetery Rd

287

Central Park Av

Tarrytown Rd

White
Plains

Bronx River Pkwy

Bronx River

Metro North Harlem Line

Hartsdale

SCARSDALE

Harney Rd

Bronx River Pkwy

Leewood Dr

Harlem Line

Bronx River

Crestwood

Crestwood
Lake

Metro North

Scarsdale Rd

Tuckahoe

Bronxville
Lake

Bronx River Parkway

Bronxville

N

1/2 mile

the Bronx River Parkway at the traffic light and head for Broadway, the village's main street. Turn right onto Broadway and continue along this street until you see the Holy Name of Jesus Church. Just beyond the church parking lot, take the faint path that heads off to the left, through balsam woods, to the Kensico Dam Plaza.

By car, the start of the hike at the Kensico Dam Plaza is about 20 miles from the George Washington Bridge. The Bronx River Parkway takes you right to it. When you see the dam, follow the sign that says Broadway/Kensico Plaza. There is a large parking lot at the dam. A per-vehicle fee is charged, with a discount for seniors.

Kensico to Hartsdale The plaza is a huge grassy area, with the dam loom-ing overhead to the left. Walk across the plaza, with the parkway on the right and the dam on the left. When you have reached the opposite side, turn right and continue across the parkway. On your left are concrete stairs that will take you to the top of the dam. There you will see a sign marking the Bronx River Reservation. This is the beginning of the north-ern end of the Bronx River Pathway. It is a wide asphalt path at this point, but narrows to four or five feet at places, particularly after White Plains. Motorized vehicles are not allowed, but bicycles are permitted and often speed by. As with all multi-use trails, you need to stay alert.

The path initially turns left, runs parallel to the parkway, then goes under an overpass and turns right; a baseball field is to the left. Soon the trail crosses the first viaduct over the railroad tracks. A plaque in the stonework of the viaduct gives details of the park's construction. The first street beyond the viaduct is Virginia Street. Here the history-minded walker can take a short detour to the left toward North White Plains and the Miller House, used as a temporary headquarters by Washington during the Battle of White Plains in 1776. The farmhouse is open from 10am to 4pm, Wednesday through Sunday, and admission is free.

After 1 mile on the path, you will reach an unexpected interruption. The route goes between a pond and a marshy area and ends at Fisher Lane. Ahead is a knoll. Don't try to shortcut across the knoll; the far side is solid with poison ivy. Instead, turn left and go toward the narrow railroad underpass, passing a parking lot entrance on the right. Just after the parking lot entrance, turn right onto the asphalt pavement that runs between the parking lot guard rail and the foot of the railroad embankment. This walkway passes the North White Plains station. The path turns right, away from a pedestrian tunnel under the tracks. Cross the service road and continue through a park-like meadow. (Incidentally, you may choose to start the walk here in North White Plains, to take advantage of the more frequent weekday train service.)

Soon the trail goes through another meadow and passes under the cavernous, steel-and-concrete bridge of the Cross Westchester Expressway. In another few minutes, the pathway reaches the parking lot of the Westchester County Center. You can go straight through the parking lot and pick up the trail at the opposite end, but it is more pleasant to follow the paved road that runs along the base of the railroad embankment to your left. Return to the path when it reappears to the right. When you reach a pedestrian underpass beneath the railroad, stay on the path as it curves to the left—don't go through the underpass—and then turn right, parallel to the railroad.

You are now at the White Plains train station. Continue along the west side of the railroad station, cross Hamilton Avenue, and walk along the platform of the former bus station. After crossing Main Street, the path continues along the left side of a Bronx River Parkway exit ramp. You will soon cross the Bronx River and continue along a narrow right of way between the river on the left and the parkway on the right.

At the south end of Chatterton Hill, an arched viaduct carries the parkway over the valley, the river, the trail, and the railroad. About 100

The hillside above the parkway here—Chatterton Hill—is the site of an important Revolutionary War battlefield. Early in the war, Washington retreated to this hillside from New York City with the British at his heels. The British were determined to gain control of the Hudson Valley and its important waterway in order to split the northern and southern colonies. To stop their progress north, Washington stretched a defensive line across Westchester as far as a millpond near Silver Lake. His inexperienced forces could not hold the line against the superior English and Hessian veterans, however, and the American army retreated again, to Miller Hill and then to North Castle. Eventually, Washington crossed to the New Jersey side and then crossed the Delaware River to consolidate his dwindling forces.

feet past the viaduct, a footbridge crosses the river. The path goes under the tracks, slants up the hill, and continues to run between the parkway (now to the left) and the river. The trail continues through the woods, on a bluff perhaps 20 feet above the river, which is rocky and fast flowing at this point. The railroad tracks are on the other side of the river. The trail finally comes down to the river's edge, and then it and the river pass under the highway. With the highway to the west, the trail again rises above the river; with houses visible to the left. Soon the valley widens, and the trail goes down to river level once more. After passing a small dam, near which a bench has been conveniently placed, the river curves back under the highway as the trail turns away from it and cuts behind the tennis courts of the private County Tennis Club of Westchester.

Beyond the tennis courts, the trail passes a small pond and soon reaches Brook Lane. Here the walk ends, since there is no improved

Photo by Don Burmeister ©2000

path for the next two miles to the Scarsdale station. Turn right and cross the bridge over the parkway. It leads directly to the Hartsdale railroad station, where you can get a train to Grand Central or back to Valhalla.

Scarsdale to Bronxville   The section of the Bronx River Pathway from Scarsdale to Bronxville provides a little more variation in scenery and, as an added attraction, has two small scenic lakes.

Directions   Do not take a car because parking in Scarsdale is restricted to permit holders, except on Sundays. The train from Grand Central Station is recommended.

The Walk   With the brochure available from Westchester's Department of Parks, this hike should pose no difficulties once you get to the trail. It is not possible to lose one's way, since the entire length of the trail is adjacent to the river, the railroad, or the Bronx River Parkway.

To get to the trailhead from the railroad station, cross over to the southbound platform on the pedestrian bridge, then descend the stairs to a small parking area. Follow the access road (Depot Place) to Popham Road, cross it, and continue straight on Garth Road. About 150 yards south of Popham Road, on Garth Road, a dirt path angles off behind the first stores on the right side of the street. Follow this path, which soon widens [and is lined with] benches. Apartment houses rise to the left. To the right, the ground drops off into a thicket, with the Bronx River occasionally visible through the foliage.

In about 0.5 mile, the path begins to run along the grassy shoulder of the parkway. The shoulder soon narrows, and, for a short distance, you have to walk along a rather narrow strip on the side of the parkway. Just before getting to Harney Road, where the Bronx River Pathway resumes its course southward, you will pass a pond on the right that is a year-round home for ducks and Canada geese. The pathway begins on the other side of Harney Road and leads without interruption to Tuckahoe. The hike ends at Palmer Road, where you turn left (east) to get to the nearby Bronxville railroad station. The trip back to Grand Central takes only about half an hour. You should be able to walk this section of the Bronx River Pathway in about two hours.

12

Old Croton Aqueduct

Distance (southern route)	10.4 miles
Hiking time	5.5 hours
Distance (northern route)	12.7 miles
Hiking time	6.5 hours
Rating	Easy

The Old Croton Aqueduct trail has long been a favorite trail for year-round easy walking. The pathway traverses pristine woodlands and meadowlands, estates, abandoned farms, and suburban as well as urban areas. Along its route, the aqueduct passes many fine examples of architecture styles found throughout the Hudson Valley. Designated a National Historic Landmark in 1992, the aqueduct offers splendid views of the Hudson River and the Palisades, which the path parallels for much of its route.

Unlike today's superhighways and industrial complexes, which often obliterate whatever stands in their way, the great engineering projects of the mid-19th century—the railroads, canals, and aqueducts—left their natural surroundings largely intact. The area crossed by the Old Croton Aqueduct has retained much of the bucolic atmosphere that prevailed before its construction. Dogwood, mountain laurel, and other shrubs are in full bloom along the trail in the spring, and in summer blackberries abound. The wooded portions include hemlock, pine, oak, birch, Norway maple, black cherry, mulberry, ash, and sassafras. Among the birds observed in the vicinity of the aqueduct are cardinals, red-winged blackbirds, robins, blue jays, crows, pheasants, and Canada geese. The alert walker may spot rabbits, woodchucks, deer, raccoons, and even an occasional badger.

The two hikes described here both use Tarrytown as the starting point. The first hike heads south from Tarrytown to Yonkers; the second leads north to the New Croton Reservoir. Each hike makes a nice day trip, and the especially energetic walker might be able to combine both for a strenuous, 23-mile hike. An informative free trail map is available by sending a self-addressed stamped envelope to Historic Site Manager, Old Croton Aqueduct State Historic Park, 15 Walnut Street, Dobbs Ferry, NY 10522. In addition, a deluxe, full-color map is available for $5.25 from the same address and is strongly recommended.

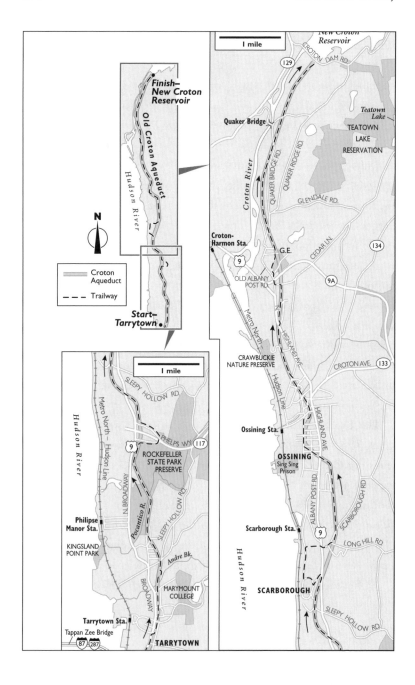

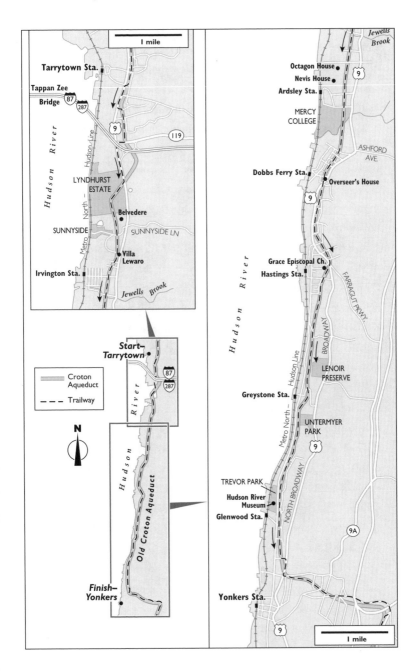

Construction of the old Croton Aqueduct was first discussed in the early 1830s, when the 280,000 residents of New York City still obtained their water from local springs and wells. A cholera epidemic in 1832 and a disastrous fire in 1835 led to increased awareness of the need for a more adequate water supply. Among the many sites considered, only the Croton River, located in the northern wilds of Westchester County, was found to be sufficient in quantity and quality to serve the needs of New York City.

This was not the first proposed solution to New York City's water problem, however. As early as 1797 the city started considering plans for an improved water supply and decided that it needed to be a municipal system, since a private corporation would profit at the expense of the city. A bill was submitted to the state legislature in Albany that proposed using public funding to build pipes to the Bronx River. Aaron Burr used his considerable political influence to get a new bill introduced, which then created his private corporation, the Manhattan Water Company. Soon residents discovered that Burr's true intent was to create a banking institution; their water needs were unmet by the woefully inadequate supply from the well that was drilled at Reade and Center Streets. Poor quality water traveled from the well through wooden pipes that headed toward only the more profitable neighborhoods. More than one-third of the city still had no water supply. The company even neglected to install fire hydrants, forcing the city to complete the essential task. The cholera epidemic of 1832 forced the city to find a real solution to its water problem.

Work was begun on the Croton Aqueduct in 1837 and completed in 1842. It was immediately hailed as one of the great engineering projects of its time. Like so many early major construction projects of this sort, it was built primarily by immigrant Irish laborers, paid 75 cents to a dollar a day for 10 hours of work. The total cost of the aqueduct, including land acquisition, was $12,500,000. The aqueduct was enclosed in a masonry structure running through ridges and valleys and over rivers;

the Croton River itself had to be tamed behind a dam before any water could be delivered to the city. Gravity fed (based on principles used in Roman times), the aqueduct dropped 13 inches per mile. Starting at the Croton Dam a little south of Peekskill, the aqueduct extended 33 miles to the High Bridge on the Harlem River, from where the water used to flow into the Yorkville Reservoir (now the Great Lawn in Central Park). From there, it went to the Murray Hill Reservoir (now Bryant Park on 42nd Street).

Although the Old Croton Aqueduct was capable of conveying as much as 100 million gallons of water a day, the phenomenal growth of New York City eventually made it obsolete. A new Croton Aqueduct, with three times the capacity, was constructed between 1885 and 1893; no trail was included in that project. When this water source also proved inadequate, it was supplemented by the Catskill aqueduct system, built between 1907 and 1917, which more than doubled the city's water supply.

Leaky and expensive to maintain, the Old Croton Aqueduct was taken out of service to New York City in 1955, although it continued to supply water to some suburban communities until 1965, when the head gates on the Old Croton were closed. (Interestingly, in 1988, the northernmost section of the aqueduct was reopened to bring water to Ossining.) In 1968, at the urging of the New York-New Jersey Trail Conference and other outdoor groups, New York State purchased both the aqueduct itself and the land on top of it in Westchester (the average width of the strip is 66 feet) from the New York City Bureau of Water Supply.

Directions The most singular feature of this trail is its proximity to an active rail commuter line—the Hudson Line of the Metro-North Railroad. This extremely scenic rail line, which often parallels the aqueduct, offers hourly service to and from Grand Central Terminal (with service every half-hour to the major stations: Yonkers, Tarrytown, and Ossining). Of course, this makes the hike convenient for those who depend on public transportation. But even those who drive to the trail can take advantage of the nearby rail line by parking their car near a station at one end of the hike, following the aqueduct for as long as they choose, and then taking the train back to the starting point. (Note that parking at many of the stations is free on weekends, but many station parking lots are by permit only and many downtown streets are metered.) Be sure to pick up a copy of the train schedule at Grand Central, or you may call the Metro-North number listed at the back of this book from one of the pay phones located in any of the towns near which you will walk. Strategic spots of the trail north of Tarrytown have been blazed with yellow disks (Taconic Region Markers), and in several locations where the hiker must leave the aqueduct right-of-way and follow city streets, the yellow disks have been placed on telephone poles.

Tarrytown to Yonkers   Those walkers arriving at the Tarrytown railroad station and wanting to walk south on the aqueduct should make their way to Route 9 (Broadway) by heading east up Franklin Street. Turn right (south) onto Route 9 and continue straight ahead, soon passing an entrance to the Tappan Zee Bridge. (The entrance is for automobiles only—walkers are not permitted on the bridge.) You will shortly come to the Tarrytown Hilton. (If you arrived by car, you might be able to obtain permission to park here; otherwise, those coming by car should park on a side street, since parking is not permitted on Route 9.) South of the Hilton, you will pass the large General Foods Technical Center. A few hundred yards further, there is an opening in the stone wall on the west side of the road, and the trail continues to the right down a dirt path. (The total distance walked from Tarrytown Station is about 1 mile.) This section digresses from the path of the aqueduct because of the obstruction of the NYS Thruway.

Here, the aqueduct trail heads through the Lyndhurst estate. You can see the American Gothic revival castle designed by Andrew Jackson Davis, though it is partially obscured by the huge beech trees shading the lawn. This was formerly owned by railroad tycoon and financier Jay Gould. It now belongs to the National Trust for Historic Preservation, which has opened the estate to the public. Please do not wander off the aqueduct path unless you pay the required fee to visit the estate.

From Lyndhurst, the aqueduct is easily followed all the way to Yonkers. Every mile or so, the pathway passes the chimney-like white stone towers that once served as ventilators and pressure equalizers. Less frequently, large square structures known as waste weirs are encountered. These contain large metal gates that were lowered to regulate the flow of water or cut it off completely so that maintenance could be undertaken "downstream." Excess waste water was diverted via spillways into adjacent "kills"—the Dutch word for streams.

South of Lyndhurst, you will pass the high stone walls of Belvedere. The French manor-style mansion—its slate roof is partially visible from the trail—is now occupied by the Holy Spirit Association for the Unification of World Christianity. The trail soon crosses Sunnyside Lane. Down the hill to the right is Sunnyside, the home of 19th-century author Washington Irving. This charming cottage, described by its creator as being "as full of angles and corners as a cocked hat," is an engrossing assemblage of gables, a tower, and weather vanes, with gardens all around. The house and gardens are open to the public for a fee.

About 0.25 mile after Sunnyside, you will pass Villa Leward on your left. This beautiful neoclassical mansion was built in 1917 and was named by Enrico Caruso. It was owned by Sarah J. Walker, an African-American who made a fortune from her extremely successful hair straightening formula and became America's first self-made woman millionaire.

A little farther south the trail passes through the town of Irvington. Just beyond the town, the aqueduct runs 60 feet above the valley on an embankment over Jewells Brook far below. The trail soon passes two architecturally significant houses, both located to the west of the trail.

The flamboyant Armour-Stiner House, or Octagon House, is an ornate structure topped by an enormous dome. The house was originally built in 1860 and was remodeled and expanded to four stories in 1872 in the then-popular French Second Empire style. Its exterior has been restored to its original hue—shocking pink. Within 0.25 mile of Octagon House stands a stately columned mansion, set back a ways from the aqueduct. Called Nevis, it was built by Alexander Hamilton's son in 1835 and is now Columbia University's primary center for the study of high-energy particles and nuclear physics.

The aqueduct crosses the campus of Mercy College, a liberal arts college. Continuing south, the trail passes the Overseer's House—temporary headquarters for Old Croton Aqueduct State Historic Park. The handsome Italianate structure dates from the 1840s and is currently under restoration. State Parks and the Friends of the Old Croton Aqueduct have begun turning the structure into an interpretive center. The nearby barn was built in the 1880s. Shortly, after Walnut Street, the trail crosses to the east side of Route 9. The train station in Dobbs Ferry can be reached by turning right on any of the small streets before crossing Route 9 and then turning left on Main Street.

In Hastings-on-Hudson, the trail passes a large park and then a five-corner intersection. Cross Route 9 and continue on the path, which is next to the driveway of Grace Episcopal Church and marked with a park sign. The trail soon passes an abandoned quarry, which has subsequently been used as a village dump. On the east side of the aqueduct, a short path leads to the Lenoir Preserve, a wildlife sanctuary with a self-guided nature trail.

At Greystone, the trail crosses Odell Avenue. Within 0.5 mile it passes the gates, guarded by marble lions, and the former caretaker's house of the old Untermyer estate. The grounds are certainly worth exploring if you have the time. The estate house was demolished years ago to build the nearby hospital, but the gardens have been partially restored. The main garden, which is far up the hill from the classical colonnade that can be seen from the trail, is one of the most significant in the country in the Beaux Arts style. It has some 40 fountains, enormous tile mosaics, and in spring, masses of blooming flowers. The gardens are open to the public and no admission is charged. The upper part of this unique park is used for weddings and concerts in the summer, but the bulk of the former estate needs attention. The city of Yonkers has begun rehabilitating parkland along the river, which will offer excellent views of the Palisades and connect with the Aqueduct trail via a reopened carriage road from the estate to Warburton Avenue.

Beyond the Untermyer estate, the trail passes a stone weir and then comes to a road, Shonnard Terrace. The nearby railroad station is Glenwood, also located near the site of Trevor Park and the Hudson

River Museum, well worth a visit. To reach the museum, turn right and continue a short distance to Warburton Avenue. Turn left and head toward the museum, in a restored Victorian mansion called Glenview, built in 1876. Glenview has been operated as a museum since 1924. A modern addition was built in the mid-1960s and houses exhibits on contemporary art, a planetarium, library, many Hudson River School paintings, and a museum shop.

To get to the railroad station, backtrack along Warburton Avenue and turn right on Glenwood Avenue. Located directly across from the station is the former Con Edison power plant. Even in its dilapidated state it is an impressive structure, with its Tudor touches and its breathtaking riverfront location.

Those continuing on the trail will come to a school parking lot at Lamartine Avenue in Yonkers. The hike ends there. Though the trail continues southeast, the areas through which it passes are increasingly urbanized and heavy with traffic.

The walker can choose to return by bus or train to New York City. A bus runs along Warburton Avenue, west of the aqueduct, and terminates at the 242nd Street subway station at Van Cortlandt Park. To get to the Yonkers railroad station, head west on Lamartine and south on Warburton Avenue and then west on Main Street to the station.

Tarrytown-North   The trailway north of Tarrytown should also interest hikers and Revolutionary War history buffs. It is a longer walk—more than 11 miles—although perhaps more picturesque than the lower half just described. It can be hiked in small pieces, like the southern half, because there are railroad stations only a few miles apart on this segment also.

Those arriving by train at Tarrytown should follow Main Street east from the station and up to South Broadway (Route 9). After crossing

South Broadway, turn left, then right on Hamilton Place. The trail is 100 yards east.

You will soon cross Andre Brook on a high embankment and reach the spacious grounds of Sleepy Hollow High School, 1 mile from the train station. The school has a breezeway on top of the aqueduct, so you will have to detour around the building. Turn right and climb the steps at the southeast corner of the building; turn left, then go north once more, walking through a parking lot between a ball field on the right and a wooded strip (the actual aqueduct route) on the left. At the north end of the parking lot, go around the gate to Bedford Avenue. (Those who are driving may choose to begin the hike at this point.)

Cross Bedford Avenue and continue along a grassy embankment. After passing a stone ventilator and crossing Gorey Brook Road, the trail enters a beautiful wooded section. To the right, the land is part of the Rockefeller State Park Preserve. Soon you will come to the burying ground of the old Dutch Reformed Church, which is the final resting place for many of the people on whom Washington Irving reputedly based his characters. The church itself, and the nearby Phillipsburg Manor (across Route 9) are worth a visit because of their historical significance. After passing the cemetery, the aqueduct curves to the left and crosses the Pocantico River on a 0.25-mile long embankment, dressed and buttressed with stone rip-rap, towering 85 feet above the stream. This is near the spot where, according to the Washington Irving legend, the headless horseman frightened Ichabod Crane. A stone weir is located just beyond the embankment.

In another 0.75 mile, the aqueduct route is interrupted by the limited-access Route 117. This road was built after the aqueduct was taken out of service and is one of only two places north of the city line where the conduit of the aqueduct has been interrupted. Here, the trail goes east along Route 117, turns left and crosses the highway on a steel bridge, then turns left again until it finally regains the aqueduct route. The trail is bordered for most of the way by high fences, so it is not hard to follow. Upon reaching the aqueduct, it bears right and soon passes another ventilator at 2.5 miles.

Shortly after the ventilator, the trail bears left (the narrow path straight ahead is a horse trail) and crosses Route 9 on a steel bridge. This road, also known as the Albany Post Road, predates the aqueduct, so when the aqueduct was constructed, it passed over the road on a stone-arch bridge. (The few houses in the vicinity were, in consequence, known as Archville.) In those pre-automobile days it was considered sufficient to construct an arch just wide enough for a single carriage to pass through. But when traffic began to increase, the arch became inadequate. In 1926 it was removed, and an inverted siphon was constructed so that the aqueduct could pass under the road. In 1997, 30 years after the establishment of the trail as a state park, a new bridge was constructed at a cost of $1.2 million. At the west end of the bridge, plaques have been installed in a monument on the right commemorating key events in the bridge's history. About 100 yards beyond, a carriage road on the left leads down into Rockwood Hall and continues along a stream to wonderful views over the Hudson River.

The trail continues through a pleasant stretch of woodland walking. After crossing Country Club Lane, it once more goes through some backyards and passes another ventilator. It reaches River Road opposite a school. Here, the aqueduct crosses under Route 9 and to avoid an unpleasant walk on this busy highway, the trail turns left and follows River Road. It turns right on Creighton Avenue, then right once more on River Road. This stretch of road walking is an interesting change of pace, with beautiful views of the river to the left. The trail turns right on Scarborough Station Road, which it follows back to Route 9. (If you wish to shorten the hike, continue straight ahead instead of turning right, and you'll soon arrive at the Scarborough Metro-North station, where hourly trains will take you back to Tarrytown.)

When you reach Route 9, you will notice a large church on the opposite side of the road. Cross the road, bear right, then immediately turn left onto Scarborough Road. Continue for two blocks, then turn right on Long Hill Road. You will see the aqueduct route crossing the road here; turn left and follow the wide aqueduct path. After crossing Scarborough Road again, the aqueduct enters a pleasant wooded section, continuing across an embankment and passing another ventilator. Tall apartment buildings soon appear to the left, after which the aqueduct curves sharply to the left, passes through a parking lot, and reaches Highland Avenue (Route 9) in Ossining (6.75 miles).

Cross the road and continue through a town park. The aqueduct cuts diagonally through the park, but walkers will probably find it easier to follow the paved path that goes along the edge. Cross the intersection of Washington and Edward Streets and go through the park, with a paved path following straight along the aqueduct route, then turn right onto Spring Street. You will notice a stone ventilator on the school grounds to the right. This one is particularly interesting because it is inscribed with the name of the contractor who built this section of the aqueduct and the date of the construction. Proceed ahead on Spring Street. Between Broad and Waller Avenues, you will see the aqueduct route leaving to the right (note the unusual triangular-shaped building that occupies the narrow space between the aqueduct and Spring Street at the corner of Waller Avenue). This section of the aqueduct has been closed and fenced at the request of local authorities, so one must continue ahead to Maple Place. Turn right here and then left, regaining the route of the aqueduct, which is a landscaped path, and reach Main Street. There are many stores along the street, most with historic facades, and the walker may wish to stop for refreshments.

After crossing Main Street, you will notice an interpretive sign to the left of the trail. You are approaching the famous Double Arch across the Sing Sing Kill—one arch carries the aqueduct; another, below, carries Broadway over the kill. (Just before the arches, you will see a path leading to the right. Take a short detour here to visit the Ossining Heritage Area Visitor Center, in the hollow to the east of the arches. It contains exhibits on the construction of the aqueduct and the Ossining Correctional Facility, commonly known as Sing Sing.) Cross the arch bridge. (It is known as the "double arch" because underneath the one carrying the aqueduct is another arch that carries Broadway over the river. The aqueduct structure contains two more arches elsewhere; one, only seven feet high, was constructed to allow an adjacent land owner to cross from his house on one side to his fields on the other.) Just beyond the double arch is a stone weir, built in 1882. The weir is one of several improvements added to the aqueduct years after its initial construction. When the aqueduct was started in 1837, the country was in the midst of a deep depression. As a result, the project was built as economically as possible.

The trail route now crosses a street and climbs a flight of steps (7.9 miles). There are several more street crossings in quick succession. The walker will notice some brick ruins to the left of the right-of-way, most likely the remains of an old root cellar. Those wishing to return to Tarrytown by train will probably want to turn left on Snowden Avenue and follow it to Water Street, which leads to Main Street and the Ossining Metro-North station (0.5 mile). Trains for Tarrytown leave every half-hour. (The next station, Croton-Harmon, can be reached only by walking along Route 9, which is unpleasant, dangerous, and not recommended.)

Those who wish to continue farther along the trail will soon come upon another stone structure in the center of the route. The purpose of this stone building, which looks somewhat like a weir, is unknown.

After crossing Beach Road, the Kane Mansion, constructed about 1843, is just to the left of the aqueduct. As you walk through the grounds of the Engelhard Corporation, the Hudson River comes into view on your left. The trail then crosses Route 9 (North Highland Avenue) for the last time. The trail crosses Piping Rock Drive and descends an embankment, at the base of which is a ventilator. At the next intersection, Ogden Road, it turns left then right onto Old Albany Post Road.

Just before the trail crosses under Route 9A, look for the Parker Bale American Legion Post on the left. This building, formerly a one-room schoolhouse for Crotonville, was the scene of the first public meeting of the Hudson River Fisherman's Association, which led the drive to restore clean water to the Hudson River.

The trail then follows the fence around the General Electric Management Institute and soon rejoins the aqueduct route. For the next 2.4 miles, the trail is completely rural. It ends at the New Croton Dam, where parking is available at the east end of the dam. There is a seasonal parking fee if cars are left below the dam in Croton Gorge Park. Those who wish to cover the section north of Ossining should plan to leave a second car at the dam, since there is no public transportation at this end of the trail, unless you plan for an expensive cab ride to either the Croton-Harmon or Ossining stations.

If you have spare energy you may use the Briarcliff-Peekskill Trailway and walk to Teatown Lake Reservation (1.9 miles) or Blue Mountain Reservation (4 miles.) To get to Teatown Lake from the end of the aqueduct trail, make a right along Croton Dam Road and follow the path blazed with green diamonds. To get to Blue Mountain Reservation, you will need to leave the park, exit onto Route 129, and head north.

13
Mianus River Gorge

Distance	5 miles
Hiking time	3.5 hours
Rating	Easy

About 35 miles northeast of the George Washington Bridge, the Mianus River Gorge Wildlife Refuge and Botanical Preserve is a peaceful, friendly, enticing retreat. Rich in historical background, geological formations, mineral deposits, and flora and fauna, it is a naturalist's preserve. The refuge grew from its original 60 acres, purchased in 1959, to 719 acres in 2000 and is still being expanded. It includes a stretch of the Mianus River, the steep-sided gorge cut by the river, a 20-acre stand of virgin hemlocks over 300 years old, a five-mile trail system discretely marked, several outstanding views, a waterfall cascading over variegated rock formations, and an intriguing patchwork pattern of old fieldstone fences reminiscent of a bygone farming era.

The Mianus Gorge Conservation Committee was founded in 1953 to ensure "the preservation of the virgin forest and abundant wildlife along the Mianus River in Bedford, New Castle, and Pound Ridge, New York." In 1964, the gorge was registered as the nation's first Natural History Landmark by the U.S. Department of the Interior, a testimonial to the committee's success in meeting its objective. The gorge was also the first preserve affiliated with The Nature Conservancy.

The gorge is open only between April 1 and November 30, from 8:30am to 5:00pm. Entrance is strictly forbidden at all other times. Between those dates visitors can savor a place resplendent with spring flowering, fall coloring, and shady summer warmth. The entrance area is the only place to eat, either in your car or on the grassy rim surrounding the parking lot, as picnicking in the preserve is not allowed in the interests of cleanliness. Also, dogs and trail bikes are not permitted. Water is available from a pump and there are composting toilets at the far end of the parking area.

Directions   Direct public transportation to the preserve is not available, but there is regular Metro-North service on the Harlem Line to Bedford Hills, six miles from the preserve. Taxis to the gorge are available.

By car from the metropolitan area, take the Hutchinson River Parkway north and onto the Merritt Parkway. Get off at Exit 34, Long Ridge

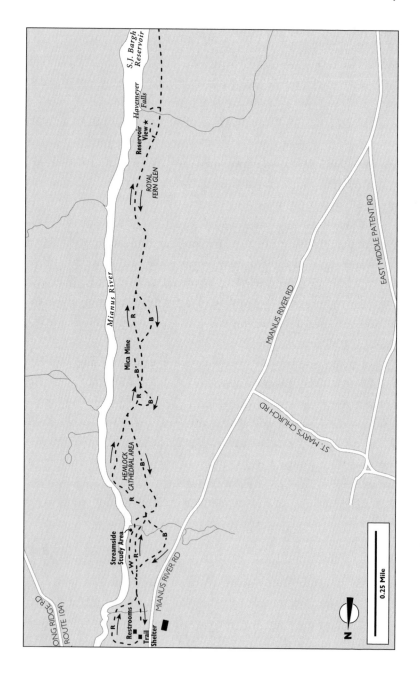

S.J. Bargh Reservoir

Havemeyer Falls

Reservoir View ★

ROYAL FERN GLEN

Mianus River

R

B

Mica Mine

B

R

B

HEMLOCK CATHEDRAL AREA

R

B

Streamside Study Area

W

R

B

R

Restrooms

Trail

Shelter

LONG RIDGE RD ROUTE (104)

MIANUS RIVER RD

ST. MARYS CHURCH RD

MIANUS RIVER RD

EAST MIDDLE PATENT RD

0.25 Mile

N

Road, and go left toward Bedford. Continue on this road for 7.7 miles to Millers Mill Road. Turn sharply left and go over the bridge to Mianus River Road, a dirt road on the left. Make a left turn and go 0.7 mile to the entrance; the parking area is on the left. Parking is free.

For an alternative route, take Interstate 684 from where it leaves the Hutchinson River Parkway near White Plains. Get off at Route 172 (Exit 4) and take a right to Bedford Village. Turn left at the traffic light, going north on Route 22; take the right fork at a grassy triangle onto Pound Ridge Road just before the business district of the village. Soon after, turn right at the gas station onto Long Ridge Road. Turn right again at the first right, Millers Mill Road, making the left turn just past the bridge and proceeding on the dirt road to the gorge parking area.

Walks The gorge is user friendly in that it is almost impossible to lose your way or fail to return to the starting point. You are bound between the river below and the road above. Only a genius of misdirection could stray from the well-trod paths. The maximum round trip is about five miles, so if your pace is leisurely, with rest stops, sights to see, and nature to absorb, allow about three and a half hours at most for the traverse and return.

At the trail shelter, pick up the brochure and trail map describing the gorge and showing you what to see and where to go to see it. The trails are generally smooth, well delineated, and well maintained, with the main trails marked in one direction. The Brink of Gorge Trail (red-blazed) is the outgoing trail to the end of the preserve at the S.J Bargh Reservoir, and the Fringe of Forest Trail (blue-blazed) is the return path—a roundtrip distance of five miles. At times they run together. The first portion of the red trail is handicapped-accessible to a bench overlooking the river.

There are three short side trails. Bank of River Trail (green-blazed) goes down to the river to the Streamside Study Area. There are hills,

Photo by Don Burmeister ©1999

roots, and rocks but no exhausting obstacles. The hemlock forest is a glory of peace and solitude. The tread is soft, and the gurgling of the river below is seductive music that emphasizes the stillness of the hemlock forest.

Another side trail goes to Hobby Hill Quarry, the remains of a mica mine. Mica is a brilliantly shiny material, shown in the photo below, once popular as insulation for high-grade radio components. Through the years, the flat pieces of loose mica have gradually wandered away; half the shimmering material is now gone. Please do not accelerate its disappearance.

The third side trail goes to Havemeyer Falls. During rainy season, water rushes down the precipitous hillside, cascading noisily over multifaceted and mossy rock formations. The trail to the river and reservoir edge is short and steep. Step carefully and avoid embedded stones and roots; watch out for wet and slippery leaves and roots.

The Mianus River Gorge Wildlife Refuge and Botanical Preserve is a major repository of flora, fauna, habitats, geology, and history. Photogenic and scenic, it is relaxing, peaceful, and stimulating.

Photo by Don Burmeister ©1999

14
Ward Pound Ridge Reservation

Distance	3.7 miles
Hiking time	2.5 hours
Rating	Easy to moderate

*T*he Native Americans called the river Peppenegheck (Cross River). Along its shores stood stone weirs, stretched with nets of woven dogbane fiber and deer sinew. Algonquin of the Mohegan nation and members of the Tankiteke tribe traveled its slow waters in birch-bark canoes. At night they slept in bark and reed shelters, cushioned on mats of evergreen needles. The land was rich in deer and other game.

Today, the fields through which the Cross River meanders are within the boundaries of Ward Pound Ridge Reservation, a 4,700-acre preserve, 40 miles northeast of the George Washington Bridge. The reservation's rolling hills look out on grassy meadowlands, with tree-lined slopes and lakes beyond. Over 35 miles of marked trails thread through the park. There are also facilities for cross-country skiing, horseback riding, sledding, and snowmobiling, although restrictions apply in some cases. Overnight permits for the 24 shelters in the park can be obtained at the superintendent's office or by calling the reservation at least two weeks in advance. The stone and timber shelters, each with a sleeping capacity of eight, are equipped with fireplaces and picnic tables. No tent or trailer camping is permitted in the reservation.

The Trailside Nature Museum, located on Boutonville Road just before the Bergfield Picnic Area, features exhibits on various aspects of Westchester's history and the reservation itself. Educational programs are offered by the museum, which is open Wednesday to Sunday from 9am to 5pm. (The reservation is open daily from 8am to dusk.) A schedule of events is available by writing to the Ward Pound Ridge Reservation, Cross River, New York 10518, or calling (914) 763-3493.

The museum is also the home of the Delaware Indian Resource Center, a library dealing with native North American culture. The area was under Native American control until 1640, only 135 years before the Revolutionary War, and several trails offer the opportunity to study the reservation's rich Native American lore. Reminders of those times are the Bare Rock petroglyphs, ancient rock drawings in the southwest part of the park on the Dancing Rock Trail. Another is in the name of the reservation itself. At the park's southern boundary, near a ridge by Raven

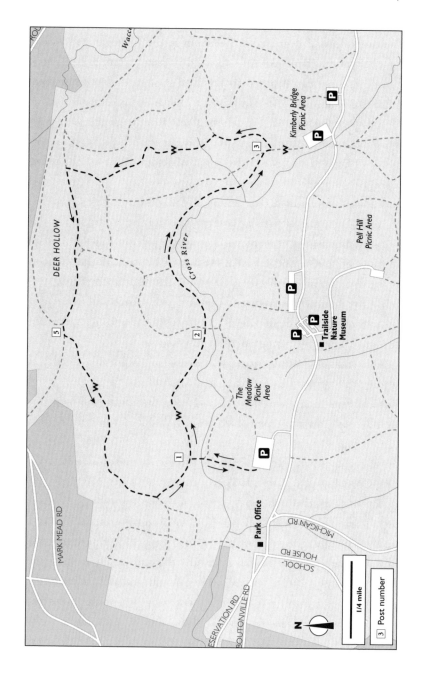

Rocks, is a natural trap. The Native Americans constructed an enclosure, or pound, here. Parties of hunters, whooping and crying, would drive their prey from the surrounding areas into the pound, while other hunters kept the animals from escaping. The "Ward" part of the name comes from William "Boss" Ward, a Westchester political power for 40 years, who fought for the establishment of the reservation.

The hike described below will be along the white-blazed trail in the northern part of the reservation. It is a loop of 3.7 miles. Like all loop hikes, one can always turn around and retrace one's steps, early in the hike. The hike starts from the parking lot at the Meadow Picnic Area, which is the first left turn on the road leading straight ahead from the tollbooth. The white-blazed trail can also be accessed or exited from several other points along the way.

This recreational sampler includes nature, culture, geology, and history that Ward Pound Ridge's lush woods and rolling hillsides provide to the solitary walker, families, and groups. Pack your enthusiasm along with a picnic lunch and come prepared for a fresh and invigorating day in the outdoors. Nature lovers and photographers should be sure to bring along field guides and cameras. The hike is along woods roads that allow hikers to walk 2–3 abreast, except in the areas with boardwalks.

Directions   Although not fully accessible by mass transit, the reservation is easily reached by car from the White Plains side of Westchester County. It is possible to take Metro-North to Katonah, and take a taxi 4.5 miles to the reservation. You may either make return arrangements with the cab driver, or call for the return trip from the park office, but be sure to do so before 5pm.

Drivers should take the Saw Mill River Parkway or I-684 to Katonah. At the junction with Route 35, turn right. Go east to the junction with Route 121 and turn right, The park entrance is on the left, just over the bridge. There is a seasonal entrance fee. Be sure to ask for the map of the park when you pay or pick one up at the Nature Museum. Rest rooms are located at the park entrance and parking lots.

The Walk   Start in the northwest end of the Meadows Picnic Area parking lot, where there is a water fountain, and follow a path through an open field into the woods. On a spring day, the open field is dotted with blue flag and hawkweed, daisies, and forget-me-nots. The air is alive with butterflies, grasshoppers, and birds. The trail enters a shrub area, which can be swampy in spring and summer and muddy in winter. After a heavy rain, it can also be filled with water.

At the first bridge over the Cross River, stop a while and, as the shallow waters ripple and babble over smoothed stones, reflect on how it was when the Native Americans fished here. Parallel stone walls with trees line the route following the bridge. The white-blazed trail starts across from the bridge. Along the route, there are numbered markers to identify places on the map. The first such marker you pass, 1, is on the tree straight ahead of you. To the left, the trail leads to the Meyer Arboretum, a 175-acre habitat of native trees and shrubs you may want to visit at the end of your hike. Take the white-blazed trail to the right. When you enter a forest of white pine, white spruce and Norway spruce, it is suddenly quieter. The canopy of tall trees and their needles cushion sound. The air is crisp with the scent of pine, and the ground is soft and springy underfoot. Look here for red-breasted nuthatches and hairy woodpeckers flitting from tree to tree.

Along the hike, you will notice the remains of low stone walls alongside the trail. Erected by farmers, the walls once served to divide croplands and define property lines. In the 18th and 19th centuries, this area was heavily farmed, until westward migration led to an eventual decline in population.

The trail returns to a deciduous forest of oaks, hickory, maple, and beech. Squirrels and chipmunks scamper through the woods. Another wet area intersects the trail, and a conduit pipe crosses it. The river meanders alongside. At marker 2, in 0.6 mile, you will come to a bridge on the right. Do not cross it; continue straight ahead, following the river.

Gradually ascending and descending as it follows the contours of the hillside, the trail continues along the river's shore. On sunny days, sunlight filters through the leafy canopy, capturing reflections in the still waters below. In places, the trail can be very muddy and eroded near the water's edge. A boardwalk has been laid down to help the hiker through the wet areas and protect the resource.

The trail comes to a T junction. Do not take the unmarked woods road that leads up to the left, but continue to bear right on the white-blazed trail. There is no identification marker. Near the bottom of the hill, the route follows the white trail heading to the left. At 1.3 miles, marker 3 is on a tree. White blazes heading down the road to the right lead to the Kimberly Bridge Picnic Area. If you wish to shorten the hike and avoid a climb, turn around and retrace your steps, for a hike of 2.6 miles.

The white-blazed trail now goes up hill, heading almost due north. There are also faded green blazes marking the trail. As the trail curves around the hill, a small pond is visible below and to the right. An unmarked trail comes in from the left at 2 miles. Stay on the white trail on your right, which begins to descend. Look for the Eastern bluebirds that call this part of the forest home. With their bright blue backs, rosy breasts, and bright chirping, they are easy to spot.

At 2.1 miles, at a T junction, marker 6, you should bear left. The long descent enters a bowl-like area, where the trail curves into pines. Continue down the hill, crossing an extensive wetlands on a causeway, and then briefly ascend. The evergreens are soon replaced by multiple stands of young beech trees. Along this part of the trail, which is wide and flat, there are intersections with unmarked trails. At the intersection, marker 5, bear left and continue down hill. Ignore the many turns

in the road, bearing left with the white blazes. Soon, you will be able to catch a glimpse of the fields and the main road of the reservation off to the right. The trail re-enters the evergreen forest and you arrive back at the first bridge. Cross it and follow the trail through the field back to the parking lot to complete the 4.7-mile loop.

There are other sections of the 35 miles of trails in Ward Pound Ridge you may wish to explore. South of the Pell Hill picnic area are the Fire Tower Trail and the Spy Rock Trail. The Fire Tower Trail is a broad road leading to the highest point in the reservation. On a clear day, Manhattan can be seen from this point, almost 1,000 feet above sea level. In June, the trail is fragrantly fringed with clusters of mountain laurel. During the Revolutionary War, Spy Rock Shelter, south and west of the tower, was used by Colonel Sheldon's Light Dragoons to observe the movements of British troops.

15

Rockefeller State Park Preserve

Distance	6 miles
Hiking time	4 hours
Rating	Moderate

*T*his lovely area has been made available to the public through a gift from the Rockefeller family in 1983. It encompasses 859 acres and is in the heart of the Pocantico Hills of Westchester made famous by the writings of Washington Irving. The aptly named Sleepy Hollow Road bisects the preserve.

The preserve has wetlands, woodlands, meadows, a 24-acre lake, and a wide variety of trails. Twenty miles of carriage paths lead to shady river lanes, intimate wooded roads, and panoramic vistas. The carriage roads were designed by the Rockefeller family to capture all the beauty of the surrounding landscape and woodlands. There is good birding in the park, especially during the spring and fall migrations. Deer can often be spotted, nearly any time of day, but most often in the late afternoon.

The park is open from 9am to sunset. Pick up a map of the trails in the park at the visitors center. You should not walk the trails without one as there are many interconnected trails. At times a compass would help. The trails are user-friendly since the map clearly indicates all the routes and their interconnections. The park has concrete [guide] posts or Carsonite fiberglass signs at most intersections, which are helpful in trail identification. Most of the posts also have a "P" with an arrow suggesting the shortest way back to the parking lot.

It is possible to combine the many miles of trails to suit your own taste and capacity. The shortest is Spook Rock Trail (0.1 mile) and the longest is the 13-Bridges Trail (2.1 miles). Don't be surprised to find that joggers far outnumber hikers either early or late in the day.

While you are in the neighborhood, you may want to visit the old Dutch Reformed Church in Philipse Manor. It was built in 1697 and was designated a National Historic Landmark in 1963. Many of the original Dutch settlers are buried in the church's graveyard. Washington Irving is buried nearby on top of the hill to the north beyond the church. Also worth seeing is the Union Church on Route 448 with its famous Chagall and Matisse stained glass windows. It is open to the public.

The hike described here will be on a variety of trails within the preserve (with the exception of one small section outside the boundaries)

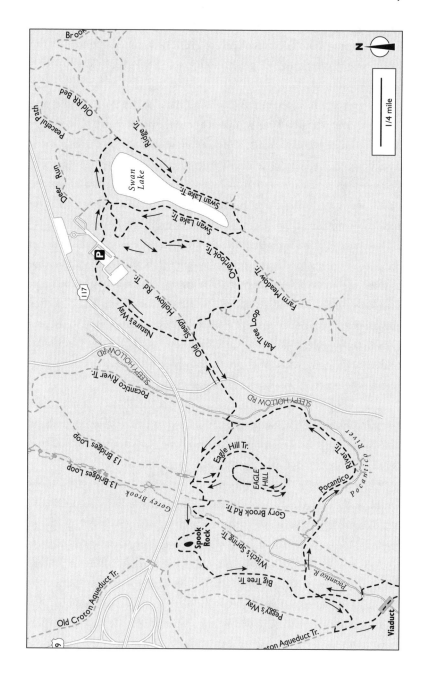

and takes in the best that the park has to offer. Although the private property of the Rockefeller family that abuts the park is open to hikers, it is advisable for newcomers to get thoroughly acquainted with the park trails first; it's quite easy to get lost outside the park.

Pick up a free plastic trash bag at the entrance to the trails. Park users are expected to carry out their own trash. And people do, for the park is always spotless—not even a cigarette butt or gum wrapper will be seen on the ground.

Directions   Metro-North trains from Grand Central Station stop regularly at Philipse Manor, the station closest to the park. Rather than walk to the visitors center (a distance of almost three miles), it is suggested that you take a taxi. They are usually waiting at the station. Another option is to take the train to Tarrytown station, which is serviced more frequently, and then a cab from there. On the return, you can use the public phones at the visitors center to call for a cab ride back to the station.

For hikers who come by car, take Route 9 north out of Tarrytown to Rt. 117. Turn right onto 117 and go about 1.6 miles to the park entrance on the right, where you will find the visitors center and rest rooms. There is a fee to park.

The Walk   Leave the visitors center on the short path to the left. You will come to your first intersection in a few minutes. Take the Swan Lake Trail left to go around the beautiful lake. It's level and ideal for strolling, and should put you in the mood to enjoy the rest of the hike. Since the Swan Lake Trail is a loop, you will return to the intersection you left. (You can omit the 1.3-mile lake walk to shorten the hike to less than five miles, if you wish, by turning right at the first intersection, onto the Overlook Trail.)

The Overlook Trail climbs steeply at first. You soon pass a number of birdhouses constructed by the park to attract bluebirds, although you are just as likely to encounter tree swallows occupying some of the structures. The trail soon levels off to provide a panoramic view of Swan Lake and surrounding woodlands. At the highest point of the hill you pass a concrete water storage facility on your right. It holds a three-day supply of water for Tarrytown.

From here, the trail descends; you will soon pass a path on your left with a triangle shaped intersection. Stay on Overlook, and soon after bear right at the next junction; descend gently downhill until you come to a T intersection with Old Sleepy Hollow Road Trail. Turn left onto Old Sleepy Hollow Road Trail, an old colonial road. There will be a small brook on your left and almost immediately ahead, on your right, will be the entrance to Nature's Way Trail (it still has a small red-circular marker on a post).

Stay on the Old Sleepy Hollow Road Trail. You will soon cross Sleepy Hollow Road, a paved two-lane vehicular road that cuts through the park. There is a bridge ahead and some wet marshland on your right. At the T junction just after the bridge, turn left onto the Pocantico River Trail and almost immediately right onto the Eagle Hill Trail.

Continue ahead uphill and cross a small wooden bridge. Shortly, on your right, the 13-Bridges Trail comes in. You can see the bridge that goes over Route 117 on this trail. Turn left onto the Eagle Hill Summit Trail. You will now be climbing gradually, in a southerly direction. The edge of the road on your left falls off steeply to a ravine below. On the right, you will pass a carriage road that is part of the circular on which you will return from Eagle Hill.

At the top of Eagle Hill there is a vista of the Hudson River, the Tappan Zee Bridge, and adjacent woodlands. On the hill at the left is Kykuit (pronounced KY-CUT), the home of several generations of Rockefellers. Kykuit was opened to the public by the Rockefeller family in 1994. Contact Historic Hudson Valley, (914) 631-9491, for information.

It is said that Spook Rock area is the site of a Native American legend. It was on the large rock here, the story goes, that 12 beautiful girls were seen dancing one day by a youth. He admired the girls from a distance until, to his disappointment, a basket materialized and whisked them into the sky. When the girls next appeared, the youth captured the loveliest of the maidens and took her home as his bride. They had a child. But within three years of her capture, the young woman died; soon her baby refused food and died as well. It is said this young mother now returns, thinking she had been gone only a moment, and searches in vain for her husband and lost baby. Strange lights and other occurrences have been reported in the vicinity of Spook Rock.

Descend on the circular road until you get back to the intersection with the 13-Bridges Trail. Turn left (west). The trail will almost immediately turn sharply left (south) downhill and then come to a T connection with another branch of the 13-Bridges Trail (it forms a loop). If you look to your right, you will see this trail going under Route 117. Go left a very short distance on the 13-Bridges Trail and take the first trail on your right—the Witch's Spring Trail. This trail will go in the direction of Route 117 and, at its closest point to the road (you will see a wire fence at the spot), will swing sharply around to go south.

The Witch's Spring Trail crosses a bridge over Gorey Brook. Shortly, you will turn right onto the Spook Rock Trail. Uphill is a large rock, where the trail turns 180 degrees to go south.

The Spook Rock Trail ends at a T junction with the Big Tree Trail, which is a circular that returns again farther down this road. Turn left onto it. Toward the end of the Big Tree Trail, you will come to an intersection with a road that, as you face it, comes in from the right and goes out to the left. Bear right on this road, which goes uphill. At the top of

Photo by Tom Rupolo

the hill the trail turns sharply right; the Old Croton Aqueduct and a cemetery are visible through the woods. Leave the trail at this point and take the narrow path to the left; it will bring you out onto the Old Croton Aqueduct at a stone building (a weir). Straight ahead is the Pocantico River Viaduct. (Notice the extensive stone work below, near the tunnel through which the river flows.)

Continue across the viaduct; walk until you see to the left a bridle path that parallels the aqueduct. Look for a short, unmarked trail (about 30 feet long) on the left and take it to the bridle path. This is private property and technically outside the park, but only for a very short distance. Occasionally you may see a sulky with local gentry on board. Turn left on the gravel bridle path; stay on the gravel path as it turns left and ignore the footpath that travels straight ahead. You soon come to an intersection just before a beautiful stone bridge that spans the Pocantico River. Note the fine stone work on the viaduct, now on your left.

Continue straight and cross the Pocantico River. You will soon be at a four-way intersection visited earlier. The Big Tree Trail, the Witch's

Spring Trail, and the Pocantico River Trail meet at this spot. Turn right and follow the Witch's Spring Trail. Continue ahead a short distance to another intersection. The Witch's Spring Trail departs on the left. Continue straight, crossing another bridge that spans the Pocantico River. Immediately, another path will come in on your right; continue straight on the Pocantico River Trail.

Within a short distance you come to a four-way intersection with a bridge over the Pocantico River on the left. Ignore this bridge and in about 50 yards take the next bridge to the left, staying on the Pocantico River Trail.

Farther on, you will see, on your right, another beautiful stone bridge—you will have noticed by now that there are many in the park. Beyond it is a small wooden bridge. The Pocantico River Trail bears left, following the field edge on the left. The Pocantico River, which in Native American language means a "run between two hills," was likely named for this spot. Eagle Hill is on your left and the river meanders on your right.

Continue on the Pocantico River Trail. You will come to the Eagle Hill Trail on your left, at the intersection where earlier you turned to go up Eagle Hill. Stay on the Pocantico River Trail. You will come to a turnoff on the right; turn right and cross a bridge over the Pocantico River onto the Old Sleepy Hollow Road Trail. You will re-cross Sleepy Hollow Road and then shortly go left onto the Nature's Way Trail. It has the red marker on the post. This trail is a regular hiker's dirt path—well trod and narrow with shrubs, grass, and plenty of poison ivy on either side. In a few minutes you will come a faint trail that leads to a huge boulder, known to geologists as a "glacial erratic." Reputedly, this stone is the largest such boulder deposited in this part of the country by the receding glacier. The path goes by a small marshy area on the right, where a pair of great horned owls is occasionally seen. You soon reach the parking lot.

16

Blue Mountain Reservation

Distance	4.5 miles
Hiking time	3 hours
Rating	Moderate

*B*lue Mountain Reservation is located in the Hudson Valley on the outskirts of Peekskill in New York. It has 20 miles of trails, which pass through the rolling hills typical of the lower Hudson Valley. The reservation has a natural beauty worth exploring; the upper pond, surrounded by trees and shrubs, is secluded and a wonderful place to rest from the busy world outside. The views from the tops of Spitzenberg and Blue mountains are enjoyable. Hemlock groves and imposing rock formations are everywhere, particularly in the northern part of the park. The forest is a mixture of hemlock and fine hardwoods, with an attractive understory of viburnum, witch hazel, spice bush, dogwood, and ferns.

A map of the reservation is available at the entrance gate and from Westchester County's Department of Parks. Call (914) 242-PARK. The map also has numbers at all intersections that correspond to routed numbers on wooden posts at the intersections, so there is rarely any doubt where you are if you have the map. A compass may be useful for orientation as the trails twist and turn a lot to keep the grade down.

Blue Mountain is a multi-use park. It is used for fishing, bathing, hiking, picnicking and especially for biking with some horse usage on selected trails. There is no hunting in the park so it is a good option during hunting season. During the winter, there is ice skating on Loundsbury Pond when conditions permit. Most of the trails are suitable for cross-country skiing. The ski trails are not maintained or patrolled, however, so the park staff recommends them only for experienced skiers. Parking is free except during the summer. A discount is available for Westchester County Park pass-holders.

The 1,600 acres of Blue Mountain Reservation were originally owned by several families, and much of the acreage was farmland. Throughout the park are stone walls dating from farming times. The Montrose Reformed Church also owned part of the current park. The Loundsbury family owned the hundred acres around Loundsbury Pond where today the picnic areas and beach are located. The family operated a general

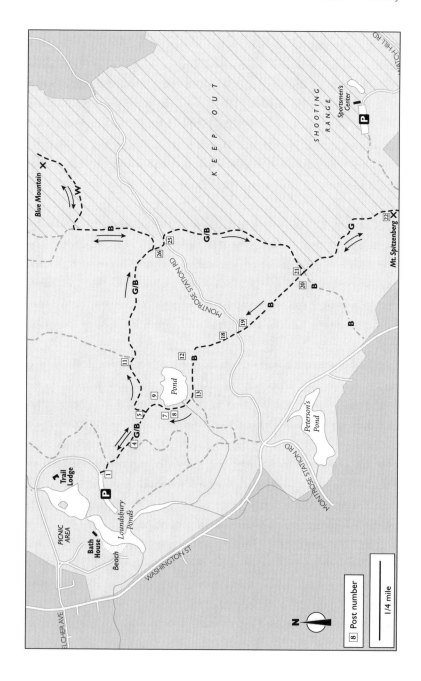

contracting, sand, gravel, cement, brick, and ice company from their property. Both New Pond and Loundsbury Pond were originally constructed by the Loundsbury family specifically for making ice. Due to a variety of natural factors, these ponds develop much more ice than most others in the Westchester County area.

The gravel pit used by the Loundsbury Company was located at the site of the present parking lot for the beach. The red brick building to the right of the road just before the entrance to the Reservation, now occupied by a company that sells sporting goods and antiques, was once a stable for the Loundsbury Company horses. In the 1920s, when demand for ice lessened (due to the advent of refrigeration), the Loundsbury family sold their land to Westchester County.

In June 1933, the Civilian Conservation Corps (CCC) made the Reservation the site of one of its camps. The CCC was an independent government agency inaugurated in April 1933 to help offset unemployment caused by the Depression.

The CCC built the fireplaces in the picnic areas, the two stone latrines near the park office, and the fire tower on Mount Spitzenberg, which was used as a ranger station for many years. Only the first story of this tower remains. The CCC also built a lean-to on Blue Mountain, 16 miles of hiking and bridle trails, and the trail lodge. The steeper sections of the trails are "paved" with rounded versions of Belgian blocks common on some roads in Europe or older parts of U.S. cities. These have kept the trails largely free of erosion problems despite the use by horses and bicycles.

The trail lodge originally housed many of the CCC workers and was going to be part of a chain of youth hostels envisioned by President Franklin D. Roosevelt. His plan fell through, and the park now owns the lodge. The lodge, which can accommodate thirty people, can be rented. Contact the Westchester Parks Department at (914) 682-2621 for an application. Blankets, pillows, and mattresses are provided.

Directions   To get to the park by car, take Route 9 along the east shore of the Hudson to the Welcher Avenue exit, about 35 miles north of the George Washington Bridge. Turn east, away from the river, onto Welcher Avenue and follow it for about a quarter mile to the entrance of the park. Just past the tollbooth, take the left fork, which leads to parking lot 3 and the trails. To get to the park by train, take the Metro-North Hudson Division to the Peekskill station. From the station, it is a two-mile walk or a short taxi ride to the park.

The Walk   One of the most interesting and beautiful walks in the Reservation begins at parking lot No. 3. The trailhead is to your immediate left as you enter the parking lot. The green blazes are the Briarcliff-Peekskill Trailway, which goes all the way across the park and then south to Teatown Lake Reservation and beyond to Briarcliff. You will follow the green and/or blue trails for most of the hike. Almost immediately on your left is the beginning of the yellow trail. Continue straight-ahead uphill. About ten minutes from the start of the hike, an orange trail goes off to the right and the blue/green to the left. Stay with the blue/green trail. (The orange may appear closer to red to some people.)

On the left is a small vernal pool that may not have any water in it, depending on the season; ahead are some fir trees. About 20 minutes into the hike, the path comes to a T junction at post 11. A red-blazed trail is to the left, while the blue/green turns right. Stay with the blue/green blazes. The path soon comes to the open area of a gas pipeline with Montrose Station Road visible ahead (25 minutes from the start of the hike). Follow the pipeline to the left (blue trail) and soon come to post 26, to which you will return after climbing Blue Mountain. Shortly the trail bears left from the pipeline.

In 5–10 minutes, or less than 0.3 mile, at post 30, a white trail turns sharply to the right to go up to Blue Mountain. It's easy to miss the turnoff. If you come to a Y fork in the road with both trails ahead of you blazed red, you've gone too far. Retrace your steps and find the white blazes. The summit of the mountain is no more than 0.3 mile from the turn in the road. Near the top of the mountain and to the left of the trail, there is a fine view from a rock ledge into the gorge where the Hudson River cuts through the Highlands. This view is worth the climb. Return to the trail and go right up a steep, fainter trail that leads to the actual summit, which is wooded. The remains of a roofless rock lean-to are near the summit, which is a bushwack off to the right.

Retrace your steps down the white trail and turn left at post 30 onto the blue trail; continue back to the gasline and post 26 (see above). Turn right post 26 and cross Montrose Station Road where the blue/green trail resumes at post 25. The trail goes steadily uphill, then levels before descending briefly to a T junction at post 21, in about 10 minutes.Turn left and continue gently uphill to another T junction at post 22 in another 10 minutes, passing some large rock outcrops. From here, the green trail turns left to descend the mountain to Briarcliff. Straight ahead you can see the 125-yard steep and rocky climb to the top of Mt. Spitzenberg. The remains of the ranger's house is on your left as you continue to the summit. The view to the south of the upper Palisades and the Hudson River is especially good.

To return, retrace your steps to the junction at post 22 and go straight ahead on the blue trail. In a few minutes a different blue trail will leave to the left. Ignore it and continue for about 10 minutes to Montrose Station Road at post 19. Pass through an open area with the same pipeline you crossed before, continuing until you see the upper pond on your left. Stay with the blue trail, which now hugs the south side of the pond. A purple trail begins at post 12 and goes around the other side of the pond. At post 13 there is an orange trail that goes to the left. Look for the very large split rock on your right near here. The purple trails returns at post 7. Continue to a T junction at post 5, where you will go left on the blue/green trail that you started on from the parking lot. You should reach the parking lot in a little over 5 more minutes.

Photo by Danielle Graham

17
Teatown Lake Reservation

Distance	3.1 miles
Hiking time	2 hours
Rating	Easy

*T*eatown Lake Reservation is a nature preserve and environmental education center in the heart of Westchester County that includes 730 acres of diverse natural beauty. Its 33-acre lake is surrounded by mixed hardwood forests, hemlock and laurel groves, grassy meadows, scenic hills, ravines, and lush wetlands. There is a small island in the lake with an unmatched display of rare and native wild flowers. The reservation is also home to a large variety of songbirds, waterfowl, and other wild creatures.

The reservation has 11 trails of varied terrain; the longest (Lakeside Trail) is 1.7 miles; the shortest (Hilltop Trail) is only 0.4 mile. However, the trails can be combined to extend a hike for many more miles. The Lakeside Trail has an abundance of birds as a result of its varied habitats. A bird blind has been built on the lake near Wildflower Island for use by birders. The access path to the bird blind is on the left at the bottom of the hill as you walk toward the boathouse.

The reservation was established in 1963 when the Gerard Swope family donated 190 acres surrounding the lake. It is a non-profit organization that depends heavily upon volunteers to help the staff maintain the buildings and grounds. It operates out of a former carriage barn that is also a nature museum, gift shop, and offices. There is a maple syrup house and a small collection of native animals, such as horned owls and hawks, that cannot be released because of disabling injuries.

Teatown offers nature classes to children of all ages and outreach programs to senior citizens and service clubs. There are weekend classes for families to discover wild flowers, listen to spring peepers, study summer constellations, identify edible wild plants and berries, and track winter wildlife.

The trails at the Teatown Lake Reservation are open dawn to dusk all year. Call (914) 762-2912 for the office, museum, and gift shop hours of operation.

Free black-and-white maps of the reservation are available at the Nature Center, but the inexpensive large colored map is recommended. It is laid out beautifully and clearly shows such details as cliffs, stone walls, marshes, and buildings.

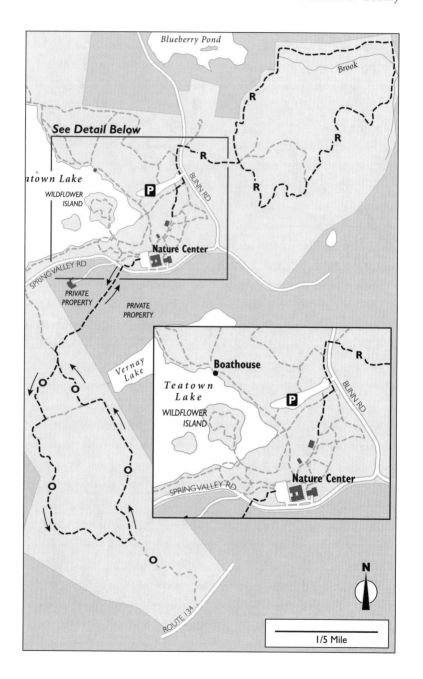

Blueberry Pond

Brook

R

R

See Detail Below

R

atown Lake

*WILDFLOWER
ISLAND*

P

BLINN RD

R

R

Nature Center

SPRING VALLEY RD

*PRIVATE
PROPERTY*

*PRIVATE
PROPERTY*

*Vernay
Lake*

Boathouse

*Teatown
Lake*

*WILDFLOWER
ISLAND*

P

BLINN RD

R

SPRING VALLEY RD

Nature Center

ROUTE 134

N

1/5 Mile

Directions   From the Taconic Parkway, exit at NY 134, heading toward Ossining. Drive west on NY 134 to the second right—Spring Valley Road; turn right onto it. At 0.8 mile on Spring Valley Road, you reach a junction with Blinn Road. A large sign indicates Teatown. Continue straight on Spring Valley Road to a large parking lot with picnic tables on the right near the Nature Center. From Route 9A, at the intersection with NY 134, drive east on NY 134 for 2.5 miles to Spring Valley Road. Continue as above. Additional parking at the Lakeside parking lot on Blinn Road provides access to the Lakeside Trail.

There is no public transportation to Teatown Reservation.

The Walk   This hike will be on two trails in two different sections of the reservation. The first will be on the Hidden Valley Trail (blazed red and 1.7 miles long) and the second on the Back 40 Trail (blazed orange and 1.6 miles long).

You can find the Hidden Valley Trail in back of the Nature Center, by the map bulletin board. The trail follows the road to the right, past the syrup house and cages for non-releasable animals donated to Teatown. It goes downhill gradually until you reach the Lakeside Parking Lot, where it turns right, goes through the parking lot, and then immediately left as the trail runs parallel to Blinn Road. It crosses the road, soon goes into an open field, and then crosses a wet area on a small bridge.

Ahead, a sign with red arrows points in two directions. Go left; you'll arrive back at this point near the end of the hike. Notice several wooden birdhouses placed here by the reservation. The trail goes back into the woods through a stone wall. You are now in a pine grove. On your right, a sign indicates "viewpoint in winter." Continue left, as indicated by an arrow and red blazes. Shortly, you'll cross a bridge over a brook and very wet area. The trail turns right. At this point, to the left, you will see the intersection with the Overlook Trail (blazed yellow), which traverses an area with spectacular rock formations. Continue following the red trail, with a very high cliff on your left and a swamp on your right. In spring, skunk cabbage and marigolds are rampant in the swamp. You will be on this most northern part of the trail for a while.

The embankment will become steadily steeper, until suddenly the trail turns sharply right to go south over a long boardwalk. The swamp is now on either side of the boardwalk. Skunk cabbage is abundant in this area. After crossing the boardwalk, you will see a red blaze ahead indicating that the trail continues to the right. A brook is on your left. The trail soon begins to climb steeply. The area is dense with mountain laurel (look for them in full bloom in June) and full of evergreens. Huge boulders soon come into view on the left, and the trail passes among some of them.

After 0.4 mile from the beginning of the steep climb, you reach a junction with a woods road. Go right on the woods road through an area of sugar maples. In February and March, you will see buckets collecting sap to be emptied into the syrup house that you passed at the beginning of the hike. Shortly, the trail leaves the road to the left into the meadow, where you soon reach the junction you saw at the beginning of the loop. A sign indicates the direction back to the Nature Center. You are now retracing your steps, crossing the small bridge, continuing on the woods road back to Blinn Road and eventually reaching the Nature Center in 0.3 mile.

To get to the start of the Back 40 Trail, go to the northwest corner of the Nature Center parking lot. A path leads past a tree with a sign that says "Back 40 Trail" (blazed orange). Almost immediately, the trail turns right to follow a stone wall and then turns left through the wall to cross Spring Valley Road. On the other side of the road, the trail uses a stile to cross another stone wall and heads uphill through open woods. There is a private residence on your right. Soon you will come to an open area for the high-power line. You'll see a "Back 40 Trail" sign and an arrow pointing left. Cut diagonally left under the power lines and you will see a sign directing you to turn right. You will be returning to this place near the end of the hike, when you will then retrace your steps to the parking lot.

Ahead, the path goes through a stone wall and turns left into a wet area. Stepping stones and a boardwalk have been laid down to help you through the wetlands. You will again see a large quantity of skunk cabbage. Shortly before the path goes uphill, you will see another "Back 40" sign and a sign to a bench to the left. You have come 0.2 mile. The initial climb is short and steep, followed by a more gradual ascent. Along the ascent, you will see two large cement and rock pillars on the left. The trail reaches a T junction with a woods road. Bear left, as indicated by another "Back 40" trail sign. On your left is another stone pillar. This is the most southern part of the trail. Now the trail heads back north and shortly crosses under the power lines in 0.9 mile. There is an open view north, unfortunately marred by the power lines.

The trail reenters the woods at a "Back 40" sign and goes steeply downhill. It turns right and leaves the wide path, continuing downhill. A private lake is to your right. At the bottom, bear right, as indicated by another trail sign. The woods become very dense. You'll reach another boardwalk, which almost immediately divides. Turn right. On sunny, warm days, look for garter snakes that sun themselves here. The trail goes gradually uphill again and goes under the power lines. Very soon you will be at the fork where, earlier, you made a turn to the right. Now retrace your steps to the parking lot.

If you have time, walk around the lake, an easy stroll of 1.7 miles on the Lakeside Trail. The rim of the lake is heavily wooded, but boardwalks or gravel have been laid down over wet areas. At the beginning of the Lakeside Trail you will see the entrance over a causeway to Wildflower Island. The gate is locked. To take a tour of this beautiful island during summer months, contact the receptionist at the Nature Center.

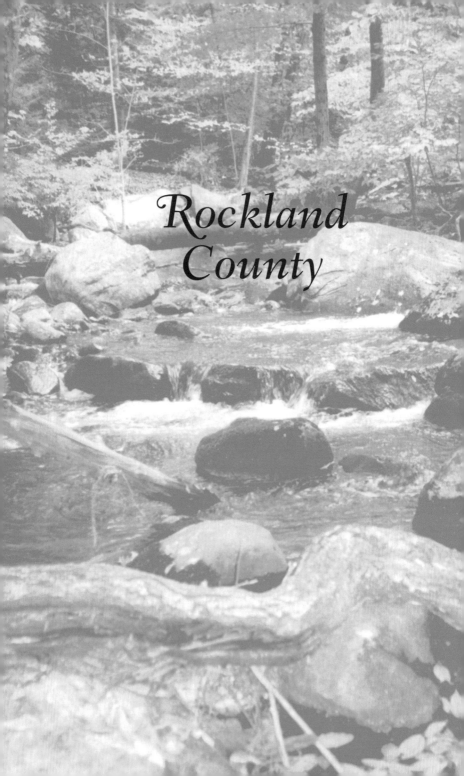

Rockland
County

ROCKLAND COUNTY
The High Hills Call

North of New York and west of the Hudson is the most mountainous terrain of the metropolitan area. The mountains nearest the city are Hook Mountain and High Tor. These are the northernmost outposts of the Palisades, which border the Hudson River from the Tappan Zee Bridge to New York Harbor before finally disappearing beneath Staten Island. The Palisades originated 180 million years ago, when molten rock was forced by intense pressure between strata of sandstone; millions of years later, this rock was uncovered by erosion. (The Watchung Mountains in Central New Jersey arose at the same time; there the molten rock flowed directly onto the surface of the earth.)

Farther north in Rockland County, and extending into Orange County, is a much larger mountainous area—the fabled Hudson Highlands. See separate chapter for several Highlands hikes. In Rockland County, Bear Mountain and Dunderberg Mountain rise abruptly more than 1,000 feet above the Hudson. Inland, streams rush through rocky gorges, and lakes nestle below wooded slopes.

The Hudson Highlands are part of a larger range. Called by geologists the Reading Prong, the range is known locally as the Housatonic Highlands in Connecticut and the Ramapos in New Jersey. Sweeping through Rockland and Orange Counties, these mountains are some of the oldest in North America; in fact, they are older than the continent itself. A billion years ago, sedimentary deposits were transformed by tremendous subterranean heat and pressure into today's gneisses, schists, and marble.

When the range was first raised, it soared upward 10,000 feet or more. In the next few hundred million years, it was eroded, ground down, raised up, and ground down again, but the rock endured. Only a few thousand years ago the highest mountains were over 3,000 feet high; but then the glaciers came.

The glaciers profoundly altered the landscape of this area. They dug out most of the lake basins in Rockland County and opened up the valleys of

Photo by Jane Daniels

the Ramapo and Hudson Rivers. They shaved 2,000 feet off the peaks of the Highlands and then pushed this enormous pile of dirt south over the coastal plains of Long Island and Staten Island. Where the last wave of gla-ciers stopped, the dirt remained: today's Brooklyn Heights, Staten Island's Todt Hill, and the hills in Alley Park in Queens are the results.

Then the glaciers began to melt. As they melted, the sea rose. Water flooded into the low river valley between present day Long Island and Connecticut, creating Long Island Sound. Salt water flowed back up the deep channel of the Hudson. Today the Hudson is tidal and brackish, as walkers along its shores in the Palisades or Hook Mountain will observe. In fact, the Hudson is not a river at all in this area but an arm of the sea.

This complex geological history has created a multitude of local habitats: the salt marsh of Iona Island, the fresh-water swamps of Harriman Park, the ocean marshes of Cheesequake, barrier beaches, glacial moraines and kettle ponds, cliffs and plains—a diversity not found in any other metropolitan area. As if this weren't enough, this region lies in a transition area between two natural zones. Here the southern, Carolinian flora like sweet gum, persimmon, magnolia, and holly can be found close to such northern, Hudsonian types as maple, beech, birch, and hemlock.

The result is a great variety of wildlife, particularly birds. The Hudson Valley is a major corridor for the migrating species that will stop off at Jamaica Bay and Pelham Bay. In Harriman Park alone, almost 100 species of birds are known to nest.

Walking is strenuous in the Highlands, but it is rewarding. Hawks ride the summer air below Hook Mountain. In winter, cross-country skiers glide through hemlock groves. The variety of fall colors is startling. But on a first visit, try to see Harriman Park in the spring. Everywhere, rhododendron and mountain laurel are bursting with blossoms. Spring freshets roar and deer abound. Henry Hudson was right 350 years ago: "It is as pleasant a land as one can tread upon."

Photo by Tom Rupolo

18

Hook Mountain

Distance	6.7 miles
Hiking time	4.5 hours
Rating	Moderate

*T*he Hook Mountain circular walk is a varied and scenic exercise that is among the most spectacular of all the hikes described in this book. The walk follows the cliffs of the northern extension of the Palisades, which fall off sharply to the Hudson. It wanders across pastures of lichens and wildflowers, through forests of box elders and 100-year-old hemlocks, and then down to the water's edge and past abandoned rock quarries along the Hudson.

Directions   Getting to the trailhead by car is not difficult. Take Route 9W, the major highway running up the west side of the Hudson from the George Washington Bridge. Hook Mountain is about 20 miles north of the George Washington Bridge. Drive to Upper Nyack, a little north of the New York State Thruway, and look for an intersection with Christian Herald Road (there is a traffic light). Stay on 9W; just beyond the intersection (50 feet or so on the right) is Old Mountain Road, which runs into 9W. There is a gas station located between Christian Herald and Old Mountain roads, and an empty lot across the street from it where you may park your car. Recross the highway and pick up the aqua blazes of the Long Path heading north along Route 9W.

Via public transportation, take the 9A Red & Tan bus to Nyack from the George Washington Bridge Terminal (be sure to call ahead for departure and return times). It is an easy and convenient 50-minute ride. Along the way you will have the opportunity to observe the charming and historic town of Tappan, passing George Washington's former headquarters, and to experience fine river views from Piermont. When you reach downtown Nyack (which you may want to explore after the hike), ask the bus driver to let you off at the Christian Herald Road stop on Route 9W.

The Walk   Begin walking north up Route 9W. The highway soon starts to climb and curves to the right. You will find aqua paint blazes on the telephone poles bordering the highway; here the Long Path runs along the road. After a few hundred yards, at the break in the steel barrier, you will come to a double blaze indicating that the Long Path is leaving

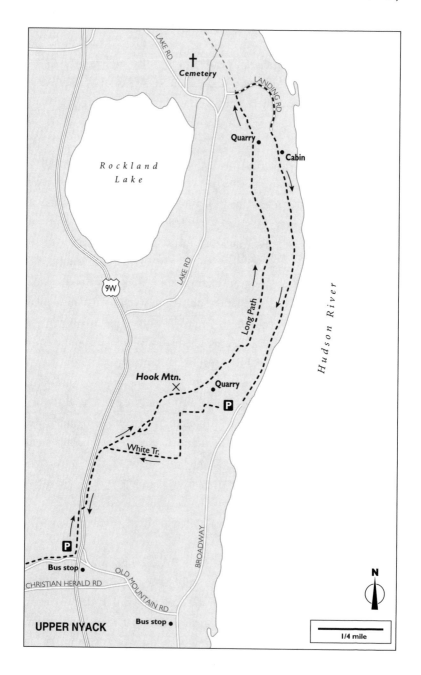

Cemetery

LAKE RD

LANDING RD

Quarry

Cabin

*Rockland
Lake*

LAKE RD

9W

Hudson River

Long Path

Hook Mtn.

Quarry

P

White Tr.

P

BROADWAY

Bus stop

CHRISTIAN HERALD RD

OLD MOUNTAIN RD

UPPER NYACK

Bus stop

N

1/4 mile

Route 9W and entering a broad path on the right. About 200 feet from the road, a triple white-blazed trail will enter from the right. You will be returning on this trail at the end of the hike. Continue to follow the aqua blazes. The Long Path hugs the contour of a hill. This was the old route of 9W; the new route is already out of sight on the left side above the trail, although cars can still be heard. To the right, a shaded, rocky slope quickly drops away; to the left, 75 feet up the hill, is the rock retaining wall for Route 9W. The trail jogs almost imperceptibly to the right and becomes somewhat rocky; if you stop and look, you can see the faint traces of the old highway curving off to the left. At the same time, the new highway overhead turns away, and the traffic noise gradually fades. The well-trodden trail descends slightly before beginning a climb, swinging around to the left. The foliage, dense up to this point, begins to thin, allowing views of the slope of Hook Mountain ahead and of the swimming pool and tennis court of a camp some 250 feet below. After circling the mountain so that you are headed toward a col in the ridge, the trail makes a sharp right and climbs steeply for 100 feet or so, coming out on the bare rock top of Hook Mountain (736 feet above the Hudson), where you are rewarded with a nearly 360-degree view. (Ignore a yellow-blazed trail that was laid out by hawk watchers to provide more direct access from Route 9W to the top of Hook Mountain.)

Hawks circle overhead here; you are most apt to see them in mid-September, when the migration south is in full swing. Seven hundred feet below, the Tappan Zee Bridge spans the Hudson. On the horizon are the towers of Riverdale and Manhattan as well as those of Newark. Just below, so close that you feel as though you are intruding, are the backyards of Upper Nyack. West are the hills of the Ramapo ridge; through the trees to the northwest, Rockland Lake can be seen. Beyond the lake is the long curving ridge of the Palisades, with the quarried side of High Tor jutting out prominently. The Hudson and the hills of Westchester County are visible over a sweeping arc from the south to the east. A badly eroded side trail allows for unimpeded southerly views. Here are examples of the rare Hudson Valley cactus that are spotted only on the occasional mountain peak. This is as far as you need to go for a breath-taking view. There are few better spots anywhere along the Hudson.

The walk continues up and down along the top of the ridge, with many more spectacular views, and then comes out into a bare area with a completely open view to the east. There is a triple-blazed yellow marker on the left; it leads down to some administration buildings of Hook Mountain State Park. Stay on the aqua-blazed Long Path. The view of a few minutes ago, from Hook Mountain, was awe-inspiring; this view is a little frightening. You are next to the edge of the upper rim of an old quarry. There are no trees, no slope, no bushes—just open air and a 100-foot drop. Small children should be kept back. Even adults should approach with caution, since the rock here, while hard, is crumbly. No one should attempt to rock climb here (moreover, rock climbing is prohibited by park regulations).

The trail goes up past the quarry and into the trees, letting your heart slow down a little. Ahead is a grassy knoll with many boulders, the last of the open views. Hook Mountain is the round-shouldered rise just south. Nyack is now farther away; the feeling is quieter, more restful.

The trail leaves the spectacular Hudson views. Descending, it passes an unmarked trail to the right that heads steeply down the wooded slope. Soon after, at some ruins (barely visible), the trail makes a sharp left. Another unmarked trail leads a few paces to the right past a concrete boundary marker to the last real view over the river.

The aqua blazes now lead down, crossing a woods road. Ahead, Rockland Lake can be seen through the trees. Then the woods road comes in again from the right and makes a switchback; the trail joins it, levels out, and heads north on a broad path with easy footing. Before long, another old road comes in from the left; the slope below the trail becomes steeper and more open, with trees far below and at times the sound of a spring.

The road begins to climb, gaining the top of a hemlock-clad ridge. Keep an eye out for the markers; the trail descends slightly, and soon an old trail leads straight ahead to the ruins of an old foundation. The markers lead left, past what appears to be a huge stone barricade or foundation of some sort. On the other side of this low hill is a clearing fringed by a variety of trees—cedar, pine, and hemlock. This is a sheltered spot to have lunch if the weather is cold. The trail then drops down through a grove of hemlock to a clove, which it crosses to run beside an old causeway; it then passes by a dark pond. You will have walked almost a mile from where the woods road begins to climb again.

Now Rockland Lake and its picnic areas are close, and on a busy day the shouts and radios of reveling picnickers below can be heard. The Long Path begins to descend, passing unmarked trails. One of these is the old route of the Long Path, abandoned because it was too steep. The slope is rocky, with few bushes, but old tall trees, including a tulip tree, which blossoms toward the beginning of May, grow here. The last 100 feet before the trail levels off are very steep and can be extremely slippery in wet weather or when there are leaves on the ground.

Just beyond the trees are two sets of very large foundations—the remains of an ice industry that flourished here years ago. Before the advent of electricity, ice was the primary refrigerant; in the metropolitan area. It was often cut from lakes and ponds along the Hudson and floated down to New York. Some of it was exported as far as the Caribbean. An ice business was started at Rockland Lake in 1831. Rockland Lake ice was considered superior; the ice houses here, along with a railroad branch, a cog railroad, and a boat landing, employed hundreds of men in season. All that is gone now, but until not too many years ago, the rotting remains of ice boats lay in the Hudson just offshore.

The trail makes a last turn and comes out on a road at a barrier. Off to the left is a firehouse. Beyond that, down the road, is Rockland Lake State Park. Ahead, just out of sight on the hill, is an old cemetery. The aqua blazes continue north past the cemetery, traversing High Tor and Low Tor mountains; ultimately the trail will cross Harriman Park and then the Shawangunks and finally the Catskills.

This walk more modestly turns right and follows the road down to the Hudson. Note the ruins, especially to the right: the diagonal rock structure is part of the conveyor that once took ice down to Rockland Landing. A little farther down, this asphalt road passes the first of several abandoned quarries. The rock spires shoot up dramatically, and the columns from which the Palisades take their name are very visible here, but the whole prospect has a raw and man-made look about it.

Quarrying began here in the 1870s. Before long, 32 quarries were literally eating up these cliffs to feed rock to New York City's houses, roads, and office buildings. When it became apparent that the cliffs could disappear altogether, protests began; money was collected and bonds were sold to buy the cliffs and put them beyond the reach of the blasters. In 1911, the large quarry near the beginning of this hike was purchased; by 1920, the last quarry in this area passed into the hands of the state.

Faint side paths now diverge north, to Haverstraw. Ahead, in the water, is the Rockland Lighthouse. Still descending, the road passes a fork to the right and the asphalt road suddenly seems to be heading straight into the yard of a private house, but this is the ranger's bungalow, and the road heads to the right and passes by it. Within 200 yards, the road comes to an intersection with another asphalt road heading downhill on the left; this is the bike path that leads to Haverstraw, three miles north. That path passes by the André historical marker, which indicates the spot where Major John André and Benedict Arnold met to plot their treason. Stay on the road to the right.

After heading downhill a short while you pass an abandoned rest room. At the bottom of the hill, jutting into the river, is the remains of a landing. It's now a grassy, tree-shaded point, with several picnic tables—a good place to stop and eat when the weather is warm.

The majority of the trail back to Upper Nyack runs right along the river and should take about 40 minutes. Built in 1932 to connect the two ends of the park, the road makes for a somewhat sterile walk despite its water's-edge location. It is partly asphalted, but mostly graveled closer to the river's edge. Still, the walking is easy, and the constant activity is entertaining. Bicycles and joggers pass by continually on the weekends. In winter, cross-country skiing is popular. (For families with young children, this stretch is a good walk in its own right. Come in from Nyack, driving north on Broadway to the end. This leads right into Hook Mountain State Park. Leave the car in the lower lot and walk north on this path.)

Notice the overhanging rock ledges above the shore path. The soft red sandstone has been eroded right out from under the more durable rock overlying it. After about 20 minutes, the road passes a roomy shelter constructed from rock. A little farther on, there are some picnic tables with a fireplace, then a few old foundations, and finally more picnic tables, which signal that the end of the walk is near. Here are the park headquarters and other facilities, including a water fountain at the near corner of the headquarters building. To avoid a road walk out of the park, follow the lower paved parking area to the end, past the parking lot entrance. Then take the asphalted path up the hill. Turn left when the path goes through an opening in a rock wall and out onto the road. Continue up the road past a tollgate (for the parking lot below) and then turn left onto North Broadway.

Those returning to the parking lot on Route 9W (1.2 miles from this point) should turn right at the first street, Larchdale. The next turn is a left at the entrance to Camp Marydell (now a faith and life center) onto Midland Avenue. Then look for a double white-blazed trail marker on the right side of this street, less than a 0.1 mile from the camp entrance. If you get to a street junction with a road coming in from the right, you have gone too far. This trail will take you back shortly to the Long Path,

Photo by Jane Daniels

where you first saw the triple-blazed white marker. [**Note:** This trail is not shown on the Trail Conference map of the area; neither are the yellow trails for which you saw markers leading off the Long Path]. It is, however, well-marked and winds generally to the left with houses within sight on the left the entire way; as it approaches the Long Path, it begins to climb steeply. Turn left onto the Long Path and then turn left again onto Route 9W. Follow 9W back to the parking lot.

Those headed for return buses from Nyack have a more interesting prospect. Rather than going back to the original bus stop, continue on North Broadway into Nyack, about a 30-minute walk. This street leads past interesting old houses, in architectural styles ranging from chateau phony to the white Victorians that so fascinated the American painter Edward Hopper (1882–1967), who was born in a house on North Broadway close to the center of Nyack.

The village of Nyack offers several attractions to visitors. The Edward Hopper House, at 82 Broadway, built by Hopper's maternal grandfather in 1858, was the artist's birthplace. It is open Thursday through Sunday from 1pm to 5pm. Hopper went through high school in Nyack and left in 1910 to study and live in New York City, but he returned frequently to visit his family and held title to the Hopper House until he died. He is buried in a family plot in nearby Oak Hill Cemetery, across Route 9W from Nyack Hospital. The actress Helen Hayes, who lived at 235 North Broadway, asked Hopper to do a painting of her house, "Pretty Penny," the only work Hopper did as a commission. The Hopper House does not contain any memorabilia or paintings by Hopper (all of his artistic estate was given to the Whitney Museum), but exhibitions of other artists' works and art-related lectures are scheduled. Call (845) 358-0774 for further information.

Nyack is also notable for its many fine craft and antique stores, particularly for stained glass and original oil paintings, and for its many restaurants and dessert places. Antiquarians can choose from a number of bookshops in the immediate area.

The first bus stop on Broadway is at a little grocery on the right, just past the Upper Nyack firehouse, but consider walking on another 20 minutes into the main business district to explore the village. When you are ready to return to New York, pick up the bus at the Tappan Zee Playhouse (a rather forlorn looking yellow brick building on the corner of Broadway and Church St.), which provides benches but little shelter. The bus will also stop at other points along Broadway.

19
Pine Meadow Lake

Distance	8.9 miles
Hiking time	4.5 hours
Rating	Moderate

*F*rom lovely Pine Meadow Lake, set in a nest of hills, runs a fast, deep stream. The stream winds its way down between steep hillsides, joins Stony Brook flowing out of Lake Sebago, and finally flows into the Ramapo River near Sloatsburg, New York. A trail follows the stream closely, leading the hiker to the waterfall and pool known as the Cascade of Slid, which is at its crest in early spring.

The trail is located within Harriman-Bear Mountain Park, a large expanse of wild property within an hour's drive from New York City. There are about 100 trails in the park (43 are marked) extending over 300 miles. The trails go up and down over varied and rugged terrain and provide a network of infinite combinations that would takes years of constant hiking to cover. There are steep cliffs, abandoned iron mines (more than 20 at one time or another), and over 240 species of birds.

On this walk, you will hike from the Reeves Meadow Visitors Center at the southern end of Seven Lakes Drive up to the Cascade of Slid and then to Pine Meadow Lake and return to the visitors center along the Pine Meadow Trail. There is a parking lot at the visitors center, which is crowded on weekends, so get there early.

This is a walk for all seasons. In spring and fall, the high water makes an endlessly fascinating spectacle as it rushes and flows over and around the rocky creek bed. In summer, the water slows down and beckons from several excellent pools. Winter brings it almost to a halt, as the rocks are glazed with ice and the snow creates fantastic forms on the rocks it covers.

Directions Car drivers can reach the Reeves Meadow Visitors Center by taking Route 17 to just north of Sloatsburg and turning east onto Seven Lakes Drive.

Public transportation from Manhattan is available to Sloatsburg by bus. Take the Short Line bus from the Port Authority Bus Terminal. The ride takes about an hour. Inquire if the bus stops at Sloatsburg (some expresses may bypass the village). Train transportation is also available from Hoboken to Sloatsburg, but is limited on weekends to one early

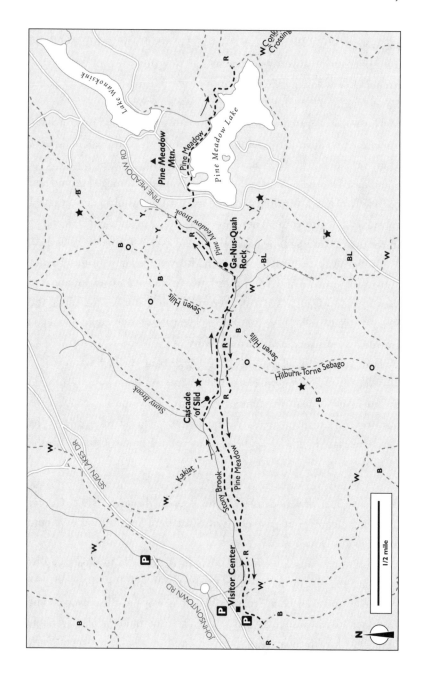

morning departure and a late afternoon return. Call New Jersey Transit for exact departure time.

From Sloatsburg one must then walk 0.7 mile north on Route 17 to the western terminus of the Pine Meadow Trail on Seven Lakes Drive. You can reach the visitors center either by hiking the trail at this point, or walking north along Seven Lakes Drive. The latter may be easier as the grading is not steep and the distance is about the same as the trail, but you would be missing a lovely little walk. The Pine Meadow Trail is blazed red on a white background. The beginning of the trail (a triple blaze) is clearly shown on the right side of a bridge that crosses a creek 100 feet or so before the sign that says "Welcome to Harriman State Park." Turn right at the triple blaze onto the trail, which runs along the edge of a private residence and curves left into the woods. It meanders frequently along the edges of the creek and has many ups and downs. The blazing is fairly clear, but be on the alert.

You cross a wide woods road under which runs a cable. Then the blue-blazed Seven Hills Trail comes in from the right. There are some misplaced blue blazes before this, but ignore them. Continue on the Pine Meadow Trail, which runs right into the visitors center parking lot. From the start of the trail to the parking lot is a distance of 0.9 mile.

At the end of the hike, retrace your route for the return to Sloatsburg. The bus stop is in town. You will have to flag the bus to make sure it stops. The railroad station is down to the left on the east side of Route 17.

The Walk   Start at the parking lot for the visitors center. Behind the center you will see a broad dirt path disappearing into the woods to the left. Follow this path, which is a continuation of the red-on-white blazed Pine Meadow Trail. Soon you will cross a spring outlet and then pass a large, deep pool on your left. Follow the Pine Meadow Trail along the side of the brook, passing groves of hemlock, laurel, and hardwood. At the 0.5-mile point, the trail branches off to the right. Go straight ahead on the unmarked Stony Brook Trail. This broad and distinct path continues to run along the brook.

In about another 0.5 mile, you will come to a bridge across the brook to your left. Do not cross the bridge but continue straight ahead on the white-blazed Kakiat Trail, which has entered from the left. After a short distance, you will come to another bridge. Cross Pine Meadow Brook on this bridge and then immediately bear right. Continue to follow the white blazes, climbing over large rocks, with the brook on your right. In about 0.3 mile, this climb takes you to the Cascade of Slid, a beautiful waterfall and pool. It's a perfect spot to sit and relax. Frank Place, author of the 1923 edition of the *New York Walk Book*, named the cascade after a fanciful character in Lord Dunsany's book *The Gods of Pegana*.

Continue on the white-blazed Kakiat Trail. Soon you will pass a bridge on your right (don't cross it). Here, an orange-blazed trail, the Hillburn-Torne-Sebago Trail, crosses. Continue straight ahead on the Kakiat Trail. You will note that some of the Kakiat blazes near this intersection have a black "K" on them, so you can be sure that you are following the correct trail. Almost immediately after passing the bridge, the Kakiat Trail reverts to the plain white blaze. In another 0.3 mile, the blue-on-white blazed Seven Hills Trail joins the Kakiat from the left. Continue straight ahead, following the white and blue-on-white blazes. After less than 0.1 mile, the two trails meet the red-on-white-blazed Pine Meadow Trail at a bridge.

Here you have a choice. You can continue on to Pine Meadow Lake—less than a mile from this spot—or shorten the hike by turning back here to the visitors center. (Those who walked in from Sloatsburg have already walked 1.6 extra miles to the visitors center and must cover the same distance on the return to Sloatsburg.)

Those who want to shorten the hike should turn right on the red-on-white-blazed Pine Meadow Trail, crossing the bridge. After the bridge, the Pine Meadow Trail then bears right and follows along the brook, approximately 1.6 miles back to the visitors center. (Refer to the end of this hike for additional details.)

Those who are continuing on to the lake should not cross the bridge. Instead, continue straight ahead on the red-on-white-blazed Pine Meadow Trail. In 0.25 mile, you will see some very large boulders on your right. This formation is called Ga-Nus-Quah Rock (the Stone Giant). Directly upstream from these rocks is a wonderful natural bathtub and waterfall, a good rest stop.

After passing this spot, you will once again leave the brook below as you head up through a gap between two hills and come to a clear area, with Diamond Mountain on your left and a marsh on your right. Here, a broad path leads straight ahead, while the Pine Meadow Trail turns left and passes a stone foundation with eight concrete columns rising from it. This is the ruin of the headquarters building for the Civilian Conservation Corps camps in the area. In a short distance, the broad path rejoins the Pine Meadow Trail.

Soon the Pine Meadow Trail turns sharply right. To the left, 0.4 mile from Ga-Nus-Quah-Rock, you will see an unmarked path that leads to the yellow-blazed Tower Trail. Continue on the red-on-white-blazed Pine Meadow Trail, which crosses a stream and heads uphill through laurel bushes. At the top of the hill, you emerge from the woods onto a dirt road. To your right is the dam of Pine Meadow Lake. From the rock ledge next to it you can get a good view of the lake. The red-on-white blazes follow the shore of the lake for a short distance until the trail cuts across the base of a small peninsula. Many faint trails branch off here, so be alert. You may notice one or two yellow circular metal blazes in this area. These signs indicate that the paths are for horses.

Shortly, the Pine Meadow Trail returns to the lakeside and stays by it for 0.5 mile or so, until it reaches the far end of the lake. Here are the remains of a stone pumphouse, designed to house pumps that would move water through the labyrinth of pipes to supply CCC camps around this and surrounding lakes. These camps were never built, however, and the pumphouse was never used.

If you continue on the Pine Meadow Trail for another 0.2 mile, you will reach the site of Conklin's cabin. Built around 1779 by Matthew Conklin, the cabin was occupied until 1930. The last inhabitant, Ramsey Conklin, was a great-great-grandson of the original builder. He was forced out when the lake was flooded by the Civilian Conservation Corps, but continued to spend his summers in the area. (The junction of the white-blazed Conklin's Crossing Trail is 0.1 mile ahead.)

From the former cabin site, the hike now retraces itself back 1.5 miles to the bridge where the Pine Meadow Trail meets the blue-on-white Seven Hills Trail. Turn left and cross the bridge and follow the red-on-white blazes of the Pine Meadow Trail. Soon the blue-on-white Seven Hills Trail goes off to the left; continue ahead, following the red-on-white blazes. The orange-blazed Hillburn-Torne-Sebago Trail will come in from the left, run along with the Pine Meadow Trail for a short distance, and then go downhill to the right. Stay on the Pine Meadow Trail. You are passing the Cascade of Slid from high on the side of the gorge; in the summer it can be heard but not seen through the dense foliage. In about another 15 minutes, the trail crosses a cleared strip (for a gas line) and goes onto a footbridge over a brook. Shortly after, the unmarked Stony Brook Trail comes in from the right. From this point, you are returning on the same trail you started on.

20

Claudius Smith Den

Distance	8.1 miles
Hiking time	5 hours
Rating	Moderately strenuous

Within the boundaries of Harriman-Bear Mountain State Park are 52,000 acres of dense woodland and mountainous terrain that have been preserved from the development that has affected much of the rest of the metropolitan area. The hiking trails in the park, among them a section of the Maine-to-Georgia route of the Appalachian Trail, meander through intimate pine forests, follow the shores of quiet lakes, and climb to rocky peaks that afford panoramic views of the surrounding mountains and valleys.

The hike from Tuxedo Park up to the hideout of the notorious Revolutionary War bandit Claudius Smith follows a circular route of about eight miles in the southwestern part of Harriman Park, 30 miles northwest of the George Washington Bridge.

Directions   Drivers can take Route 17 to Tuxedo Park. Parking is permitted in the parking lot at the train station on weekends. It is more convenient to leave cars at a larger parking lot just north of the train station that can be used every day of the week. It is advisable to inform the police that you are parking there.

For users of public transportation, Short Line buses make regular runs to Tuxedo Park from the Port Authority Bus Terminal (call Short Line for exact departure times). The ride takes about an hour to the parking lot alongside the Tuxedo railroad station. There is a bus shelter directly across the highway, which is the pickup point for the bus on the return trip. Although it is cheaper to purchase a round-trip ticket at the Port Authority, bus tickets for the return trip can be bought at the IGA supermarket, about 500 feet south of the bus shelter on Route 17. (**Note:** The supermarket closes at 3:00pm on Sundays.)

Tuxedo Park can also be reached by the New Jersey Transit and Metro-North Commuter Railroad trains, which depart from Hoboken, New Jersey. Connecting trains of the Port Authority Trans-Hudson line (PATH) depart from 33rd Street and the World Trade Center in Manhattan. The train from Hoboken takes about 50 minutes to get to Tuxedo. As of this writing in 2001, on weekends there is one morning departure from Hoboken, and one late afternoon return train.

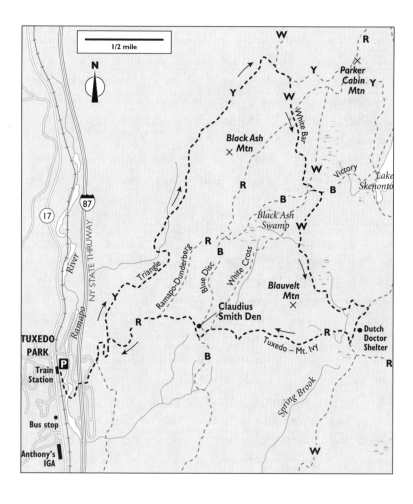

Just north of the train station on the west side of Route 17 is a 5,000-acre private-gated community known as Tuxedo Park. Now a year-round residence, it was once a famous weekend and summer resort for the wealthy from New York City. It was founded by Pierre Lorillard V (of the tobacco family) in 1885 from purchased and inherited land. Tuxedo Park was intended originally as a private club limited to the more notable of the Who's Who in The Four Hundred. It soon outranked many other New York resorts and rivaled Saratoga and Newport for the carriage trade. Today it clings to its old reputation, but like many other old-time resorts, has been bypassed as the automobile and the airplane have made other areas more accessible.

The Walk   Walk south from the parking lot for a short distance along the railroad tracks past the train/police station. You are now following the route of the Ramapo-Dunderberg Trail, the first trail in Harriman State Park to be built by the New York-New Jersey Trail Conference (then known as the Palisades Interstate Park Trail Conference). This trail winds all the way across the park to the Hudson River. The first trail marker, a red dot on a white background, appears on a telephone pole along the tracks. Follow the markers across the tracks and down to the footbridge over the Ramapo River. About 400 feet beyond the footbridge, you will turn right on a paved road (East Village Road.) Follow it under the New York Thruway and then turn left onto Grove Drive. About 750 feet up this road, follow the red-dot-on-white markers to the right, up into the woods of Harriman State Park. The white trail coming in from the extreme right down the woods road is the Kakiat Trail, which leads to Kakiat County Park in Montebello.

After an uphill hike of about 200 yards, look for three yellow triangle blazes on a tree to the left. This indicates the start of the Triangle Trail. You have walked 0.65 mile from the train station. Turn off the Ramapo-Dunderberg Trail and follow the yellow triangles as they wind uphill. The Triangle Trail continues to climb for a short distance, then levels off and passes through a stand of birch before descending into the shadows and patches of sunlight beneath pines. About 20 to 30 minutes' walk beyond, about 0.5 mile, at the intersection of a telephone line with a firebreak (a north-south corridor, 30 yards wide and cleared of trees), there is a clear mountain stream, two feet deep in places, off the trail to the left and down the corridor.

If you walk down to the stream, note the old roads you cross on the way. The park is filled with these woods roads; they once connected the mines, furnaces, forges, and charcoal pits that were scattered throughout these mountains. Some of the woods roads were in existence during the Revolutionary War and were used by the Americans to transport munitions and supplies to avoid British detection.

Returning to the trail, follow the telephone line uphill briefly and then turn to follow the woods road to the right. In about 300 yards, you will come to a pretty stream cascading over stone ledges. The stream comes down from the right and crosses the roadway. Continue along the woods road until you meet the telephone line again in another 0.3 mile. Cross the right-of-way and continue on the woods road. The Triangle Trail turns sharply left and soon crosses Black Ash Brook; it then turns right onto another woods road, which leads through a passage where outcrops of stone rise 20 to 30 feet above the trail on both sides for about 100 yards. At 1.25 mile on the Triangle Trail, it crosses Deep Hollow Brook and then begins to ascend gradually. Soon the trail levels off. For the next 1.0 mile or so, the trail continues through a valley, with Black Ash Mountain to the right. There are a few ups and downs and several minor streams to be crossed.

Finally, after crossing another stream, the trail turns right, climbs a slope, and turns right again onto the route of the White Bar Trail, marked with white horizontal blazes. The distance to this point from Deep Hollow Brook is 1.35 miles, so count on about an hour to cover this part of the hike. The Triangle and White Bar trails coincide for about 750 feet, with a low ridge of outcropped bedrock on the left. The large boulders that sit isolated on top of the ledge are "erratics," rocks that were picked up and carried along by glaciers. When the glaciers melted, the rocks were left here, far from the place of their origin.

Stay on the White Bar Trail as the Triangle Trail bears left toward Parker Cabin Mountain. Just a few hundred yards ahead, the White Bar

Trail crosses the Ramapo-Dunderberg Trail. The terrain along the White Bar Trail continues level for a while, with a silhouette view of the distant mountains to the east. Then the trail descends for about 0.15 mile into a valley, at the bottom of which is the extensive Black Ash Swamp. On the way, the path crosses the White Cross Trail.

The White Bar Trail turns left and crosses the swamp on a natural causeway. The Victory Trail (blue V on white) joins briefly, but stay on the White Bar Trail as it leaves the causeway and climbs through thick bushes up the other side of the valley—the steepest climb of the day. The view from the top of the slope is magnificent. Straight ahead to the south is Blauvelt Mountain, 1,177 feet high; to the northeast, behind you, is Parker Cabin Mountain, 1,200 feet; and to the northwest, so close that individual trees and rocks are discernible on its slope, is Black Ash Mountain, 1,044 feet. You might see hawks or turkey vultures circling between the mountains as they search for prey in the swamp below.

The White Bar Trail soon begins to descend. It winds around a patch of swamp, follows a stream alongside large boulders, and then circles to meet the end of the Triangle Trail, which has swung back from Parker Cabin Mountain. Stay on the White Bar Trail as it turns right. About 700 feet ahead, you will see the Dutch Doctor Shelter on the left, a short distance up the slope from the trail. Overnight camping is permitted in the open lean-tos, such as Dutch Doctor Shelter, that are scattered throughout the park.

About 500 feet beyond the shelter, the White Bar Trail runs into the Tuxedo-Mt. Ivy Trail (hereafter called the T-MI). This trail is blazed with a red dash on white —not to be confused with the Ramapo-Dunderberg blaze, a red dot on white.

Turn right (a sharp horseshoe turn) onto the T-MI, which heads northwest at first and then west toward Tuxedo Park. A little over 0.25 mile ahead, opposite a small patch of marsh reeds, a 30-foot-high outcrop of bedrock appears on the right side of the trail. Weathering has

From 1776 to 1778, Claudius Smith and his band of British sympathizers, among them his three sons, William, James, and Richard, terrorized residents of the Ramapo Pass. At first, as Loyalists, they stole only horses and cattle and sold them to the British troops, but later they raided homes and farms for whatever valuable booty could be had. They would sometimes burn the homes and murder the occupants. Following a night raid, the gang would return to the caves. The upper chamber was their hideout, while the lower one was used to stable the stolen animals. This was only one of their hideouts; at other times they used Horse Stable Rock, about a half mile from Route 202 near Wesley Chapel. Eventually, New York Governor Clinton offered a $1,200 reward for the capture of Smith. Since $1,200 in those days was a huge sum of money, Smith fled to Long Island and placed himself under British protection. There a supporter of the Revolution recognized him, formed a posse to capture him, and collected the reward. Smith was tried and, on January 22, 1779, hanged at Goshen, New York.

Smith and his band were not the first to use the caves for shelter. The Minsi Native Americans on their hunting expeditions returned every season to this and other protected campsites in the Highlands; pottery shards and arrowheads have been found nearby.

broken large chunks from its side to expose wavy bands of light and dark rock; these were once horizontal sedimentary strata subsequently twisted, bent, and hardened under tremendous compression.

In another 0.75 mile, immediately after intersecting the White Cross Trail, the T-MI makes a sharp left. For the moment, bear right and go to the edge of a large rock outcrop. You will find yourself standing on the edge of a cliff, overlooking the forest and hills stretching out in front of you like a carpet.

Photo by Tom Rupolo

Return to the T-MI and follow it down a narrow, rocky gorge. On the way down, you will cross the Blue Disc Trail (blue dot on white). The T-MI passes a small cave in the side of the cliff and another larger one at the bottom. These cliffs, or overhangs, are known as Claudius Smith Den, after the rampaging bandit who used them as a hideout.

About 0.35 mile farther on, the Tuxedo-Mt. Ivy Trail ends at an intersection with the Ramapo-Dunderberg Trail (red dot on white). Take the Ramapo-Dunderberg left (west) and stay on it the rest of the way, 1.25 miles, back to Tuxedo Park. The trail descends and then climbs to the left, passing an excellent viewpoint at Smith Rock, from which one can see west to Tuxedo Park and the train station. From here the trail rapidly descends to the road. Follow the Ramapo-Dunderberg blazes along the road, under the Thruway, across the river, and back to the station.

Drivers who parked north of the train station should turn left off the trail onto Grove Street and then right onto East Village Road where, a short distance ahead, the parking lot is located.

Photo by Tom Rupolo

21

Bear Mountain

Distance	9 miles
Hiking time	5.5 hours
Rating	Strenuous

*T*his circular hike on four trails in Harriman–Bear Mountain Park includes a gorge walk along a rushing stream, a steep climb to and from the summit of Bear Mountain, and superb views of the Hudson River and nearby mountains. It is for the stout-hearted and the very fit.

Note: As described, the steep climb to and from the top of Bear Mountain come close to the end of the hike, which can be difficult for many hikers. Directions for reversing the hike, so that the steepest climb is closer to the beginning, are included at the end of this chapter.

Directions   The hike starts at the Bear Mountain Inn, located on Route 9W in Rockland County just south of the Bear Mountain Bridge. Bus transportation is available to Bear Mountain from Port Authority in New York City. Schedules change frequently, so be sure to call for exact departure times; see the Park and Transportation Information section at the back of this book. Car drivers should park at the Bear Mountain Inn. It is best to get an early start since the parking lots adjacent to the inn can fill up in nice weather. There is a parking fee on weekends. See the end of this section for an alternative parking area and start for those with cars.

The Walk   From the inn, look for the white blazes of the Appalachian Trail (AT). Follow them as they head north on the east side of Hessian Lake. Approximately half way along the lake, the AT turns right to cross Route 9W. Continue on the trail as it passes through the Bear Mountain Park Zoo (there is a small fee to walk through the zoo in season) and to the tollbooths of the Bear Mountain Bridge at a crosswalk. Take the crosswalk to the north side of the road and then turn west (left) to follow the sidewalk as it follows the traffic circle counter-clockwise and then north on the continuation of Route 9W. After leaving the traffic circle proper and walking for about 100 feet, look across the road for three red-dot-on-white triple blazes marking the start of the Popolopen Gorge Trail. The trailhead is 50 feet south of the 9W bridge over the gorge on the west side of the road.

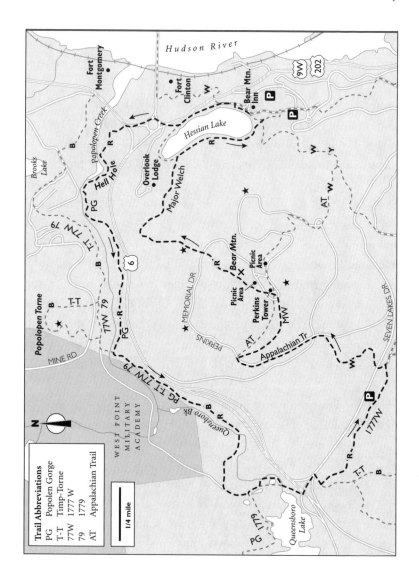

Two Revolutionary War era forts, both burned to the ground by the British army in their effort to gain control of the Hudson River, once stood near this spot. Fort Montgomery was just north of Popolopen Gorge and to the east. Fort Clinton was located just east of Hessian Lake; all evidence of this fort was removed during the construction of the Bear Mountain Bridge.

Hessian Lake was originally known as Lake Sinnipink, then Highland Lake, and now Hessian Lake. The bodies of some of the Hessian soldiers killed in the fight for the two forts were dumped into this lake; their blood so reddened its waters that at the time it became known as "Bloody Pond."

The Popolopen Gorge Trail starts out on an old woods road and follows the south side of the gorge, eventually descending to water level. The road is the course of old Route 9W. At a clearing about half way down toward the water is the site of the former bridge across Popolopen Creek. The clearing sits on top of rockwork supporting the south end of the bridge. The northern support is easily visible on the other side. You will soon come to a spillway over an old dam with deep pools and cascades below. It is best seen from the ledge to the right of the trail, facing the falls. This scene is especially beautiful in the spring when the water gushes over the dam at full strength. In summer the area is a popular picnic destination. Though the pools have long been used by swimmers, Hell Hole, as the spot is known locally, has its dangers, and there have been several deaths here. The trail ascends briefly from here before finally dropping to near water level.

As you continue to hike beyond Hell Hole, watch for more pools and old roadways, huge rocks, hemlocks, and sycamores along the banks of the creek, as the trail gently rises from the banks of the creek through a series of more ups than downs. About 0.3 mile from the dam, the trail turns left and climbs steeply to the old Bear Mountain Aqueduct, away from the gorge, which continues to be visible from above. Follow the aqueduct's surface as it slowly climbs. In 0.1 mile, the trail turns right, away from the aqueduct path, and heads downward toward the creek again. In a further 0.15 mile, it joins the Timp-Torne Trail (blazed blue) and two revolutionary-era trails—1777W (red 1777 on white diamond) and 1779 (blue 1779 on white diamond). The 1777W trail marks the route taken by the British in their attack on Forts Clinton and Montgomery, while the 1779 trail is the path taken by General Anthony Wayne in 1779 to defeat the British at Stony Point. Both of these trails were inaugurated in 1976 for the Bicentennial celebration. From the start of the hike at the inn to this junction of four trails is a distance of 2.2 miles—about an hour's walk.

The four trails continue together as they head west along the bank of Popolopen Creek, following an old woods road for part of the way as they skirt the West Point boundary. After rising and descending again to water level, the trails top a small rise and reach Queensboro Brook. The four trails cross the brook on the very narrow concrete surface of an old aqueduct. Many parts of the hand railings were washed away during Hurricane Floyd, and the Park officials removed the rest. Only the aqueduct itself remains. Across the aqueduct, the trails turn to follow a sometimes muddy woods road. This road meets at a T junction with Fort Montgomery Road, a gravel road. It is still in use by park officials for vehicle traffic. Turn left onto the road. A short distance from the intersection, it is closed to hikers to accommodate a State Park Police firing range; a big sign warns, "Caution, Pistol Range, Stay on Marked Trails." The trails split here. Go left and stay with the Timp-Torne/1777W trails. (The Popolopen/1779 trails go to the right.) You will soon pass the firing range and picnic tables on the right and a stream on the left; after them, the trail rejoins the gravel road and turns left onto it. The road becomes paved just as it reaches a water treatment plant at Queensboro Dam. Continue on the pavement until it reaches the exit ramp for Major Welch Drive as it joins the Palisades Interstate Parkway at Exit 19. Turn left to cross the parkway via the overpass, staying on its south side. At the barrier, turn immediately right. On the other side of the barrier you will see the blazes of the Timp-Torne/1777W trails and yet another road. Cross the road and look for similar blazes.

As you enter the woods here, notice that the Timp-Torne and 1777W trails divide. Timp-Torne goes straight ahead toward West Mountain. You go left on the blazed 1777W trail which, in this stretch, parallels Seven Lakes Drive. A short way up the trail is a swampy area that can be very difficult to cross when wet. In 0.6 mile from the turning point, you will come to a small parking lot. Look for the 1777W Trail marker at the other end of the parking lot and follow it a short distance until you reach the white blaze of the Appalachian Trail (AT); turn left onto the AT.

The AT crosses Seven Lakes Drive, then reenters the woods. From here the top of Bear Mountain (1,350 feet high) is a distance of 1.6 miles. The trail climbs steeply for a short distance and then more gradually; you pass a woods road and come to Perkins Memorial Drive; turn left onto it. Follow the white blazes uphill on the left side of the road, facing traffic. The road can be quite busy at times; beware of drivers distracted by the views. As you hike up along the road, watch the trees on the right side for the blaze of the Major Welch Trail (red-circle-on-white square). A few feet beyond that marker is the white blaze of the Appalachian Trail. You can take either trail up Bear Mountain; they converge at the top.

(If you do not feel like climbing any more, continue on Perkins Memorial Drive, walking beyond a viewpoint to catch the Major Welch Trail coming down the mountain. Look for its red-circle-on-white-square blaze on the left, and follow it down to return to the Bear Mountain Inn, as described further below.)

The views from the top of Bear Mountain on a clear day are spectacular. Truly clear days with no haze in the distance are rare; you will be well rewarded if you scout the weather reports for a good day. The stone tower on the summit is a memorial to George W. Perkins, Sr., first president of the Palisades Interstate Park Commission (from 1900 to 1920). Here also is a plaque fixed on a stone just below the summit in honor of Joseph Bartha, Trails Committee Chairman of the New York-New Jersey Trail Conference from 1940 to 1955.

When you are ready to continue, head north on the Major Welch Trail (red circle on white), which connects with the Appalachian Trail at the summit. The Major Welch Trail runs past a large outdoor restroom and continues on the road for about 75 feet. Look for a very large boulder, more than half buried, on your left. The blazes take you to the right of the boulder along the edge of a small road and then immediately into the woods behind the boulder. The trail descends very steeply for 900 feet, crossing Perkins Memorial Drive approximately 20 minutes (0.5 mile) from the Perkins Tower at the top. The trail shifts left on the road approximately 50 feet before reentering the woods. Continue down the trail. You will come to an open, rocky area, where there are good views of the meandering Hudson River to the north. Follow the marker at the left of the rocks to continue the steep descent. The trail levels off on a 400-foot contour on the northeast of Bear Mountain, then resumes its drop for about half a mile before coming out onto a woods road. Almost immediately, it veers to the left, then finally emerges at the north end of Hessian Lake, where a comfortable bench awaits you. In the winter and spring it can be very wet here. Turn right onto the paved path and walk back to the Bear Mountain Inn.

This hike can be done in reverse. From the Bear Mountain Inn, find the Major Welch Trail (red circle on white) by taking the paved path on the west side of Hessian Lake and watching for the left turn near the north end of the lake. Climb to the summit of Bear Mountain and

proceed down the south side on the Appalachian Trail (white blaze) to the 1777W Trail. Take this trail north all the way to the junction with the Popolopen Gorge Trail (red dot on white), which splits off to the east (right). Take the Popolopen Gorge Trail east to Route 9W, then cross the Palisades Parkway to get back to Hessian Lake and the Bear Mountain Inn.

Car drivers can also start this hike on the 1777W Trail from a free parking lot on the south side of Seven Lakes Drive. A narrow, roughly paved road, 0.2 mile west of where Perkins Drive turns to go up the mountain, takes you to the lot, which is less crowded than those at the inn. Walk in either direction.

Clockwise or counter-clockwise, this hike makes for an exhilarating and scenic experience.

Hudson
Highlands

HUDSON HIGHLANDS
Nature's Landscape

The mountainous area through which the Hudson River flows between Newburgh and Peekskill—a distance of only 15 miles—is known as the Hudson Highlands. At the northern end of the Highlands, Breakneck and Storm King Mountains stand as guardians of the serene riverscape of the upper Hudson. At the southern end, known as South Gate and easily viewed from Peekskill, the river flows past Dunderberg Mountain, Bear Mountain, and Anthony's Nose. The Bear Mountain Bridge anchors on Anthony's Nose and links Highland parks and roadways on either side of the river.

This is a land of romance, where fairies cavort on Crows Nest and forest spirits haunt eerie ravines. Painters of the Hudson River School have celebrated its architecture of rugged mountains and sublime riverscapes. The views from the mountains in this area—some of which are well over 1,000 feet high—are among the best in the world.

Efforts to preserve the beauty of the Highlands began in 1922 when Ernest Stillman gave about 800 acres in the Storm King Clove (a "clove" is a chasm or valley) to the Palisades Interstate Park. Stillman was also responsible for preserving the area now known as Black Rock Forest, which he donated to Harvard University in 1949; the forest was later acquired by a not-for-profit consortium that promotes scientific research and education and ensures the continued preservation of the area for hiking. Black Rock, which is on the south side of Route 9W just southwest of Storm King Mountain, includes many reservoirs that supply water to local communities and refreshing vistas for hikers. On the east side of the Hudson, efforts to acquire land for preservation began only in 1938 but accelerated in the 1960s. In 1992, with the assistance of the Lila Acheson and DeWitt Wallace Fund, Scenic Hudson Trust acquired 845 acres in the Fishkill area. The property is managed as an extension of Hudson Highlands State Park, in which most of the other hiking trails on the east side of the Hudson River are located.

Photo by Jane Daniels

The Highlands were a strategic area during the early years of the Revolutionary War. General Washington feared that the British navy might try to cut off all transport between the northern and southern colonies by gaining control of the Hudson River. He urged that the area's defenses be strengthened. Washington's fears were justified when in 1776 and 1777 the British launched two campaigns to control the river. In their second effort, in 1777, the British landed at Stony Point and advanced overland along a route that today is marked by the 1777 Trail in Bear Mountain Park. In bitter and bloody battle at Popolopen Creek, the British destroyed Forts Montgomery and Clinton. They then had clear sailing up the river to Kingston, the provincial capital, which they burned. But when the Americans defeated General Burgoyne at Saratoga in October 1777, a turning point of the war, the British withdrew to Manhattan to protect their flanks. They had held the Highlands for only 20 days. The scene of war shifted to the south shortly thereafter.

The Highlands were once considered a refuge from the epidemics that ravaged New York City during the 19th century. Tuberculosis was widespread; outbreaks of cholera and malaria were frequent. Doctors recommended mountain air to escape the bad "miasma" gas of the city, which they felt contributed to the spread of these diseases. The nearest mountains were in the Highlands. Cornwall, just north of Storm King, became one of the most popular health spas in the area.

After the Civil War the Highlands attracted railroad barons and other wealthy people. They built castles on the shores of the Hudson, which became known as Millionaire's Row. Railroads were built on both sides of the Hudson River to make the area more accessible. This development, which skyrocketed property values, and the growth of industry, especially the manufacture of iron, changed the character of the Highlands significantly.

We are fortunate that these same millionaires later contributed much of their property to the cause of preservation and the creation of parklands in the Highlands.

Photo by Jim Morgan

22

Camp Smith Trail

Distance	3.8 or 3.9 miles
Hiking time	4.5 hours
Rating	Moderately strenuous

*E*xcellent viewpoints along the way to Anthony's Nose provide broad panoramas of the Hudson River as it snakes its way south toward Stony Point and Haverstraw Bay. Since the trail often passes close to busy Route 6/202, expect traffic noise to accompany this hike. In addition you may hear gunshots from the National Guard's rifle practice at Camp Smith. The views, however, more than make up for these noisy interruptions.

Volunteers from the New York-New Jersey Trail Conference and students in the National Guard's ChalleNGe program at Camp Smith constructed the trail on property then owned by the camp. (Camp Smith is a unit of the National Guard and the site is heavily used for training throughout the year.) In 1998, the summit of Anthony's Nose, four acres surrounding the tollhouse, and 50 feet on either side of the trail became part of Hudson Highlands State Park.

The full length of the Camp Smith Trail, which is blazed blue the entire route, is 3.7 miles from its start at the old tollhouse on Route 6/202 to its intersection with the Appalachian Trail beyond Anthony's Nose. The trail rises and falls relentlessly, traversing steep slopes. Three long flights of well-constructed rock steps help hikers ascend and descend the steep areas. The easiest section of the trail to hike is in either direction from the U bend where the road is farthest from the river to the first viewpoints.

Directions   The Camp Smith Trail can be accessed from Route 6/202 (located east and south of the Bear Mountain Bridge) or from Route 9D. There are parking areas and access routes at three places: the southernmost one is at the start of the trail next to the tollhouse on Route 6/202, 0.7 mile north of the entrance to Camp Smith; the second, also on Route 6/202, is 2.2 miles north of the Camp Smith entrance (roughly midway between the tollhouse and Anthony's Nose), at a U bend, where the road is farthest from the river; the third is along Route 9D near Anthony's Nose, just north of the Bear Mountain Bridge.

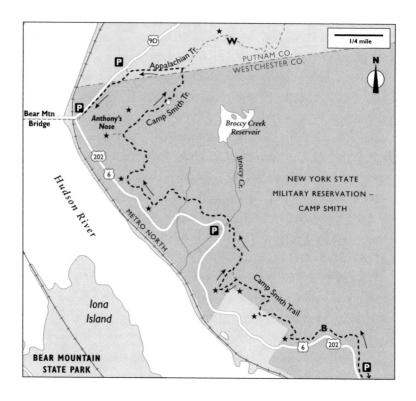

Public transportation is available by taking a taxi 2.5 miles from the Metro-North station in Peekskill to the tollhouse trailhead. At the end of the hike follow the Appalachian Trail over the Bear Mountain Bridge to the Bear Mountain Inn to catch the Short Line Bus back to the Port Authority. Alternatively, on weekends and holidays, catch one of two late afternoon Grand Central-bound trains that are scheduled to stop at Manitou, if the conductor sees you (check Metro-North schedule).

The Walk   The Camp Smith Trail starts at the tollhouse on Route 6/202 and proceeds to Anthony's Nose and the Bear Mountain Bridge. Those with a car parked at the tollhouse may want to retrace their path from the summit back to the tollhouse for a total distance of 6.2 miles. There are several exit points on the trail, as described above, for those who want to shorten the hike. The triple blue blaze of the Camp Smith Trail is on a tree behind and to the left of the tollhouse. The area is full of poison ivy and near rifle ranges (the land to the east is actively used by the National Guard for training exercises), so stay on the trodden path.

The trail starts uphill almost immediately. Ahead is the first of four registers (sign-in sheets) on the trail. Soon after, you reach the first set of stone steps. The trail goes down over many rocks as it hugs the side of huge boulders and parallels the sights and sounds of Route 6/202. At 0.6 mile, about 20 minutes from the start of the hike, you will reach the second set of stone steps. The ascent is short but arduous. You come to the first viewpoint looking down the Hudson River. The Indian Point nuclear plant is in front of you. The body of water to your left is the Annsville Creek. The Hudson flows south along its S curve toward Stony Point in the distance.

Annsville Creek, visible from the Camp Smith Trail, is joined in a bay at the east shore of the Hudson by Peekskill Hollow Creek, a long stream that drains much of Fahnestock State Park. (The bay is crossed by the railroad and frequently has swans swimming and breeding in it.) During the Revolutionary War, there was a little hamlet near Peekskill Hollow Creek called Continental Village. It was so named because the village was a depot for Continental, or government, cattle and stores. These were destroyed in 1777, right after the capture of Forts Clinton and Montgomery, by Hessian mercenaries hired by the British to quell the rebellion of the colonies. General William Tryon, the British commander and former governor of New York State, ordered every house in the hamlet burned to the ground. Tryon had already devastated Danbury and several towns on Long Island in the same way. It is only fair to point out that these marauding expeditions were condemned by the British public and censured by the opposition in Parliament.

Photo by Tom Rupolo

The trail now heads slightly downhill over some rocks and then up through a more forested area to another viewpoint called Two Pines view. (Actually, there are three pines, but you will not see the third one until you reach the viewpoint.) Two Pines is about 45 minutes from the start of the hike, or 0.9 mile. The trail continues its uphill course to more points that offer improving views of Iona Island and Dunderberg and Bear Mountains across the Hudson.

The path soon heads downhill, and you will encounter the second register. After the register, the trail veers close to the highway (Route 6/202), which you can clearly see. A path from the U bend parking area joins the Camp Smith Trail at this point. Stay on the blue-blazed trail as it veers right. The climb is again uphill through thicker woods. The third register is ahead, and the climb continues to another magnificent viewpoint overlooking Iona Island. This spot is 2.5 miles from the tollhouse.

Iona Island was a strategic defense post during the Revolutionary War. In the mid-1800s it was a thriving vineyard, which also contained 2,000 to 3,000 pear and other fruit trees. It was reported that the vineyard produced more grapes and other fruit than all other such establishments in the United States combined at that time. The Iona grape takes its name from the island.

In the early 1900s the island was a resort for picnickers from New York City. They would come up by barge or via the railroad that skirts the island's western, inland border. The island is separated from the mainland by a marshy inlet that was called Doodletown Harbor. There was a port here that served Doodletown, a small village, located about a mile inland from present Route 9W. The site is part of Bear Mountain State Park. The buildings presently on Iona Island are remnants of extensive facilities used to store naval supplies during both world wars. The island is now a wildlife refuge. Bald eagles winter on the southern part of the island. If you face west, Dunderberg Mountain (1,100 feet) is on your left, Bear Mountain (1,350 feet) is straight ahead, and Popolopen Torne looms up on the right beyond the Bear Mountain Bridge.

The width of the Hudson at Iona Island is only 3/8 of a mile, the narrowest point of the river below Albany. Here the water is deep and the tidal currents are so swift and dangerous that this stretch of the river was once called "Devil's Horse Race."

From this viewpoint the trail continues relentlessly uphill another 0.4 mile to the top of Anthony's Nose (899 feet). The summit is reached in about 30 minutes from the third register. A small, round, metal plaque placed on the rock by the U.S. Geological Survey marks the top. Walk north, down from the summit, about 50 feet and turn left; a viewpoint overlooking the Bear Mountain Bridge is just below. This is the best

Photo by Tom Rupolo

place for lunch. The view from here is broadly panoramic and stunning. Across the Hudson were the two forts destroyed by the British in the early days of the Revolutionary War. The few remnants of the northern fort, Fort Montgomery, are very difficult to reach, but there has been talk of restoration. All evidence of the southern fort, Fort Clinton, was removed during the construction of the Bear Mountain Bridge. Directly across the river is the lake where the bodies of some of the Hessian soldiers killed in the fight for these forts were dumped. Their blood so reddened its waters that it became known as "Bloody Pond." The lake was originally known as Lake Sinnipink, then Highland Lake, and now is known as Hessian Lake.

The Camp Smith Trail continues ahead on an old woods road and, in 0.6 mile, it ends at the intersection with the Appalachian Trail. The fourth and last register is on your right; just past it turn left on the white-blazed Appalachian Trail and head south. In 0.6 mile you will reach Route 9D. Hikers taking the train from Manitou will turn right on Route 9D and walk 1.0 mile to Manitou Station Road, on your left across from South Mountain Pass Road. Then walk 0.6 mile downhill to the station. Those taking the bus will turn left, following the Appalachian Trail 1.5 miles southbound and across the Bear Mountain Bridge to the Bear Mountain Inn. The view from the bridge is an opportunity you should not miss, even if you only walk out a short distance and return.

23
Canada Hill

Distance	7.7 miles
Hiking time	5 hours
Rating	Moderate

The southern portion of Hudson Highlands State Park just above the east side of the Bear Mountain Bridge offers a smorgasbord of hikes to satisfy almost any taste. The varied terrain includes steep climbs, long stretches of level ground, and moderate ups and downs. Many viewpoints overlook the Hudson River. The laurel groves on Canada Hill are delightful, especially when in bloom in June. Just off the top of Sugarloaf Hill are colonies of prickly pear cactus, thriving on rocky sandy sites with a southern exposure.

Directions   Public transportation to the hikes in the southern Hudson Highlands is via Metro-North's Hudson Line to Manitou. Trains will stop at Manitou in the morning on weekends and holidays. You must tell the conductor that you want to get off here. Two return trains are scheduled to stop in the late afternoon (check Metro-North schedule), if the conductor sees you. The train stops in Garrison once each hour on weekdays, weekends, and holidays. Garrison is a better choice for a return trip as trains are more frequent.

For those coming by car, parking is available at three spots: at the Appalachian Trail crossing on South Mountain Pass Road, on Route 9D at Manitoga, and at the Castle Rock Unique Area, one mile south of the intersection of Routes 403 and 9D.

The Walk   Starting from the Manitou train stop, walk 0.5 mile up Manitou Station Road, turn left on Route 9D, and walk 0.1 mile to South Mountain Pass Road. Turn right onto this road and walk uphill another 0.5 to the white-blazed Appalachian Trail (AT). Turn left and go north on the AT. The trail switchbacks its way up Canada Hill. When the path begins to flatten out and you need to stop to catch your breath, make use of a viewpoint to your right. Across the way, on the side of Mine Hill, you will notice an open area. It is an old mine opened in 1767 and operated by Peter Hasenclever, a German iron master trained in England. Hasenclever operated numerous iron mines in what are now Ringwood

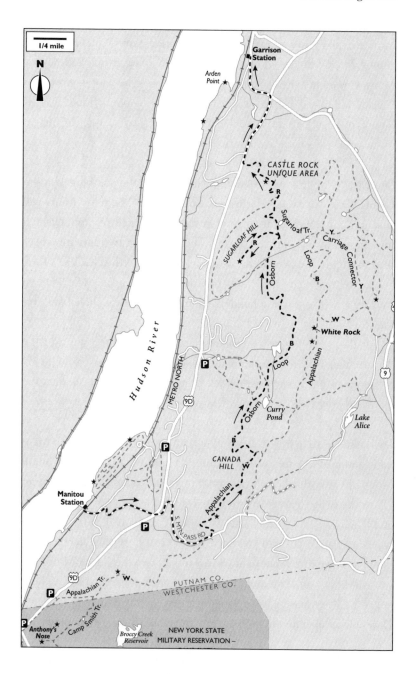

and Sterling Forest state parks. This mine contained iron pyrites and some copper, but was later mined for sulfur.

Continuing up the hill, but less steeply, the AT reaches the blue-blazed Osborn Loop; it is 1.0 mile after the South Mountain Pass. The Osborn Loop honors the family that donated the land to the state. The family has long been associated with the conservation movement. Henry Fairfield Osborn was president of the Museum of Natural History. His son, Fairfield, wrote *Our Plundered Planet*, one of the first books on the need for world-wide conservation, and served as president of the New York Zoological Society.

Turn left onto the Osborn Loop and begin to descend along the carriage road. In 0.7 mile, pass a trail to the left; it goes to Manitoga and a parking lot on Route 9D. Manitoga was the home of designer Russel Wright and means "spirit ground" in the Algonquin language. The trails on the property have different themes illustrating various aspects of nature. Stay on the Osborn Loop trail. You will come to an intersection with another carriage road; to the right is a wooden sign indicating the yellow-blazed Curry Pond Trail. Continue straight on the blue-blazed Osborn Loop, heading toward Sugarloaf Hill. In 0.2 mile the trail turns right off the carriage road and passes thorough laurel. Over the next 0.6 mile, you cross numerous streams on large stepping stones as you ascend the flank of Canada Hill. The seasonal view of the Hudson River provides an excuse to stop; you have hiked 3.6 miles from the Manitou train stop.

Continue on the trail and turn right onto a carriage road in 0.3 mile and then right again in 0.2 mile. When you come to a third intersection, look to your extreme left to find the red-blazed Sugarloaf Trail; it steeply ascends 0.5 mile to the top of Sugarloaf Hill. (Take care while on the rocks at the top not to step on the prickly pear cactus. You can find many colonies of this sun-loving succulent in the surrounding woods.) The view from Sugarloaf to the south toward the Bear Mountain Bridge is

beautiful, especially when glints of sunlight bounce off the waters of the Hudson River. To the northwest is the village of Highland Falls and West Point. To the east is Graymoor Christian Unity Center. Like Lorelei, Sugarloaf tempts hikers to stay forever. When you are ready to leave, retrace your steps 0.5 mile downhill.

Once down Sugarloaf Hill, stay on the red-blazed trail as it heads 1.1 miles down carriage roads toward Route 9D. Pay attention at the turns for the blazes, as red is hard to see in the dense shade of the hemlocks. Once the trail levels out, a field stretches before you. If you shortcut across the field before reaching a gazebo on the right, you will miss a lovely view toward West Point. The red trail ends on Route 9D at the stone pillars, one bearing the inscription "Wing & Wing." Hikers heading toward the Garrison train station need to turn right and walk 1 mile along the road. At the traffic light, turn left onto Lower Station Road. By the time you have walked the last 0.5 mile to the train station, you have hiked 7.7 miles.

24

Bull Hill and
Cold Spring

Distance	5 miles
Hiking time	5 hours
Rating	Strenuous

Above Cold Spring and Nelsonville rises a mountain that the local residents call Bull Hill. Hikers know it by its highbrow name, Mount Taurus. No matter what you call it, a hike to its 1,420-foot summit provides breathtaking views over the Hudson River.

The start of this hike is in Cold Spring, a charming place that seems more like a town in the Berkshires than a commuter suburb. The village center is a National Historic District with 19th-century buildings. The town attracts a literary coterie from New York City, which spends weekends and summers there and has been dubbed "Bloomsbury-on-Hudson." Cold Spring is a very visitor friendly town and offers numerous places to eat. However, as described by people who live there: "It's easier to buy antiques than groceries." On beautiful weekend days the sidewalks are crowded with visitors—a good excuse to head for the hills.

Directions   Public transportation is available via Metro-North's Hudson Line, with hourly trains to Cold Spring on weekends. The trailhead, on Route 9D north of the village, is a 0.8-mile walk from the train station (less than a mile from the village for those with cars). From the station, walk up Main Street. At Fair Street, opposite the village hall, turn left. When Fair Street ends at Route 9D, turn left. Ahead on the east side of the road is a small parking area, gate, and the trailhead.

As you head north on Route 9D from Cold Spring you will notice a bridge over the railroad tracks. This is almost directly across the highway from the trailhead and goes out to Little Stony Point, a small scenic peninsula that is crisscrossed by trails. The views of the Hudson Valley from Little Stony Point are superb, with Crows Nest and Storm King looming skyward across the river. On the southern portion of the peninsula's beach are the remains of an old iron mine shaft. Use the bridge over the railroad tracks to access Little Stony Point.

Bull Hill   A triple white blaze marks the beginning of the Washburn Trail. Go uphill, following the road; it leads into an old quarry, opened in 1931 by the Hudson River Stone Corporation. The grass, sparse

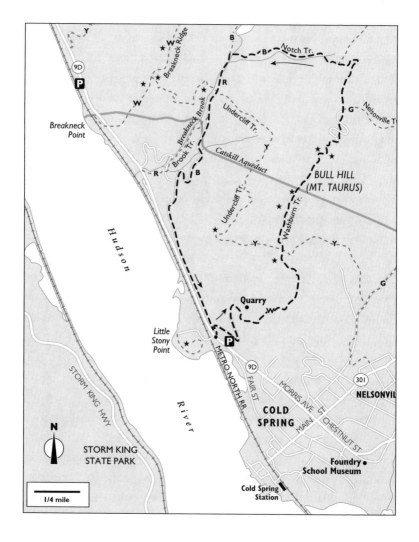

undergrowth, and small trees on the quarry floor may remind you of a savanna. At 0.4 mile, just before the road enters the quarry, look for the white blazes of the Washburn Trail; it veers sharply to the right and goes along the southern rim for 0.1 mile. Cuts in the rocks and pipes are all that remain from the quarry operations, which closed in 1967.

Turn right, leave the quarry rim, and begin to ascend Bull Hill more steeply. In another 0.1 mile, there is a viewpoint 30 feet to the right overlooking Cold Spring and the Hudson River. The trail continues to climb steeply for another 0.6 mile, offering two more viewpoints, where you can stop and catch your breath. In clear weather these views to the west—of Storm King, Crows Nest, and the Hudson River—are picture-postcard delights.

At the end of the steep section and 1.2 miles from the trailhead, you cross the yellow-blazed Undercliff Trail. Stay on the white-blazed Washburn Trail. In the next 0.7 mile, the path ascends, dips slightly down, and ascends again several times. When the trail reaches a rock face and turns left, stop and scramble up. The excellent view down the Hudson Valley includes West Point, the Bear Mountain Bridge, the Tappan Zee Bridge, and the Manhattan skyline. The easy route down from this vantage point is to retrace your steps. In another 0.1 mile, the Washburn Trail joins a woods road that circles the tree-covered summit.

Photo by Tom Rupolo

When the woods road turns sharply left, an unmarked trail to the right leads to views into Fahnestock State Park. Descending slightly, the woods road then reaches a spectacular view in 0.1 mile. The view extends over Breakneck Brook valley and ridge, Lake Surprise, the Newburgh-Beacon Bridge, the Shawangunks, and the Catskills.

Continue downhill along the woods road for 0.2 mile. Follow the white blazes of the Washburn Trail as it turns right off the woods road, descends steeply, and crosses the road twice. At the third intersection with the road the Washburn trail ends and the blue-blazed Notch Trail begins. Continue straight ahead on the Notch Trail. Do not take the green-blazed Nelsonville trail to the right, as it ends on the opposite side of the mountain in Nelsonville.

From the junction of the Washburn and Notch Trails, it is 1.0 mile to the valley floor, with a 200-foot drop (out of 700 total) in the first 0.2 mile. When the slope lessens, keep your eyes open for the blue blazes as the Notch Trail joins and leaves old farm roads, evidenced by numerous stone walls. Once on the valley floor, turn left onto the red-blazed Brook Trail; the triple blazes are on a tree to the left. (You have stayed on the Notch Trail for 0.1 mile too long if you reach the ruins of a large stone dairy barn and farm buildings. The farm was owned and operated by the Cornish family until the mid-1940s.)

Follow the Brook Trail down the road toward the Hudson River. In 0.2 mile, the yellow-blazed Undercliff Trail crosses as it goes south to Bull Hill and north to Breakneck Ridge. Stop at the bridge over Breakneck Brook and enjoy the sound of the rushing water. Along the Brook Trail are ponds and pump houses that once served the dairy farm. Bear left in 0.1 mile at a Y junction to follow the blue-blazed Cornish Trail along a woods road. In another 0.1 mile, cross the Catskill Aqueduct. Completed in 1916, the aqueduct carries 500 million gallons of water per day from the Ashokan Reservoir in the Catskills. After passing a large cement cistern, the woods road becomes concrete. Over the next 0.7 mile, wind your way down the mountain, passing stone steps, stone walls, and numerous large boulders. The Cornish Trail turns left just before the gate at the stone pillars. Paralleling Route 9D, the trail ends in 0.2 mile near the trailhead for the white-blazed Washburn Trail, where you started the hike.

Cold Spring If you are not too tired from the hike up Bull Hill, there are several short jaunts in Cold Spring that will introduce you to some local history.

In 1817, Cold Spring was the site of the then largest and most modern iron foundry in the United States. The location was ideal: abundant iron mines were nearby, the surrounding forests offered a source of charcoal, and the Hudson River was a convenient route by which to transport the products to market. The foundry's mainstay was the U.S. government's purchase of weapons and cannonballs. The Parrott cannon, invented and produced here, is credited by many historians as the gun

Downstream, the river narrows between West Point and Constitution Island. It was here that during the Revolutionary War a great iron chain supported by long booms stretched across the river. Its purpose was to prevent British warships from sailing up the Hudson with supplies and reinforcements for General John Burgoyne, who was operating between Fort Ticonderoga and Saratoga. If the British had succeeded in traveling up the Hudson, they would have split the colonies in two. The iron for the chain was mined in areas that are now Harriman and Sterling Forest State Parks in Orange County and Fahnestock State Park in Putnam County. Surviving sections of the chain and boom are on display at West Point and at Washington's Headquarters State Historic Site in Newburgh.

that won the Civil War for the North. In 1911 the foundry closed. To learn more local history, take time to visit the Foundry School Museum or Foundry Cove. The museum was originally a school for children of foundry workers, but now houses exhibits and a library of local, county, and Hudson Valley history.

To reach both the museum and the cove, walk 0.4 mile up Main Street from the train station, then go south 0.3 mile on Chestnut Street, which at this point is also Route 9D. When Route 9D hooks to the left, continue straight ahead. The Foundry School Museum is one block on your right. Call (845) 265-4010 for its hours. To reach the trail down into 85-acre Foundry Cove, continue on Chestnut Street to the stop sign. The blue-blazed trail starts just beyond three parallel concrete barriers (the purpose of which is unknown). Once down in Foundry Cove you can return to the train station by walking 0.6 mile along the gravel road that skirts the cove. An alternative route to the cove is to walk up Main Street and turn right onto Kemble Avenue. It is then 0.5 mile to the cove. A left turn takes you to the ruins and a right turn heads you back to the train station.

Photo by Jane Daniels

Photo by Jane Daniels

For another trip to the river's edge, you need to start at the former Cold Spring train station, now a restaurant, just north of the current train station. Go under the railroad tracks, then straight to the dock and bandstand. From the dock, walk south along New Street, which swings left. Turn right on Market Street and head toward the Chapel of Our Lady, situated high on a bluff right across from the station parking lot. This early 19th-century Greek-revival style church faces the river rather than the road. The owner of the foundry built the church for the use of the Irish foundry workers in 1833. It remained in use until the congregation built a newer and larger church on Fair Street. In 1932 the building was badly burned and was sold by the Roman Catholic church. Later restored, it is owned by Chapel of Our Lady Restoration and is open to all faiths for weddings, recitals, and special events. Its grounds afford magnificent views of the mountains and the Hudson River.

It is unlikely that a visitor can sample all of Cold Spring's delights in one day. Hikers can stay at one of the several bed and breakfasts in town or save some of Cold Spring's history, dining, or shopping for another day.

25
Breakneck Ridge

Distance	5.7 miles
Hiking time	6 hours
Rating	Strenuous

*B*reakneck Ridge is part of the 4,200-acre Hudson Highlands State Park, a network of public lands stretching along the eastern shore of the Hudson River from Anthony's Nose to Beacon. Be forewarned, Breakneck's 1,200-foot vertical climb is very steep. It requires scrambling over rocks and passing close to the edge of cliffs. Good hiking boots with non-slip soles are a necessity. Do not underestimate how rigorous this hike is. Although one could hike 5.7 miles much faster than six hours, take time to savor the views along the ridge and resist the urge to speed. The crowds decrease the farther along the ridge one hikes, and there are three points where one can exit for shorter hikes.

This area of the Hudson Valley has been described as "one of the grandest passages of river scenery in the world." Karl Baedecker (1801–59), the noted German publisher of travel guidebooks, was the first of many to describe the river as "grander and more inspiring" than the Rhine. For much of this hike, there are unparalleled views of the surrounding Highlands and the river. Vistas such as these inspired 19th-century landscape painters known as the Hudson River School. Their impressive landscapes displayed in precise detail a romantic love of nature.

Directions   Public transportation to Breakneck Ridge is via Metro-North's Hudson Line. Two trains on weekends and holiday mornings (check the Metro-North schedule) will stop at the Breakneck Ridge train stop, if you have told the conductor. Two return trains will stop there in the evenings, if the conductor sees you. The train stop is north of the tunnel. For those arriving by car, there is ample parking 200 yards north of the tunnel on the river side of Route 9D, two miles north of Cold Spring.

The Walk   The white-blazed Breakneck Ridge Trail starts on the north side of the tunnel, on the river side of Route 9D. It turns toward the river and, on rocky ledges, almost immediately offers its first view. The magnificent scenery of the Hudson River Valley unfolds in all directions.

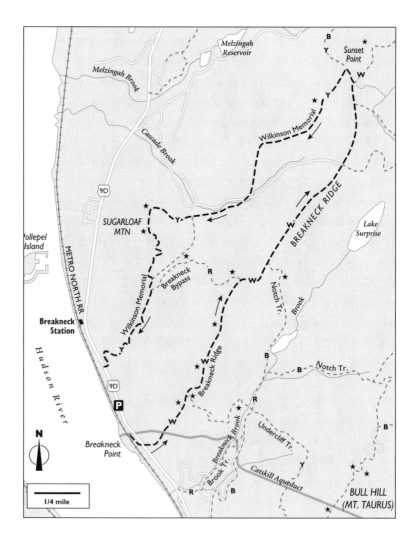

Directly across the river is the impressive hulk of Storm King Mountain, scarred horizontally by the Storm King Highway. Downstream lie Constitution Island and West Point. Upriver is six-acre Pollepel Island, also known as Bannerman's Island.

Francis Bannerman was a major dealer in second-hand military weaponry and ammunition. In 1900, he erected a Scottish-style castle on Pollepel Island north of Cold Spring. His baronial island estate doubled as an arsenal. Powder exploded in 1920, destroying the stored munitions and leaving the castle in ruins. In 1969, a fire started by vandals added further destruction. Although Pollepel Island is part of Hudson Highlands State Park, it is not open to the public. Home to snakes and poison ivy, the island is best viewed from afar. The Bannerman Castle Trust (PO Box 843, Glenham, NY 12527) is working to preserve the structures.

The stone edifice near the eastern shore of the Hudson River is sometimes erroneously referred to as a pumping station, but it is actually a cover over a 1,100-foot deep shaft that is part of the Catskill Aqueduct. Water flows through the aqueduct from the Ashokan Reservoir in the Catskills to New York City entirely by gravity. The aqueduct reaches the Hudson River near Storm King Mountain on the west bank and drops nearly 1,100 feet below the surface of the river to reach bedrock before it rises again under this building. Water courses through this U shaped section of the aqueduct by siphon effect, unaided by pumps. The aqueduct continues in a tunnel under Breakneck and Bull Hill as it heads south to New York City.

Turn away from the river and head east, following the white blazes as the trail crosses over the railroad and highway tunnels. Almost immediately you begin to climb an open ridge, the most rugged in the Hudson Valley. You will need to use your hands as the climb is very steep. Take time to catch your breath and look out over the river. Each viewpoint seems to be increasingly spectacular and panoramic. Raptors and vultures frequently soar over the rocks. In good weather the river is alive with pleasure boats, especially on weekends. Tugboats push and pull barges. Seagoing cargo ships and tankers make their way to and from ports as far north as Albany. On the railroad tracks below, passenger trains rush by, while on the western shore the entire length of a freight train can often be seen. This area is busy and popular year round. Expect to encounter many hikers in almost any weather.

Keep following the white blazes uphill over a series of bumps, some with views. The descents are followed by steep rises. Alternative routes, marked with an X, are for those who want to avoid exposure to the cliffs. At 0.7 mile, you will pass the start of the yellow-blazed Undercliff Trail. (If you follow the Undercliff Trail down to the right, you will reach the red-blazed Brook Trail shortly after crossing Breakneck Brook on a bridge. From here it is 0.7 mile down to Route 9D and then a short walk back through the tunnel.) At 1.5 miles, the Breakneck Bypass will be on your left. Its three red-on-white blazes are on a rock to the left and are easily missed. The bypass leads 0.8 mile to the yellow-blazed Wilkinson Trail, which then goes 0.5 mile (left) to Route 9D. Stay on the white-blazed Breakneck Ridge Trail.

As the Breakneck Ridge Trail continues in a northeasterly direction, there are occasional views to the south of the valley formed by Breakneck Brook. At about 2 miles, the blue-blazed Notch Trail comes in from the right to join the Breakneck Ridge Trail. (If you wish to shorten the hike, turn right and go downhill on the blue trail; follow it 0.3 mile downhill to the red-blazed Brook Trail. Take the Brook Trail 0.9 mile downhill through the valley back to Route 9D and then a short walk along the road through the tunnel to the parking area.) Follow the joint trails over the next 0.7 mile. When the trails divide, follow the blue blazes to the left. In about 300 yards, the yellow-blazed Wilkinson Trail crosses the Notch Trail. Turn left and follow the yellow blazes. After climbing and descending two peaks, you will reach the summit of Sugarloaf Mountain in 2 miles. The rocky outcrops on Sugarloaf afford

Photo by Tom Rupolo

the last good vantage points to enjoy the scenic beauty of the Hudson River.

Descending from Sugarloaf Mountain, you will cross a stream in 0.4 mile and shortly meet the red-on-white-blazed Breakneck Bypass Trail. Stay on the Wilkinson Trail and continue descending to reach Route 9D in 0.6 mile. The parking areas are to your left and the Breakneck train station to your right.

26
Crows Nest and Storm King

Distance	7.2 miles
Hiking time	5 hours
Rating	Strenuous

The Stillman Trail on Storm King Mountain has been long favored by hikers for its tough climbs and unsurpassed views of the Hudson Highlands. The valley between Storm King and the north point of Crows Nest contains wild ravines, clear mountain streams, and rich foliage that delight the eye. Its soft hue is in contrast to the ruggedness of Storm King and Crows Nest. By hiking into the ravine and to the North Point of Crows Nest on the Howell Trail, one gains opportunities to enjoy additional views. If desired, both mountains can be hiked separately by those who want to walk at a more leisurely pace.

In the summer of 1999, there were extensive fires on Crows Nest, which could not be effectively fought by the firefighters because of the exploding ordinance left over from many years as an artillery practice range. By the time you read this, the area will have been thoroughly swept for any remaining ordinance, but the trails may not have been completely repaired and may differ in detail from what is described here.

The two major trails honor men who loved the area. The Howell Trail is named after William Thompson Howell, a fervent hiker who had unbridled enthusiasm for the Hudson Highlands. He started a fierce campaign for the preservation of the Highlands in 1908, but never lived to see the results of his efforts. Ernest Stillman donated the land that eventually became Storm King State Park.

Storm King was dubbed Boter Berg (Butter Hill) by the early Dutch river captains because they thought its semi-circular shape resembled a huge lump of butter. This injustice to the king of the Highland mountains was rectified by renaming it Storm King (although a small western portion of the range still retains the original name). The Hudson River School of painters loved the mountain for its sublime scenery, and poets rhapsodized over it.

Storm King became a rallying ground in 1962 when Consolidated Edison announced that it would build a pumped-storage power plant at the foot of the mountain. The legal battle to save the mountain ended in 1980 when the utility dropped its plans. The outcome set a precedent for U.S. environmental law. Every plan for development of this scope is

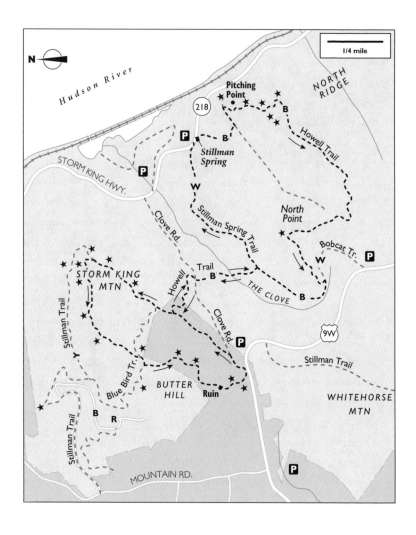

now forced to consider its esthetic impact. Storm King has become, even more than in the past, a symbol of the Hudson's grandeur.

Directions   The trail starts from the large parking lot on Route 9W along the side of Storm King at the turn just before the highway descends to

Cornwall. Heading north, this is the third parking lot on the right of Route 9W after the turnoff to Central Valley via Route 293. There is no public transportation.

Crows Nest   The hike begins on an unmarked woods road at the northeast end of the parking lot. After the road drops moderately for a short distance, there is a Y junction where you take the left fork to contour along the side of Storm King Mountain. In about 0.4 mile, the blue-blazed Howell Trail will come in from the right and continue with the woods road you are on. Be alert: You want to turn right onto the Howell Trail, and this turnoff is easy to miss. If you begin to see blue blazes without having turned right, you have gone too far; turn around and follow the blue blazes as they leave the woods road. The initial descent on the Howell Trail is steep and over many rocks and boulders, so be sure of your footing.

In 0.9 mile after the turnoff, you will reach the bottom of the clove. You will cross some small brooks and very shortly come to the white-blazed Stillman Spring Trail on your left. This turnoff is also easy to miss, particularly when the trees are fully foliated. If the trail starts to ascend, turn around; you have gone too far. Turn onto the Stillman Spring Trail and follow it down to Route 218. Turn right and walk along the road to the start of the Howell Trail (a triple blue blaze). It is to the left of a spring that flows off a ledge a few feet above the west side of the road. The walk from the start of the hike to this point should take just over an hour.

From the road, it is all uphill 1.8 miles to the top of Crows Nest's north peak, also called North Point. The grading varies from steep to moderate with few level areas. About 20 minutes up from Route 218, stone steps ease your way up the steepest parts of the climb. There are several good viewpoints on the way up. From the view at 1.4 miles (from the road) you will see Sugarloaf Mountain, Breakneck Ridge, and Bull

Hill across the Hudson. To the right are the village of Cold Spring and Constitution Island. Farther to the right, you can see part of West Point.

Rest, savor the view, then continue walking along the Howell Trail, which gradually climbs for a short distance. You will come to another beautiful view of the Hudson Highlands. As you descend at the far end of the ridge, you will see Storm King to the north, across the clove. Soon, coming in from the left, will be the white-blazed Bobcat Trail, the access route to the parking lot south of the one where this hike started. Stay on the Howell Trail. In 0.4 mile you will come to the junction with the Stillman Spring Trail that you used earlier to descend to Route 218. Continue on the blue-blazed Howell Trail, retracing the route you came down.

In 0.9 mile from the Stillman Spring Trail, you will reach the unmarked woods road on which you started the hike from the parking lot. At this point, if you wish to shorten the hike, you can turn left and return to the parking lot. It is roughly at the mid-point of the hike, and you would have covered over four miles in about three hours. To continue on the second half of the hike—a distance of about three miles that includes the top of Storm King—turn right and follow the Howell Trail north as it continues uphill. Continue until the trail turns left at the junction with the white-blazed By-Pass Trail. Follow the directions below from the *.

Storm King   To do just this half of the hike, walk in 0.4 mile on the unmarked woods road from the parking lot as described previously, to the junction with the blue-blazed Howell Trail. Continue straight, following the blue blazes until the Howell Trail turns left at the junction with the white-blazed By-Pass Trail. * Follow the By-Pass Trail, which goes uphill toward the brow of Storm King. It passes views of Crows Nest and the Hudson River and ends in 0.4 mile at the yellow-blazed Stillman Trail, which is joint with the teal-blazed Highlands Trail. From this junction, an excellent view of the whole Hudson River Valley is about 100 yards to your right. You must retrace your steps back to this point and then follow the ridge along Storm King Mountain, with multiple views to the north and west of Schunemunk, the Shawangunks, and Catskill Mountains. If you begin to descend steeply along a narrow path, you are going the wrong way on the Stillman Trail; turn around.

In 1.1 mile, you will come to Butter Hill, where there are views similar to those seen earlier from Storm King. From here back to the parking lot, the descent will be rocky, steep, and close to the edge of precipices. It is not dangerous, but be sure to maintain a good footing, and put your walking stick away so your two hands are free to assist in going down. You will be through most of the tough part in 15 to 20 minutes. You will be able to see Route 9W on your left on the way down. The trail passes stone pillars and the remains of Spy Rock House, the summer cottage of Dr. Edward L. Partridge (a Palisades Interstate Park Commissioner), and a viewpoint that provides a splendid view of the valley below and the Hudson River in the distance.

Whichever hike you choose, you are sure to experience some of the finest views in the Hudson Valley. Thanks to the efforts of numerous preservationists, Storm King was spared an unfortunate fate, and the public is now assured that its grandeur will be there to enjoy for many years to come.

Northern
New Jersey

NORTHERN NEW JERSEY
Native American Paths

After the last glacier retreated, the first settlers began to arrive in what is now the metropolitan area. Various Native American tribes settled Long Island. The Wappinger Confederacy eventually gained control of the east bank of the Hudson. West of the Hudson dwelt the Leni Lenape, "original people." The Leni Lenape nation was made up of smaller groups; the group in northern New Jersey and nearby New York were the Minsi, "people of the stone country."

The Minsi recognized no central authority. Each settlement was self-governing, with its own defined areas for farming, hunting, gathering, and fishing. Permanent villages of 60 to 100 inhabitants dotted the lowlands, particularly the Passaic River basin. Maize, beans, and squash were planted in nearby fields. In spring and summer, small groups left the villages to live and fish along the rivers.

After the fall harvest, hunting bands would head into the hills. Often they would return year after year to the same shelters to hunt and, in bad weather, to work on stone implements. In spring, the bands would return to the lowland villages to help with the planting and farming.

Over 350 generations, the Minsi had evolved a stable lifestyle, one that ensured their existence by preserving the environment that made their existence possible. Then the Europeans came. They drove the Leni Lenape westward, out of this area. Then they began to build. In the short span of 15 generations, the plains and lowlands have been buried under landfill, roads, homes, factories, dumps, and shopping centers.

For a time, development also seemed to be the fate of the hills. The rock was rich in iron ore. The ore was magnetite, which was so concentrated that 18th-century technology was able to devise simple methods for smelting it into iron. By the time of the Revolutionary War, the Hudson Highlands and Ramapo Mountains were producing 15 percent

of the world's iron. Roads were built throughout the hills. Forests were decimated for the production of charcoal. Streams were dammed and canals dug for water.

Iron mining continued strong right through the Civil War in the 1860s. However, the opening of the Erie Canal and then the coming of the railroad meant that the poorer but much more abundant ores of the Midwest would gradually replace Highlands iron. By the beginning of the 20th century, most of the Highlands were reverting to forest. Much of it passed almost painlessly to state ownership. In New Jersey, the iron-making families donated the Wyanokie plateau to the public. In New York, a gift from the widow of railroad financier Edward H. Harriman formed the nucleus of Harriman-Bear Mountain State Parks.

So the mountainous areas, at least, are near to the condition in which the Minsi left them. Still, they are not safe from development. The Ramapo Mountain State Forest has now been split by the construction of I-287. The Watchung Reservation lies conveniently in the path of I-78; only continual community action has saved the reservation thus far from the fate of Van Cortlandt Park, in which three major highways meet.

If you should go to Watchung Reservation, think about the effect of development as you stand in the quiet of the glen. Consider the effect of 65,000 vehicles a day passing perhaps half a mile up Blue Brook, just on the other side of Surprise Lake. And then think about the names of these places. So often they are the old Minsi names. Watchung means "hill" in the Algonkian dialect spoken by the Minsi. Ramapo is "place of the slanting rock." Wyanokie means "place of the sassafras" (Wanaque is another spelling of the word.) Even Windbeam Mountain has a Native American root; it comes from wimbemes, or "lone tree mountain."

27
The Palisades

Distance	4.5 miles
Hiking time	3 hours
Rating	Easy to moderate

The long and spectacular cliffs of the Palisades line the west shore of the Hudson River all the way from the Tappan Zee to New York Harbor. These cliffs were once the home of Native Americans and later the Dutch, some of whose descendants continued to farm their lands in the area until they were bought out by the Palisades Interstate Park Commission (PIPC). The commission was established in 1900 by the states of New York and New Jersey. Its purposes were to acquire land in the Palisades to prevent the expansion of quarrying and its ruinous effects on the environment and to develop parks and other recreational facilities. The cliffs were a major source of the brownstone used to construct the facades of many private homes in Manhattan at the end of the 19th and the beginning of the 20th centuries.

The land was acquired by PIPC through private gifts, with notable contributions from George W. Perkins, Sr.; J. P. Morgan; and, in 1933, John D. Rockefeller, Jr. The latter expressed the hope that a scenic parkway might be developed through the properties. The parkway was eventually built and inaugurated in 1958, running from the George Washington Bridge to the traffic circle at Bear Mountain. Its completion significantly expanded access to the recreational facilities of Harriman and Bear Mountain parks.

Two trails run the length of the Palisades from the George Washington Bridge to the New Jersey-New York state line. The Long Path (aqua blazed) runs along the top of the cliffs between the parkway and cliff edge and continues beyond the state line toward the Catskills and beyond. It is mostly level in this section of the park. The Shore Trail (white blazed) generally hugs the shore of the Hudson River and is also fairly level. It is about 11 miles in length, but to walk the whole trail in a day may be too strenuous for most hikers, particularly the second half of the hike, which involves some difficult rock scrambles.

The section of the Shore Trail from the Alpine Boat Basin to the state line—about 4.5 miles—passes through the most scenic and least developed areas of the park. It offers challenges enough for even a seasoned hiker. The section of the Shore Trail southward from the Alpine Boat

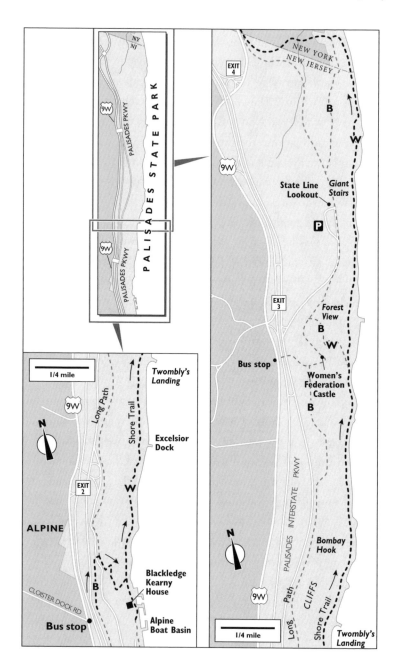

Basin to the George Washington Bridge has splendid views of the Hudson River and New York City and is worth exploring another time. The Shore Trail continues south past the George Washington Bridge for about another mile into Fort Lee Park.

The trails in the New Jersey part of the Palisades—the Long Path and the Shore Trail—are interconnected by many woods roads and unmarked trails that can be combined to offer a variety of scenic and challenging hikes. You can obtain maps from the New York-New Jersey Trail Conference.

Directions The described hike is a through walk, not a loop. It is especially suited for public transportation since hikers coming by bus from Manhattan can return to the city from a point several miles north of the start of the hike. Buses to Alpine are available at the George Washington Bus Terminal or Port Authority in Manhattan. The trip takes less than half an hour and service is frequent. For bus information, call the number for the George Washington Bridge Bus Terminal or the Port Authority listed in the Park and Transportation Information section in the back of the book.

Alternatively, hikers can add approximately eight miles to the hike and enjoy thrilling views and the southern Palisades by walking approximately two miles across the George Washington Bridge from the 181st Street subway station, then north six miles to Alpine.

Bus riders to Alpine will leave the bus at Cloister Dock Road. About 50 yards north of the stop, a tunnel on the east side of Route 9W takes pedestrians under the Palisades Interstate Parkway. On the far side, pick up the path curving left and running parallel to the parkway. Note the aqua blazes of the Long Path. Follow the Long Path through an underpass under a paved road, which is the park drive down to the Alpine Boat Basin. Just past the underpass, turn right on a woods road. A few hundred feet later, another woods road heads down to the left. Turn downhill on this, which is the Old Alpine Road. (In 1776, it is believed the Old Alpine Road was used by British troops on their march to cut off an isolated American garrison in Fort Lee after the main American force under Washington had made its retreat to distant White Plains.)

Via a series of sweeping curves, the cobblestone road descends toward the Hudson. At times, the docks and picnic area below can be seen through the foliage. Near the bottom, the Old Alpine Road runs into the white-blazed Shore Trail, which has a chain-link fence on the far side of the road. The hike turns left at this point onto the Shore Trail.

Those with cars need first to consider how they will return to their vehicles. They have three choices. The first is to return to the beginning of the walk by bus. The second is to convert the walk to a loop. (One option is to go as far as Forest View and then return to Alpine by the Shore Trail or the Long Path.) The third is to use two cars, leaving one at the northern end point of the hike and driving south in the other to the start at Alpine. You may leave a car at the parking lot at State Line Lookout (exit the Palisades Parkway at Interchange 3 and follow signs to the lookout and scenic view) or at a much smaller parking area just south of Camp Alpine (BSA) on the east side of Route 9W; an overpass over the parkway links the Route 9W parking area to State Line Lookout. Signs at State Line Lookout say that parking is limited to two hours, but the police have indicated they would not ticket cars exceeding this limit. Part of the reason for their tolerance is that parking in another small lot, in front of the Lamont-Doherty Observatory, where the hike ends, is no longer permitted. The lot is now a bus stop.

Those arriving at Alpine by car should leave the Palisades Interstate Parkway at Interchange 2 and drive down a long road to the boat basin. There is a fee for parking in the summer.

The Walk   The entire length of the Shore Trail is well blazed, and hikers should have no difficulty in finding their way. Begin heading north on

Before starting on the Shore Trail, you may want to take a short detour down to the picnic tables of the marina to the right. A simple white house sits at the edge of the picnic area under the cliff at the Alpine Boat Basin. Houses like this lined the river shore back when roads were poor and the river was the main transport route. Now only this house remains, preserved because British General Cornwallis was said to have relaxed here for a few hours while his troops toiled to pull wagons and cannons up Old Alpine Road. Now known as the Blackledge-Kearney House, the building has been restored and contains period furnishings as well as exhibits on the history of the area. The house is open to visitors several days a week in the spring and summer.

the white-blazed trail, which angles up the slope along the fence, passing the end of Old Alpine Road. The trail soon passes a waterfall and crosses a gorge on a massive stone bridge. Beneath, a tiny stream trickles over moss-covered rocks. The trail is already some 50 feet up the slope from the Hudson. Soon after, the path leaves a set of steps and comes to a fork. A picnic area is ahead on the left; turn right and follow the Shore Trail down to the water's edge at Excelsior Dock, which juts out slightly into the river.

Now that the trail has returned to the shore, it will stay close by the water for more than 1.0 mile. The path is level and wide, and the footing is mostly hard dirt. Towering above is the isolated cliff column known as Grey Crag. The shore curves in and out, with reeds on the points of land.

Twombley's Landing (0.4 mile from Excelsior Point) is a square landfill, with the ruins of a pier jutting out into the Hudson. It is named for the family that once lived here. Grey Crag looms directly overhead. Just around the point, the Tappan Zee Bridge comes into view (on a clear day). Another 0.5 mile ahead on the left is another crag, Bombay Hook. Its name comes from the Dutch word boomje, meaning "small tree." This stretch of cliffs between Grey Crag and Bombay Hook is the longest uninterrupted stretch in the Palisades. Many people, hearing of trails in the Palisades, imagine an airy cliffside adventure. In fact, much of the Palisades is wooded from top to bottom. The trails up and down the cliffs use these wooded slopes. There are no trails on the open cliffs at all, because the rock is too fragile to support them.

Beyond Bombay Hook, further sections of cliff rise above the trail in isolated splendor. Finally, the path comes around a bush-covered point with a large weeping willow over the water. High bramble bushes crowd the trail. This is Forest View, once a popular picnic area. Now, picnic tables float in a sea of brambles.

At Forest View, the wide path ends. A triple-blazed blue-and-white marked trail turning uphill leads to the Long Path and to the parking lot and refreshment stand at State Line Lookout. To avoid the rough walking ahead on the Shore Trail (including a long rock scramble), some hikers may prefer to take this cut-off, continuing to the state line bus stop by turning right near the top of the climb and following the Long Path or the abandoned portion of Route 9W. Or if you feel you've had enough, drivers can simply terminate the hike at the parking lot at the State Line Lookout (if the second car is parked there). Bus riders and drivers parked at the parking lot opposite the Alpine Boy Scout Camp can turn left near the top of the climb and follow the blue-and-white trail past the Women's Federation Castle, built in 1929 to commemorate the preservation of the Palisades. The blue-and-white trail then turns right and continues over the parkway to Route 9W, where you can catch a bus back to New York.

If you've decided to continue along the Shore Trail, go straight ahead on a footpath parallel to the shore. The pleasant walk through Forest View ends abruptly at a pile of giant boulders that extends to the water.

Photo by Mary Jo Robertiello

Here the tough hiking begins. Put away your hiking stick, as you will need both legs and two arms to secure your balance and footing. A walking stick may be dangerous to rely on over these boulders; it could easily disappear into the small crevices along the way and you could lose your balance.

Without crossing the rock slide, the trail makes a sharp turn left and heads uphill. Continue to follow the white blazes. Here are round white markers; the stones have been moved into a stairway to make climbing easier. The trail keeps making jogs to the left, away from the direction it "should" be going. Finally the path leads over a stone retaining wall and heads to the right. At this point the trail is above the boulder field, perhaps 60 feet up from the water.

For the next 0.5 mile, the trail goes from rock to rock. In the half hour that this rock hopping requires, take extra precautions about safety. Proceed slowly. The path finally leaves the boulder-filled woods and leads out onto open rocks. The jumble of boulders is faded to a reddish tan by exposure; the red comes from the iron contained in the Palisades rock. The path descends on a rock stairway, through a grove of trees, and then out onto another set of rock stairs that crosses an enormous rock slide. The descent is called the Giant Stairs (1.0 mile from Forest View). The trail continues north through the woods on the other side of the rock slide. It descends another 30 feet to the edge of the Hudson. Here water can be heard dripping under the huge boulders that extend to the shoreline.

The smell of salt water is strong here. The trail passes a marshy area; bushes along the way have dry pods that rattle when touched. The Tappan Zee is now close, and the trail has crossed the state line into New York.

The trail now continues along the shore for another 0.4 mile until it reaches Peanut Leap Falls. Here are a wonderful cascading waterfall and the ruins of a pergola from the 1890s. This area is the former estate of Mary Lawrence Tonetti, an artist and sculptor who formed an art colony for up-and-coming artists of the era. Make sure you take a look at the remains of this fantastic area as you take a step back in time.

The trail climbs steeply now as it follows the stream uphill. After the climb, the trail enters Skunk Hollow, known for its freed Black community over a century ago. Here, three white blazes indicate the end of the Shore Trail, 2.0 miles from Forest View. At this intersection, the Long Path is finally reached. Here bus riders should continue straight ahead onto the Long Path north (drivers see below) for the 0.5-mile walk to the observatory. The Long Path continues straight for a while and then turns right and goes up a hill. Soon, a road (the old 9W) can be seen on the left. Continue to follow the Long Path until you reach Route 9W, and then walk left to the front gate of the observatory. (Note the big "Welcome to New York" sign on the highway.) The bus back to New York will stop at the gate when it is flagged down.

Drivers should turn left off the Shore Trail, when it ends, onto the Long Path south (do not go straight ahead onto the Long Path north). This will lead directly back to the parking lot at State Line Lookout, about a mile to the south. If your car is parked on Route 9W across from Camp Alpine, continue walking past the State Line Lookout parking lot to the blue-white blazed trail that leads to the overpass across the Palisades Interstate Parkway.

28
Ramapo Mountain State Forest

Distance	7 or 8 miles
Hiking time	4.5 hours
Rating	Moderate

*F*rom north to south, the 2,340-acre Ramapo Mountain State Forest extends over six miles between Pompton Lakes and Oakland. The park is in the most easterly of New Jersey's mountain ranges. The Ramapos have more open spaces and gentle valleys than their neighbors—the Wyanokies—to the west. Here the mountains are not especially high or craggy. The centerpiece of the park is Ramapo Lake, a beautiful and quiet area, ideal in the summer for picnics and lazy walks in the woods. Water lilies straight out of a Monet painting cover a nearby pond.

Fishing is permitted at the lake, but swimming is not. The only roads still maintained provide access to private property in the southern part of the park and to the district ranger station on the west shore of Ramapo Lake.

The trails in the state forest were planned by Frank Oliver, a member of the New York-New Jersey Trail Conference, and were cleared by high school students in the Youth Conservation Corps during the summers of 1977 and 1978. The trails have been laid out to provide gradual ascents to rocky ledge viewpoints from which the land may drop off sharply. Two are through trails; the others are loops.

One of the through trails is an old Conference path. Originally called the Suffern-Midvale Trail, it has been renamed the Hoeferlin Memorial Trail in memory of William Hoeferlin, a famous hiker, trailblazer, and mapmaker.

Another through trail is the rediscovered historic Cannonball Road. The road originated at Pompton Lakes, where there was an iron furnace predating the American Revolution. To avoid interception by the British, cannonballs were transported by wagon to the northeast behind the sheltering Ramapo Mountains. Iron mining and smelting began in the Ringwood area, just north of the park, in 1740. The industry thrived through the Civil War, but soon after could no longer compete with the lower cost open-pit mines of the Midwest.

Hiking in this area can be done throughout the year. In the section south of Skyline Drive, hunting is prohibited because of the private holdings. If there is sufficient snow, the deteriorated estate roads can

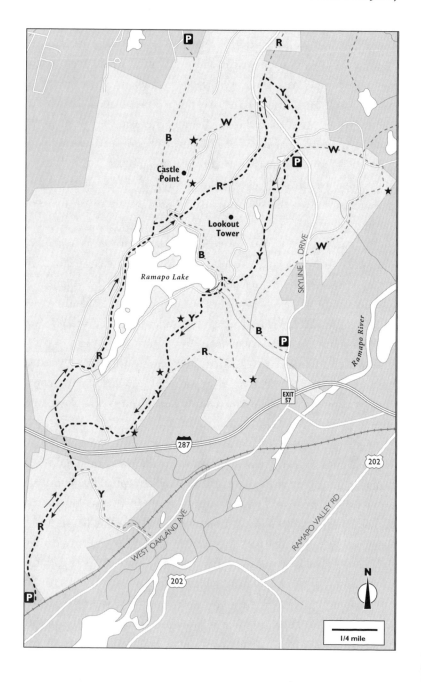

1/4 mile

serve as ski touring routes in winter. All motorized vehicles are prohibited in the park, and no fires or camping are permitted. However, this is
an area serving both hikers and mountain bikers. In many places, the
trails are severely eroded, a condition particularly evident in wet
weather, and at all times the hiker needs to be aware of bikers coming
up from behind.

The hike described here will serve as an introduction to this area.
The combinations of trails and roads make possible a variety of walks—
from short strolls along level roads to lengthy exercises over rocky ledges
and crests.

Directions   There are a number of access points to the trails, but only
one of these—to the Cannonball Road at the southern end—can be
reached by a short walk from public transportation. Originating from the
Port Authority Bus Terminal in Manhattan, NJ Transit Bus 197 stops at
the former railroad station on Wanaque Avenue in Pompton Lakes. This
stop is also served by NJ Transit buses from Paterson (P-86) and
Newark (75). Be sure to call or check the NJ Transit web site (phone
numbers and web sites are listed in the back of this book) for current information. After leaving the bus, cross the tracks and go north on the
blacktop Cannonball Road, paralleling the tracks. Turn right on DuPont
Lane. The second left then leads to Barbara Drive. Go to the end of this
road, where the Cannonball Trail starts.

By car, take I-287 and get off at Exit 57 (Skyline Drive). If coming
from the north, turn left off the ramp. Almost immediately you will
come to a traffic light. Do not turn left, but proceed straight ahead for
about 2.1 miles (the street you're on shortly becomes Colfax Avenue);
turn right on Schuyler Avenue, cross the tracks, turn right onto Barbara
Drive to the parking lot at the dead end. If coming from the south on
I-287, turn right at the traffic light at the end of the exit ramp. Then proceed for 2.1 miles, as described above.

The Walk   The trail begins at the parking area on the left side of Barbara Drive. From this lot, the Cannonball Trail (intermittently blazed red with a "C" on it) heads off to the left, crosses an abandoned railroad spur, and enters a large ballfield. It crosses the left side of the field and enters a well-defined path, which heads sharply uphill. At the fork, take the left path and follow the trail toward and then parallel to the DuPont plant fence below. (Note that this entrance to the trail can be confusing because the blazes are far apart and biking has divided the trail into many competing paths. Stay as far to the left as you can, and follow the fence line.)

The trail joins a woods road, which comes in from the left at a locked gate in the plant fence. This is the route of the historic Cannonball Road.

About 1.0 mile from the soccer field, the yellow-blazed Hoeferlin Memorial Trail joins from the right, and both trails cross I-287 on a pedestrian bridge (about 25 minutes from the start of the hike). Just past the bridge, the Hoeferlin Memorial Trail leaves to the right. Continue uphill on the Cannonball Trail. In this area, you will also see a white-blazed trail that goes off to the left. Ignore it and stay on the Cannonball. About 1.5 mile from the beginning of the hike, the trail meets a gravel road. Look for the Cannonball Trail blazes on a rock across the road. Turn right and then, after about 200 yards, turn left at a fork. The Cannonball now follows the west shore of Ramapo Lake. The time to reach this point from the beginning of the hike is less than an hour.

The road at the lake is very wide and goes past a former ranger station. The Cannonball continues around the northern part of the lake across a stone bridge. On the left is a large pond, where you will see the water lilies in season. Ahead is a double-Cannonball blaze, indicating a left turn shortly thereafter onto another road. In 200 feet or so, the Cannonball reenters the woods on the right. The MacEvoy Trail (blue blazed) also enters here and follows along with the Cannonball Trail for a very short distance to a paved road, where the MacEvoy turns right and the Cannonball goes left up a hill.

At the top of the hill, the Cannonball reenters the woods. You can't miss the "C" on red blazes on either side of the trail at the point where the road goes off to the left. Stay on the Cannonball Trail. It shortly climbs up and comes out onto another paved road, which you cross over and then again enter the woods to the right. Almost immediately the blazes tell you to get back on the road. (The Cannonball used to continue straight through a field to a woods road at this point, but it has been slightly rerouted.) Continue along the paved road past the driveway of the private residence on your right; here the Cannonball reenters the woods. The trail remains in the woods only a short time before it returns to the paved road. It then crosses Skyline Drive.

North of Skyline Drive, the trail follows a woods road. In 200 yards, the yellow blazes of the Hoeferlin Memorial Trail come in from the right—2 hours, 45 minutes from the beginning of the hike. The joint trails head north from here to Bear Swamp Lake in Mahwah. You, however, will turn right and go southeast on the Hoeferlin Memorial Trail, which leads, in 0.33 mile, to a parking lot off the Skyline Drive. This is an alternate access point to the Ramapo Mountain trails. (Hikers with two cars may want to arrange to leave one car here. When they reach this point, they will be able to drive back, rather than walk to where the first car was left.) But if a single car was left at Barbara Drive or if the hiker has arrived by bus, several alternatives are possible.

An easy route back to Barbara Drive is to follow the Hoeferlin Memorial Trail to the outlet dam of Ramapo Lake. It will take about 30 minutes to get there from the parking lot on Skyline Drive. Follow the yellow-blazed gravel road from the parking lot a short distance to a pond on the right. Across from a pumphouse, the yellow blazes turn left into the woods. (Soon thereafter, the trail can become confusing. You will come to a large downed tree. Skirt it to its left; when you have reached the end of the tree, take an immediate right and look for two yellow blazes about 100 feet ahead.) Continue following the yellow-blazed Hoeferlin Memorial Trail until you reach a spillway crossing one section of the lake.

Follow the yellow blazes across the spillway and then follow the gravel road. Keep left at the fork at the end of the lake and in 0.25 mile watch for the yellow blazes of the Hoeferlin Memorial Trail as it enters the road. Turn right and follow the Hoeferlin Memorial Trail, which shortly joins the Cannonball Trail. Turn left and cross I-287. At the far end of the pedestrian bridge, a red painted arrow points to the left; ignore it and follow the Cannonball Trail straight ahead to Barbara Drive.

A more scenic, but more strenuous, return trip would be to continue on the yellow Hoeferlin Memorial Trail past the dam. Around a bend, the trail leaves the road and climbs a rocky ridge with three wide lookouts. At 0.33 mile farther, the trail climbs a rocky pinnacle overlooking Ramapo Lake. A second lookout amid scrub pine comes up after another 0.33 mile. Dropping down the rocky ledge, the trail arrives at another lookout and then descends to a brook. Climbing, it reaches a gravel road swinging in from the right. Cross the gravel road and follow the yellow blazes to a junction with the red-blazed Cannonball Trail, then turn left, cross I-287, and proceed as above to Barbara Drive.

For the longest but most scenic return route, follow the Hoeferlin Memorial Trail back to the dam. Then take the red-blazed Lookout Trail, which takes off from the south end of the dam (look for three red markers) and proceeds down the south side of the outlet brook. It is difficult see the red blazes on the trees, and you can easily go off the trail, which in many sections of the woods is not at all well defined. The trail soon climbs about 250 feet, sometimes over large rocks, to a fork in the road, about 1.0 mile from the dam (20 minutes of hiking time). The Lookout Trail continues to the right, but to the left is a narrow path to some viewpoints. The views from here are hardly scenic. Down below is the heavy and noisy traffic on I-287; in the distance the greenery is crowded out by a heavy concentration of houses and industrial buildings. But the area on the top of the viewpoints is delightfully rustic and craggy.

Return to the fork in the trail and proceed west. In 20 minutes you will come to the yellow-blazed Hoeferlin Memorial Trail, where there is a rock ledge with views west toward the Wyanokies. Turn left and follow the yellow blazes south. You will come to a woods road, which is fenced in to the left. Proceed right and follow the yellow blazes. Shortly the trail goes off to the left of the woods road. The yellow Hoeferlin Memorial Trail will soon run into the red-blazed Cannonball Trail very close to the pedestrian crossing over I-287. This will be less than hour from the fork in the road at the viewpoints. Turn left, cross I287, and proceed as above to Barbara Drive.

The total mileage covered by the hike, if you return on the Lookout Trail, is about eight miles. It should not take more than 4.5 hours to walk. The total mileage, if you take either of the other two alternate return routes, is less than seven miles.

Photo by Fred Halale

29

Paterson/Garrett Mountain

Distance	5 miles (excluding city sightseeing)
Hiking time	3.5 hours
Rating	Easy

*P*aterson offers the walker a unique opportunity to retrace in a few hours the development of urban America and then take a walk on a mountaintop, which looks down on the historic district of the city. The walk in the historic district, including side trips, is approximately three miles; the round trip to and from Garrett Mountain is five miles. It passes through many ethnic neighborhoods, where there are restaurants, delis, and bakeries. The entire walk should be measured not only in miles, but also in the contribution that it makes to your appreciation of the early growth of industrial America. In this walk, one can experience Paterson's still unspoiled natural beauty as well as its industrial growth, decline, and ongoing rebirth.

The walk will begin at the corner of Market and Church Streets, one block from City Hall (a neo-Renaissance building with a distinct domed tower in the center of it.) Walkers arriving by either public or private transportation will have to make their way to this intersection.

Directions   Paterson is easily reached by train, bus, or car. Use the Port Authority Trans-Hudson line (PATH) to get to Hoboken, where there is frequent train service to Paterson (less than a one-hour trip); the train lets you off at Market Street. Walk northwest on Market Street to Church Street, which comes in from the right. NJ Transit Bus 126 from the Port Authority Bus Terminal in Manhattan will drop you off at the Broadway Terminal in Paterson, the last stop. This bus runs frequently and on a regular schedule. Or you may take NJ Transit Bus 171 from the George Washington Bus Terminal. From the Broadway Terminal, walk up Broadway past Main Street to Church Street; turn right to Market. Call the numbers for NJ Transit listed in the back of the book for exact departure times.

Drivers can take I-80 west from the George Washington Bridge to Exit 57C, which indicates "Downtown Paterson." At the end of the exit ramp, make a left onto Main Street. Follow Main Street to Market Street; turn right and proceed to Church Street (on the left). There is plenty of off-street parking in the vicinity, as well as municipal parking lots and garages.

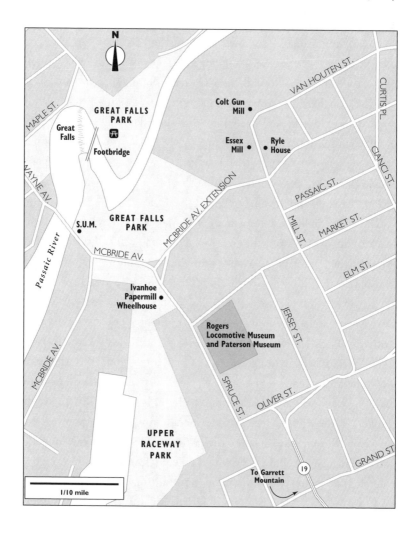

Historic Paterson   The main walk will begin at the intersection of
Church and Market Streets, but for an interesting and brief detour, first
go up one block on Clark Street (across Market from Church Street) to
Ward Street. On the far side of Ward Street is an unusual-looking building in Flemish Renaissance style. It was formerly a post office, but is

now an annex of the Passaic County Courthouse located just beyond it (a superb example of a neoclassical structure, also worth a look).

Go back to Church Street and begin a six-block walk along Market Street to Mill Street. Along Market Street, you will pass City Hall (rebuilt in 1902–03 after a fire destroyed the original 1896 building), stately banks, stores, churches, and neighborhoods.

At Mill Street, the last street before Market Street makes a jog to the left, turn right and walk north on the west side. This is the beginning of the historic district, designated a national landmark in 1975 "in commemoration of its national significance to the history of the United States of America." A short distance up and across the street is a refurbished schoolhouse, built in 1873 in Victorian gothic style. Much of the area is in various stages of restoration, so when you visit you may see many changes. Up farther to the left of the sidewalk you are on, you will see part of the canal system that supplied the water that turned the waterwheels of the local textile mills. Originally, water ran along these watercourses at the then great speed of 25 miles an hour, hence the term "raceway." The mills were built over the races, as you will see when you visit some of them on Van Houten Street. Today the races are simply ditches.

Just past Ellison Street, on Mill Street at the corner, you will see on the right an old two-story brick-faced house with gables. This is the Ryle House, which was constructed in the early 19th century by John Ryle, a founder of the Paterson silk industry. On the same block, next to the Ryle House, are the restored Thompson House (1833) and Argus Mill (1878). Almost directly across Mill Street is the Essex Mill, now an apartment house for many of the city's artists. Throughout the 1800s, in a process typical of many Paterson mills, its various sections were built, rebuilt, demolished, and then added to. A section of the original building, dating from the early 1800s, can be seen at the rear of the present structure.

During the Revolutionary War, George Washington, Lafayette, and Alexander Hamilton were encamped in this area and almost surely marveled at the beauty of the falls. After the war, Hamilton returned, not for the beauty, but for the potential of the falls as a source of power. In 1791, the Society for the Establishment of Useful Manufactures (S.U.M.) was organized with the help of Hamilton and New Jersey Governor William Paterson to encourage and organize the planning of industries around the falls. Although the fledgling federal government was unwilling to fund the project, William Paterson came to Hamilton's rescue, and in 1792 Paterson was incorporated as a city—the first planned industrial city in the United States. It owed its establishment to the falls and literally grew up around it.

At the end of Mill Street, where Van Houten Street comes in, are three partially destroyed buildings, the result of an arsonist's fire. Two mills and the 1836 Colt Gun Mill, where the Colt revolver was first produced, were damaged. Between Mill Street and Curtis Place on Van Houten are many other mills. One of these—the Phoenix—has been transformed into an apartment house. Part of the building was erected in 1816 and the extension was put up in 1826. It is the earliest extant textile mill in the historic district. The finest silk in the world was once made on this site. As you return to Mill Street, look at the raceway all along Van Houten Street.

From the end of Mill Street, walk to McBride Avenue, the first street on the right as you go back toward Market, and turn right up the hill for one long block to Haines (Overlook) Park (there is a parking lot there with a two-hour limit). It is on the right side of the block before you come to Spruce Street. Here is the best view of Great Falls.

Great Falls is a breathtaking sight, a natural waterfall that is 77 feet high and 100 feet wide. After heavy rains a rainbow will sometimes form in the gorge over the thundering cascade. In cold weather the spray freezes on the surrounding rocks to create a vision of shimmering, crystalline beauty.

Before you continue any farther, go to the Great Falls Visitors Center, at the head of McBride Avenue and Spruce Street. The center is open all year, Mondays through Fridays, 9am to 4:30pm and Saturdays noon to 4pm; from April to Sept 30 it is also open Sundays, noon to 4pm. Call (973) 279-9587 to confirm open hours. The attendants are very helpful. They can arrange group tours and provide you with maps of the historical district and other informative material. If you are planning to go to Garrett Mountain, pick up a map of the Garrett Mountain Reservation.

Cross McBride Avenue to the beginning of Wayne Avenue, where you will find an entrance to Great Falls Park. This leads to a footbridge that crosses the Passaic River high over the chasm at the base of the falls. In a small park on the other side of the river are benches. Occasionally, the walker may be lightly sprinkled with spray from the falls, refreshing on a hot day.

After lingering a while at the Great Falls, return to Spruce Street. At the head of the street to your right is Raceway Park, which contains S.U.M.'s upper raceway (1827–46) and a park. The sign at the entrance tells the story of the raceway. It was originally designed by Pierre L'Enfant, who created the plans for Washington, DC, but was later revamped to reduce the expense of construction. There is also a short trail through the park; you can obtain information about it at the visitors center. The building on the right, farther down on Spruce, was the wheelhouse for the Ivanhoe Papermill (1865). It is next to a little park overlooking a small waterfall. Here power was generated for the mill using the water from the raceway above. Behind the building is the middle raceway.

Farther down Spruce Street, at Market Street, is the locomotive complex. The largest building, the one on the left just past Market, once housed the Rogers Company, which produced steam locomotives from 1837 to 1913. At its peak, in 1873, the works could produce one locomotive every second day. Today, it is the Paterson Museum. Inside are models of machinery, a photographic exhibit of Paterson's industrial history, and the second submarine made by John Holland, the inventor of the submarine. To enter, turn left onto Market Street, then right into the parking lot just beyond Engine 299, the last of 100 locomotives made here for use in building the Panama Canal.

In the middle of the block between Market and Oliver streets, on the right, is the beginning of a trail—Old Stony Road—an early Native American trail that connected Paterson and Little Falls, to the west.

Continuing on Spruce to Grand past other mills, turn left onto Grand and walk four blocks east to Main Street, passing through a neighborhood occupied formerly by millworkers and presently by Paterson's newest immigrant groups. On the far corner of Main and Grand Streets stands St. John's Cathedral. Dedicated in 1870, this imposing brownstone building houses an impressive altar and beautiful stained glass windows; it seats over 1,700 worshipers.

Turn right on Main Street and continue 0.75 mile to Barclay Street, again passing various ethnic neighborhoods. Barclay Street begins opposite St. Joseph's Hospital; turn right onto it.

Garrett Mountain Reservation   Continue on to Valley Road (an extension of Barclay) across the Route 19 overpass. Almost immediately you will come to an access road on the right; it goes up to a turreted castle that stands on the crest of a hill: Lambert's Castle. This was built in 1891 by Catholina Lambert, an immigrant who had become a wealthy silk manufacturer. The castle now houses the offices of the Passaic County Park Commission and the Passaic County Historical Museum. It is open Wednesdays through Saturdays, 1–4pm; call (973) 247-0085 or (973) 247-0087 to confirm open hours. Tours of the building are available.

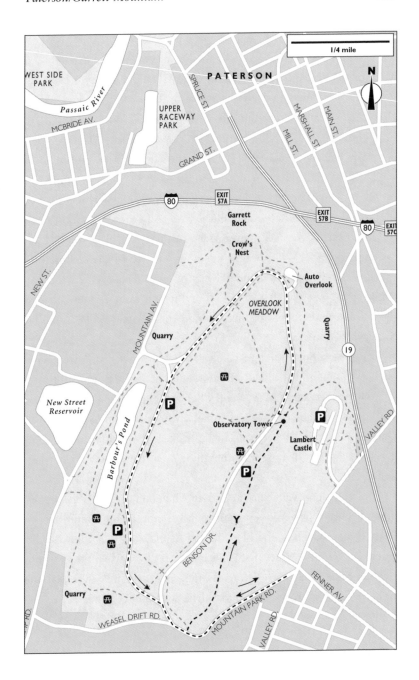

Proceed along Valley Road to a traffic light. At the right of this intersection there are two roads; the first is Fenner Avenue and just ahead is
Mountain Park Road. Walk along the grassy shoulder up Mountain Park
Road. The first road on the right is Benson Drive, the entrance to the
Garrett Mountain Reservation. Just before Benson Drive, on the right,
is an entrance to the yellow trail, which goes along the cliff to a tower,
described below, and continues through the woods of the reservation. If
you prefer to walk along the road, continue along Benson Drive; you will
encounter many side paths. Here you can picnic and enjoy the quiet of
the woods. Up a hill to the right of the road and opposite a parking area
is a tower on an overlook that provides good views of Paterson and the
historical district. This tower, a tall stone medieval looking structure,
was used by the castle's original owner as an observatory. From it, you
can hear the roar of traffic from I-80, but retreat along Benson Drive to
the more secluded areas of the park and you will feel as if you are far
from civilization.

Continue around the drive, always bearing left, until you come
back to Mountain Park Road. From here retrace your steps to Paterson
and the intersection of Market and Church Streets. The round trip from
the corner of Main and Grand Streets, where you started walking to
Garrett Mountain, is five miles. The walk in the historic district, including side trips, is approximately three miles from the start to Main
and Grand.

(You can drive your car to Garrett Mountain and on the circular
around Benson Drive. If you want to drive, proceed on Main Street to
Mary Street, which is one block before Barclay. (At this point Barclay
Street is a one-way street that you can't access from Main Street.) Turn
right on Mary Street, then left onto Marshall Street and continue to the
next traffic light. Turn right onto Valley Road and continue across the
Route 19 overpass.)

Photo by Fred Hafale

If you are walking, to return to the bus or train, retrace your steps down Mountain Park Road, Valley Road, and Barclay Street to Main Street. To get to the bus stop, go north on Main Street to Broadway. Turn left on Broadway and head toward the bus terminal. For those returning by train, go north on Main Street for just under 1.0 mile to Ward Street (three blocks beyond Grand Street). Turn right on Ward Street and walk four blocks to the railroad station.

30
Watchung Reservation

Distance	7.5 miles
Hiking time	5.5 hours
Rating	Moderately strenuous

Watchung Reservation is surrounded by a heavy concentration of suburbia. Yet within its boundaries there are glens and forests of tall dense pines, laurels, and brooks, and one can easily succumb to nature's charms and mysteries here. Only minutes from the trailhead there are deep gorges with cascading water over rocky bottoms.

Although the highest point in the reservation is less than 600 feet above sea level, it all feels much higher. The Watchungs are volcanic in origin, like the Palisades. But, unlike the Palisades, where molten rock formed a layer underground that was subsequently uncovered by erosion, the Watchungs are a result of surface flows of lava that created a double ridge from above Mahwah in the north almost to Somerville in the south.

The reservation, which covers 2,000 acres, is owned by Union County. It straddles the first and second Watchung Mountains surrounding Blue Brook Valley. In addition to the hiking trails, there are large park areas with picnic tables and walks, along which you may see many strollers.

Many walkers hike the reservation in spring, when the flowering dogwood and rhododendron are at their peak bloom. Try going as well in winter; when so many local areas look stark and bare, the hemlocks of the glen will still be verdant, tranquil, and timeless.

The Watchung Reservation offers many activities. Nature and scientific shows are put on at the Trailside Nature and Science Center, a modern building a short distance west of the parking lot. Beyond the center, on the other side of the trees, is a large playing field with a refreshment stand that is open in season. At the back of the parking lot is a modern concrete building that serves as a visitors center. A museum is located in the rambling brown wood structure on the left. Free maps of the trails are available in either building. Trailside is a nature center; its diverse habitats are home to a large variety of wildlife, displayed in both buildings. There is also a small planetarium on the grounds. The visitors center is open daily from 1pm to 5pm all year; the museum is open only on week-ends from 1pm to 5pm from the last week in November through the last week in March; otherwise, its hours are the

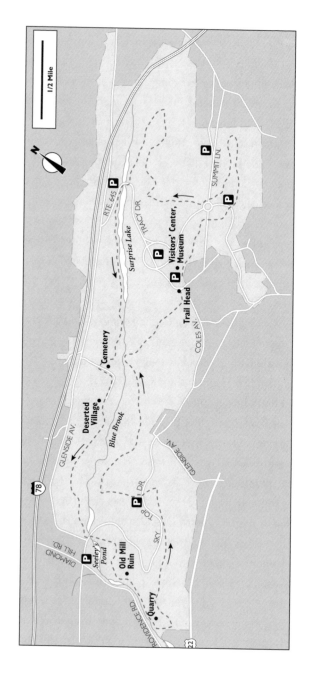

same as the visitors center. The trails are open all year. For information and to confirm hours, call (908) 789-3670.

Directions   Drivers should travel on I-78, which can be accessed from I-287 from the west and the Garden State Parkway and the New Jersey Turnpike from the east. If traveling east on I-78, turn off at Exit 44 (New Providence/Berkeley Heights). At the traffic light, turn left on Glenside Avenue. After 1.2 miles, turn right into the Watchung Reservation (Route 645) and pass Surprise Lake and its picnic areas. At the traffic circle, take the first right and proceed to the Trailside Nature and Science Center, passing suburban neighborhoods along the way. Trailside is located across from Coles Avenue. There is a small sign at this corner directing you to the visitors center.

If traveling west along I-78, turn off at Exit 43. At the traffic light, turn right onto McMane Avenue, then turn left at the next traffic light onto Glenside Avenue. From there, follow the above instructions.

Bus riders should take NJ Transit Bus 114 from the Manhattan Port Authority Terminal. Get off at the intersection of New Providence Road with Route 22 in Mountainside. From here it is about a 40-minute walk to Trailside. Go over the pedestrian overpass and follow New Providence Road uphill. You will come to a fork in the road at which New Providence Road veers sharply to the right. Take the road to the left of the fork. This is called Deer Path. Go past Tracy Drive to Ackerman Avenue. Turn right and continue to Coles Avenue, where Ackerman Avenue ends. Turn right and walk to the end of Coles Avenue, where New Providence Road comes in again. At the corner of these streets, straight ahead of you, is the Trailside Nature and Science Center.

The Walk   To get to the trails, go to the parking lot entrance and turn right on a narrow paved road. A short distance down this road, on the left, is an overhead sign reading "Nature Trails." The hike begins here.

There is only one loop trail—the white-blazed Sierra Trail—which covers 11 miles and takes in about everything you'll want to see in the reservation. (Another trail—the red-dot-on-white trail—covers a smaller part of the reservation. It does not start at the same trailhead and is difficult to find.) In addition to these trails, there are three very short nature trails that are colored green, orange, or blue.

This hike will be almost all on the white-blazed Sierra Trail, but will be shortened by diverting to the blue-blazed nature trial before completing the loop. The hike will be about 7.5 miles long. When you enter the trailhead, you will see two blazes—the white, along which you will walk, and a green, which is the shortest of the nature trails. Follow both the white/green blazes down a set of steps and over a wooden bridge. (Along this way you will cross many boardwalks laid over marshy areas.) The human world is soon left behind. Shortly, the green trail goes off straight ahead to return to Trailside. Turn left. Very shortly, the white-blazed trail turns sharply right and joins the orange trail coming in from the right. Turn left and follow the white/orange blazes. The orange trail will turn to the right at an intersection with three posts with orange blazes. Stay on the white-blazed Sierra loop trail.

Ahead, an unmarked path (there are many in the reservation) goes off straight ahead. Avoid these paths; they are woods roads or bridle paths. If you take them, you will probably get lost unless you are familiar with the area. For this walk, stay on the white-blazed trail unless indicated otherwise.

Soon you will come to the Brook Scenic Gorge. Here the deciduous forest begins to give way to conifers—mostly eastern hemlocks—and through the foliage to the left one can see, at first dimly and then more clearly, the scenery that makes the Watchungs so special. The brook, at this point, runs almost south/north for a long distance; at the bottom of the hill it is joined by the run-off from Surprise Lake. Here the gorge is only several feet deep, but follow the trail as it veers to the right and you will see that it deepens considerably. The scene is idyllic. The hillside across the gully is steep—dizzyingly so—and heavily wooded. As you descend, note the blue-blazed nature trail coming in from the right. It will stay with the Sierra Trail for a while, and both trails will cross the brook to your left. You will be heading uphill for a short distance and then both trails will go downhill.

At the bottom of the hill, close to where the brook is joined by the run-off from Surprise Lake, the blue trail veers to the right to return to Trailside. The white trail, which you should follow, goes to the left and heads back uphill. It crosses several brooks; depending on the time of year these may be filled with water or look like dry gullies. On your left you will see many private homes on Glenside Avenue, which here abuts the trail. The route heads downhill again to a bridle path. Turn left and look for white blazes on the left, about 200 feet or so down the road. Turn left into the woods. It is peaceful here as you walk over pine cinders. It is a short hike uphill across a bridge to a picnic area with tables outside as well as inside a sheltered Quonset-type hut. Sky Top Drive runs at the edge of this property. There is limited parking at the roadside. It is another access point to the Sierra Trail.

The white-blazed trail crosses the drive to a dirt road, which will hug Sky Top Drive for over 0.5 mile. You will pass many intersections before you come close to the top of the first Watchung summit. At a viewpoint downhill from here, you can see a working quarry. An escarpment will be on your right and the Green Brook on your left. Farther along, about 4.0 miles into the hike, are the ruins of an old mill, which used the waters of this brook to turn its mill wheels. The trail heads uphill again to a rock outcrop from which you can see I-78, which cuts through the northwest edge of the reservation. (In return for the loss of land to the highway, the reservation received an equivalent amount of adjacent quarry land and $3.6 million for the upkeep and development of its properties.)

From this point, the trail heads gradually downhill toward Seeley Pond. Be alert here. The markers go around the pond to the right and then veer left toward the northwest. The markers end at the road before a bridge. Cross the bridge and the road and turn right to the trail, which goes back into the woods. The trail stays close to Glenside Avenue and soon turns back down toward Blue Brook.

Just before reaching an old village called Feltville, you will cross an unmarked path heading downhill to the brook. It is an alternative to visiting Feltville; the views and atmosphere along the brook are wonderful. If you choose this route, be careful to stay on the left side of the brook. Do not cross the first wooden bridge you come to. Continue along the path, which will soon narrow and meander up and down, until you see a white blaze on a tree on the left at a paved road. Turn right and cross the stone bridge, at the end of which is a fork. The road to the left leads to Surprise Lake, where there are picnic tables and a nice view of the lake. Take the road on the right, where you will shortly see a blue-blazed nature trail. Follow it to the orange-blazed nature trail, which will then take you to a gate and paved road. Walk up a few hundred feet to the parking lot of Trailside.

Those hikers who want to visit Feltville should stay on the white-blazed trail, which continues from the unmarked side path. You will pass a beautiful pine grove on your right, from which you can see the unmarked path below. Within minutes you come to the first houses in Feltville, often called the "deserted village." (This is about 6.0 miles from the start of the hike.) The road here is paved. The village was founded around 1845 by David Felt, a New York merchant, who operated a paper mill on Blue Brook. On the hill are two rows of old houses. Workers at the paper mill once lived here. Now these buildings are classrooms, where short courses in nature study are taught to groups from the Union County schools. The grounds of Felt's mansion are down the road to the right. Past a bend in the road are the former school and church/general store of the settlement. When the mill closed, the area became Glenside Park, a Victorian retreat with lawn tennis and pure water. It was a mini-resort between 1882 and 1916.

Felt departed in the 1860s and took the secret of prosperity with him. As you stand by the river, the sunlight filters down through tall conifers. The stream is so clear that the rocks on the bottom can be counted. The hillside is steep and the foliage is dense; it's difficult not to be reminded of the Adirondacks. Perhaps most remarkable is the quiet. There are other spots in the metropolitan area that look primeval, but few that fool the ear as well. Here, the ridges deflect the usually inescapable urban hum.

At the end of the village, the trail turns sharply left and then right, where it goes off the paved road. Here there is an old Revolutionary War cemetery. The descendants of Peter Willcox, the original settler of this land, are buried here. The paved road continues to Glenside Avenue and thus offers another access to the Sierra Trail.

After the cemetery, the Sierra Trail turns left and continues almost level until it begins to descend to meet a woods road. You will leave the Sierra Trail at this point. Turn right onto the woods road and at the bottom cross the stone bridge over the brook. From this point, the instructions are the same as those given above to those who turned off before Feltville.

The Sierra Trail—its full loop is 11 miles—continues beyond the woods road for another four miles, staying on the north side of Surprise Lake, where it goes in a southeasterly direction through the north end of the reservation. It then continues south to the traffic circle, goes east again, and then returns west to the Trailside. If you have the time, you will undoubtedly find it rewarding to hike the rest of the Sierra Trail.

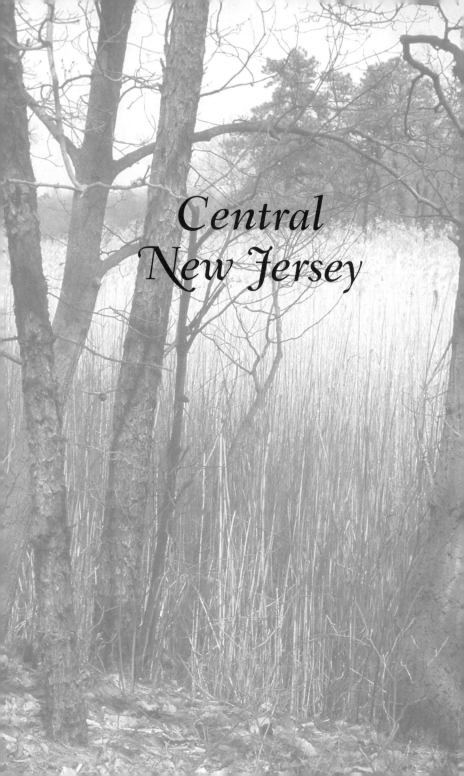

Central
New Jersey

CENTRAL NEW JERSEY
THE VIEW FROM HERE

The countryside north and west of the metropolitan area is rich in contrast-the vast yellowing columns of the Palisades, the lofty gray ledges of the Ramapos, the boulders of Blue Mountain, the hemlock-choked gorges of the Watchungs, the rugged shoreline of Pelham Bay Park.

To move south into central New Jersey is to leave all this behind. The topography here is flat, a coastal plain sloping gently to the sea. This is a countryside of estuaries, fields, low hills, and slow-flowing streams. Typical are Cheesequake State Park and the Delaware and Raritan Canal. At Cheesequake, sandy roads skirt marshes that teem with life; the canal glides peacefully past farms and villages. Compared to the rock ledges and tumbling brooks of the north, there is a different pace of life here-more leisurely, less demanding, simply less hard.

Many walkers will never visit these unspectacular points south. Others will seek them out, with their *Day Walker* or *New Jersey Walk Book* in hand, because for them diversity is one of the great pleasures of the life afoot.

The spectacular will always gain our attention; but diversity is what holds it in the long run. The teenagers shoulder their backpacks on their way to Harriman Park or the more distant Catskills or Adirondacks. The young adult turns lightweight strider, burning up the miles on the Croton Aqueduct, with every muscle glowing in rhythmic harmony. The parent watches the youngster frolic on a sunny path in Muttontown Preserve. One person goes forth to explore; another returns a hundred times to a single special corner-a holly forest on Fire Island, a piney knoll in the Wyanokies. Over a lifetime of walking, the metropolitan walker can be every one of these people.

31
Cheesequake State Park

Distance	3.5 miles
Hiking time	2 hours
Rating	Easy

Cheesequake State Park lies just inland from the northernmost end of the New Jersey shore and some 40 miles south of the George Washington Bridge. Within a relatively small area, Cheesequake contains many habitats—the predominant sandy-soil upland woods; a meadow full of wildflowers, and, in the lowlands, salt-water and fresh-water marshes and a cedar swamp. Borderlines between habitats are abrupt, often surprisingly so.

The salt marsh extends from the north and west corners of the park, and is one of a string of salt marshes that lie along the Jersey coast and indeed along the whole eastern seaboard—the most notable (or notorious) in this area being the Hackensack Meadowlands. Traditionally, salt-water marshes have been maligned and mistreated: they have been diked, drained, filled, and used as garbage dumps. Cheesequake offers an opportunity to visit a salt water marsh and experience its natural undisturbed beauty.

Although the marsh covers relatively little of the area of the park, it contributes much to the park's quality: Hooks Creek Lake, the unique plants and the wildlife, the peaceful and solitary atmosphere of the grasslands. Salt-water marshes occur when low-lying land is periodically flooded by tidal creeks (in this case a network of creeks), which vary the salinity of the water according to the rising and falling tides. The plants we are familiar with from woodland hikes could not exist in such a habitat because they could not tolerate either the amount of salt or the variation in salt content in the water. Therefore, the plants and animals that populate the salt marsh are specially adapted to this environment. A visitor to Cheesequake may expect to find blue herons, snowy egrets, muskrat, turtles, and diamond-backed terrapin around the marsh, and plentiful fish in Hooks Creek Lake. Oysters, clams, and crab live in the marsh, and many kinds of commercially important fish spend part of their lives in the tidal waters.

The dominant plant that you see as you look out over the marsh is Spartina, a fine grass once harvested for salt hay, a food for farm animals. From colonial times to the 19th century, farms near the seashore were

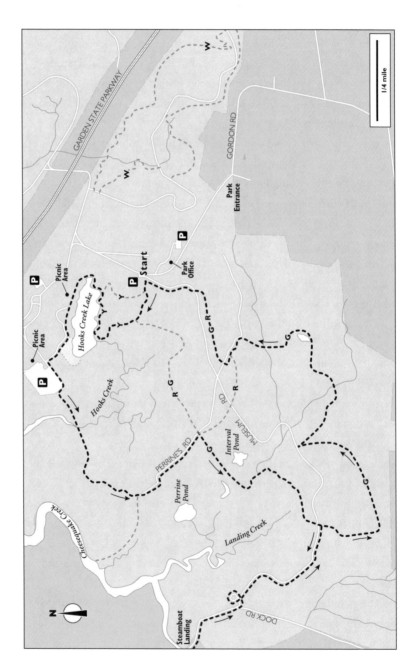

particularly prized if they contained salt marsh acreage. You won't be able to see this grass close-up as it is far out in mud as deep as 15 feet or more. Rather, you'll see phragmites, a tall reed with an arched, feathery head, which grows along the edge of the marsh. It can be found in almost any wet patch along a highway. Phragmites can grow to almost 20 feet when conditions are right. It plays an integral part in urban ecology by serving as a filter for pollutants as well as preventing soil erosion. It has been used as a cure for fevers, as roof thatch, for breathing tubes, and for elegant reed flutes. But the most fascinating use of phragmites is as a sharpened reed pen for drawing. Rembrandt used one over 300 years ago.

There is a good trail system at Cheesequake, and the trails are easy to follow. Each trail is coded a different color; the beginnings of trails are marked with wooden archways, and the trails are well blazed with colored rectangles mounted on metal posts. There are also a number of unmarked paths, fine for exploring. As one would expect in a marsh area, some of the park trails are quite muddy, no matter what the season; both insect repellent and appropriate footwear are strongly advised. And that attractive ground cover that grows along the side of sand roads and over some old horse trails is likely to be poison ivy—beware!

Cheesequake offers recreational opportunities besides hiking, including lifeguard-supervised swimming, family and group camping, and a picnic area. These facilities are much more heavily used than the farther reaches of the hiking trails.

The expansive silence of the woods sometimes loses out to traffic noise from the nearby highways. The sandy woodland foliage is not nearly as dense and lushly green as those of us might expect who are used to walking in Westchester or New England. Instead, the beauty of Cheesequake is most often small and discrete—an ornamental grass head silhouetted against the sky, a few lady's slippers along an old service road, a red fox streaking away, a ray of light filtered through cedar branches, a single blue-gray muscular trunk of an American hornbeam tree. Cheesequake is a wonderful winter walk on a clear day, when there are few visitors and even fewer insects.

The park's former farmlands were made into a park during the 1930s by the Work Progress Administration. The trail system, however, is relatively new. The paths were first cleared in 1977 with the aid of the Youth Conservation Corps. The recommended walk winds through woodlands and fresh-water swamp areas. It offers occasional glimpses of the salt marsh. Trail maps may be obtained at the visitors center. A parking fee is charged from Memorial Day to Labor Day.

Directions   The park is just off the Garden State Parkway at Exit 120; from either north or south, signs from the exits direct you to the park. Coming south off the exit ramp, turn right and continue to a traffic light; the cross street is Cliffwood Avenue on the left and Morristown Road on the right. Turn right and proceed to the first traffic light (Gordon Road). Turn right onto Gordon Road and follow it as it veers sharply to the left, to a tollbooth and visitors center. If coming north on the Garden State Parkway, get off at Exit 120; at the end of the ramp turn right and continue to Cliffwood Avenue. Then follow the above instructions.

You can take a New Jersey Transit train to the Matawan train station and then take a taxi to the park. Call the New Jersey Transit number listed in the back of the book for information.

The Walk   This walk is a loop. There are a number of points along the way at which you can turn back to the start, making routes of varying lengths. The entire hike, start to finish, is about 3.5 miles long and should take an average walker up to two hours, not counting time for lunch, rests, photographs, and exploring.

Start at the visitors center just past the tollbooth, where there are rest rooms and trail maps are available. Then either drive or walk to the nature trails parking area, a short distance down Gordon Road on the left. There is a wooden trail map at the side of the lot closest to the visitors center and signposts for the red, green, yellow, and blue trails. (Note that as of January 2001, the blue trail is not marked on park maps. It will not be mentioned further in this description.) All trails begin together. This walk for the most part follows the green markers; these are located on metal poles (sometimes on trees also) and are easy to follow. At times, you will see numbers on trees or posts; these corresponded to numbers on a nature trail system that is no longer maintained. There are, however, informative plaques at many locations along the trails.

Soon after the start, the trails fork. Follow the left-hand trail, which goes slightly downhill and is blazed in red, green, and yellow. Shortly you will come to another fork. The yellow trail goes straight ahead while the red/green-blazed turns left. Follow the green blazes. In spring, huge stands of fiddleheads and skunk cabbage are found at this turn. Cross the first of many boardwalk-type bridges and climb uphill, noting the highbush blueberries, whose white bell-shaped flowers bloom in June and yield waxy berries in July. At the top of the rise, on your left, is the Nature Center (also called the Interpretive Center on some park signs), which is open Wednesdays through Sundays from 8am to 4pm.

Follow the red and green blazes along the ridge to an overview of the salt marsh, ringed with phragmites. This view, which is very impressive in winter and spring, is not visible during the height of summer growth. Continue downhill, following the blazes to a bridge and wooden boardwalk system. The trail then climbs a set of steps up a steep rise. Just after the top, the green/red trail bears left. Soon another path intersects the trail from the left. This side path leads to a road that returns, left, to the parking lot.

Continuing on the green-and-red-blazed trail, you will pass through a miniature pine barrens environment. The sandy soil on this ridge allows rainwater and nutrients to drain away rapidly, resulting in a relatively poor site for plant growth. The pitch pine growing here and throughout the vast forest of the southern New Jersey Pine Barrens is well adapted to these dry, acidic soils.

Continue walking for a few minutes, crossing a bridge and sections of boardwalk over muddy areas. Near the bridge, you can observe a variety of forest shrubs growing under the open canopy of this section of the forest. Mountain laurel (with its thick, leathery, dark green leaves), highbush blueberry (the shrub from which commercially cultivated blueberries were developed), and sweet pepperbush (common in much of the park) can all be seen. All three of these shrubs produce white blossoms in summer; the sweet pepperbush is characterized by spikes of small, five-petaled flowers with a delicate scent.

Soon, you will come to a sand road—Perrine's Road. Beyond the road, the red trail turns left; if you take the red trail here, you will return to the parking lot. To continue the hike, follow the green trail. In a few minutes, you will come to the top of a ridge. Here the trail bears slightly to the left and descends steeply along a fence line; do not take the path to the right at the crest of the hill. The trail skirts a beautiful stand of tall phragmites, goes left up a steep rise, then down steps to a boardwalk over a fresh-water marsh. Jewelweed grows in this area and can be distinguished by its bright orange flowers, which appear in July. It is claimed that juice from the stem of this plant can relieve the itching of poison ivy. It might be best, however, to avoid the problem in the first place by remembering the old adage, "leaves three, let it be"; keep clear of all contact with the widespread, and at times lush, growths of poison ivy at Cheesequake. There are benches near the far end of the boardwalk for rest, lunch, or just enjoying.

On the other side of the fresh-water marsh, the trail again forks. To end your hike here, turn left, and, at the four-cornered intersection, go straight ahead, returning to the parking area. To continue the hike, go right at the fork; a moment later, the trail divides again. Follow the green arrow and head right, descending some steps onto a boardwalk that winds pleasantly through a corner of a tiny cedar swamp—a dark, wet area, with beautiful lacy cedars looming overhead. At one time, there was no boardwalk here and in all but the driest season the trail was at best extremely muddy and, at worst, impossible to find. It's lovely now. The reason for the stark difference between the cedar swamp and the adjacent upland hardwood forest is the contrasting soil moisture content. A layer of clay beneath the surface of the swamp prevents downward movement of water. The moist, acidic conditions mean that many species that thrive in the adjacent upland area cannot survive here.

Returning to primarily deciduous woods and following the green blazes, you will arrive at a sandy road (called Museum Road), not open to vehicle traffic, in about five or ten minutes of walking. If you want to visit the salt marsh, you may wish to turn right here. Museum Road leads to Dock Road, which in turn leads to an area known as Steamboat Landing. This is a good place to relax, have lunch, or simply watch the tide flow in or out. It is also a good place for birding. Afterward, retrace your steps to return to the blazed trails, which are clearly marked with a large wooden sign.

Photo by George Garbeck

Enter the woods again on the other side of the road, still following the green blazes. Along the trail are several large white pines, with their fluffy-looking, five-needled clusters. These trees are estimated to be up to 150 years old and, owing to their size, they make excellent nesting sites for hawks and owls. After a few more minutes of gentle climbing, turn left, following the green arrow, and cross a stepped bridge over the eroded mud. Near the top of the rise, follow the green arrow and turn left again. Here in late August and early September your nose may alert you that sweet pepperbush is nearby. After a few minutes, the trail follows an S curve to cross several bridges.

Follow the green markers along a level stretch of trail, over several bridges, and then to the left, where an unmarked trail forks right. The trail then winds through small groves of pine trees over stark buff sand. Note an enormous patch of ground pine to the left of the path. Its resemblance to miniature Christmas trees and resulting wholesale use in Christmas decorations has made this an endangered species—so look, but do not pick. A little farther on, mountain laurel borders the trail, surrounding it in early June with puffs of pink-to-white blossoms. After a few minutes, you will come to a fork, in the middle of which are the ruined foundations of a building—only some cinder blocks remain from an old museum, for which Museum Road is named. Built in the late 1930s, this museum was never used, and it was destroyed in the early 1950s.

Follow the green blazes. At the next split in the trail, you can take the left branch of the fork and return to the parking lot by turning right on Museum Road, for a total hike of approximately 75 minutes. Or you can follow the green blazes to the right and extend your hike another 30 to 45 minutes. After about 10 minutes the trail splits: right and sharply left. Take the latter. The trail at this point is essentially a sandy stream bed. Cross a bridge, then follow blazes past more mountain laurel. Follow the green arrow when the trail turns right. Straight ahead of you, at the turn, is a stand of Japanese knotweed. This plant, with its hollow, bamboo-like stems and triangular, veined leaves, appears to be a tall shrub but is really an herb that dies back to the ground each year. Its drooping sprays of white flowers in late August and early September readily distinguish it. Japanese knotweed, an introduced, or "exotic," species, has become a serious problem in the park and is forcing out the native plants such as jewelweed.

Soon the trail begins to skirt a fresh-water marsh to the left, full of ghostly dead trees standing in a pool of cloudy water. The trees were killed years ago by chemical dumping outside the park, now halted, which settled into this low area. Vegetation is growing once again, and the contrast between the stark tree trunks and the grasses and vibrant flowers is quite startling. Explore the marsh if you like and if the water conditions permit, noting especially the many beautiful grasses. Then follow the trail around the marsh. The trail crosses a number of bridges, then re-enters the woods and goes uphill. After five minutes, it comes out on a road. Green arrows indicate a left turn. After the turn, a large meadow appears on the right. This is Gordon Field, formerly an Indian campground. Arrowheads found here are on display in the park office. Walk along the road about 300 feet, until you come to a wooden arch on the right marking the red/green trails. Turn right here, skirting the field. The open area allows more sunlight into the bordering forest edge, resulting in an increased growth of grasses and shrubs under the trees. Follow the red/green-marked trail until it ends on Museum Road. Bear right onto this dirt road and follow it past a turnoff to the Nature Center and then back to the parking lot, where the hike started.

The Nature Center is well worth a visit (Wednesdays through Sundays), especially if your group includes children. Hooks Creek Lake is one of the most beautiful areas in the park and should not be missed. The yellow-blazed trail from the parking lot takes you straight to it. The trail takes you over high ground that affords good views of the lake and the salt marsh to the northwest.

32
Delaware and Raritan Canal

Distance	5 miles
Hiking time	3 hours
Rating	Easy

*T*his five-mile stroll on the towpath of the Delaware and Raritan Canal from Kingston to Princeton will take you back to the past. A strong sense of history permeates the region.

It was through this part of New Jersey that Washington retreated in 1777 with the British at his heels, crossing the Delaware at Trenton. Then, in a daring reversal, he recrossed the river to defeat the Hessian contingent that was in pursuit. Washington next struck the British rear guards at Princeton, defeating three regiments and forcing Cornwallis, the English commander, to fall back in panic to protect his stores. Washington moved back up to Morristown to go into winter retreat. In these brief campaigns, Washington regained New Jersey for the Americans. From that point, the tide began to turn for the emerging republic.

With the British connection severed, American commerce and industry began a long period of expansion. This made it necessary to improve the extensive inland waterways of the country along which this commerce was conducted before the days of the railroad. In the early 1800s, there was a boom in canal construction that, along with the building of roads, bridges, and turnpikes, was to have a major impact on the economy and on social life generally. Of the new canal systems, the most notable was the Erie Canal in New York, completed in 1825. Its success encouraged the construction of others, such as the Delaware and Raritan Canal, completed in 1834.

In connecting the two rivers, the D&R provided a fast, safe route between Philadelphia and New York. Until its construction, trade between these two cities was by way of the open sea via voyages that took as long as two weeks. The canal cut this to two or three days. The main cargo was coal. In 1843, steam-powered tugs were introduced to pull the barges along the canal, and gradually they replaced the mule teams that were first used. The canal's heyday was in the 1860s and 1870s, but by the end of the 19th century, when railroads were fast taking over the transport business, its use had declined substantially. The last year in which the canal was profitable was 1892, though the D&R remained operational until 1932, when the State of New Jersey took it over.

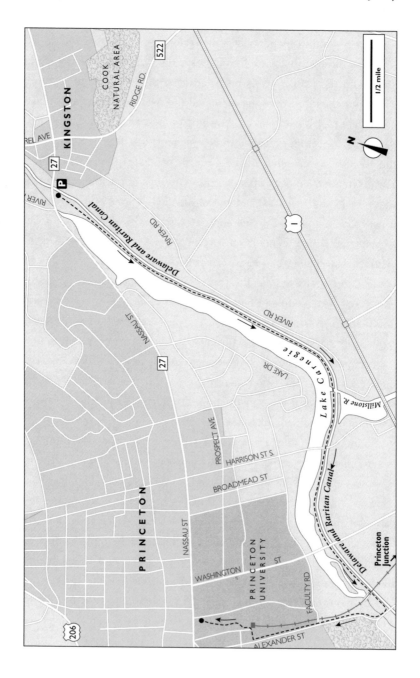

Originally the main canal was 44 miles long and ran from Trenton to New Brunswick. A feeder canal to supply the water by gravity to the main canal was built along the Delaware River to Trenton. The main canal was 7 feet deep and 50 feet wide, and it was dug by hand labor with pick, shovel, and wheelbarrow, since it was built before the existence of large mechanical earth-moving equipment.

The men who did the work were mostly Irish, many brought directly from Ireland for the work. As many as 3,000 men worked on the canal at one time, and under very difficult conditions. They labored from sunrise to sunset, six days a week, living in tents and without medical or sanitation facilities. In 1832-33, an outbreak of Asian cholera sickened and killed hundreds of the workers, many of whose bodies were buried on the banks of the canal. The pay was $1 a day, but those who pulled out tree stumps received 25 cents a day more. Skilled workers built the locks, aqueducts, and bridges.

It is difficult to envision what life was like back then. The tranquility and beauty of the place crowd out the memory of those early days. Birds and ducks add to the rustic setting as do the many wildflowers and shrubs that now grow alongside the canal. When operational, the banks of the canal were kept clear of any growth so as not to interfere with the towropes pulled by the mule teams.

The State of New Jersey converted the D&R Canal to serve as a water supply system. In 1973 it was entered on the National Register of Historic Places. In 1974 over 60 miles of the canal and adjoining land were made into a state park. Nearly 36 miles of the main canal and 22 miles of the feeder canal were left intact. There are a number of access points to the park, with parking facilities, including some along the path of this hike. The pedestrian path is shared by walkers, runners, bicyclists, and those who fish. It is appropriately wide to accommodate all these uses. The path is completely level and is handicapped-accessible and useable by those using a sturdy wheelchair. Canoes are available for rent.

The New Jersey Division of Parks and Forestry of the State Park Service has prepared a very interesting and informative map of the D&R Canal State Park, which shows the full route of the canal and its feeder. Many vendors along Canal Road or stores close to the canal should have free copies. Or you can write to the park office as follows: D&R Canal State Park, 625 Canal Road Somerset, NJ 08873. Don't try to drive to the office. You will never find it. And even if you do, there will probably be nobody there, as the park rangers are almost always out patrolling the canal. You can try to call (732) 873-3050. The office is daily, 8am to 4pm.

Directions   The hike will start at Kingston and end in Princeton. There are frequent buses departing from the Port Authority Terminal in Manhattan for Princeton with a stop in Kingston (Suburban Transit line 100). Alternatively, Amtrak has trains that go directly to Princeton from Penn Station Newark (accessible from Manhattan via the PATH trains). From the Princeton station the hiker can then walk 0.5 mile up to Palmer Square in the center of town and take the New York-bound Suburban Transit bus to Kingston or simply follow this hike in reverse. In Kingston, the Suburban bus from either direction stops on Route 27 at Heathcote Road (called Laurel Avenue on the east side of Route 27), less than 0.25 mile from the canal. Walk from the bus stop down the hill along Route 27 (toward Princeton and keeping to the left of the traffic island) until you come to the canal and the entrance to the state park on your left.

Drivers from the metropolitan area should go south on Route 1 to the Kingston turnoff onto Ridge Road (Route 522). Turn left onto Route 27 into town. Pass through town, where Route 27 goes downhill. At the bottom, on your left, is an entrance to the park, with a large parking lot that abuts Route 27. At the end of the hike, drivers can walk or take a bus back from Princeton to the Kingston parking lot.

The Walk   As you walk out of the parking lot toward two white park buildings, the towpath of the canal is directly in front of you; for the moment, though, divert to the right along the road to a stone bridge over the Millstone River. To your left is Mill Pond; farther upstream is the dam across the Millstone River that forms Lake Carnegie. The red building on the right of the river is a gristmill built in 1755. This area is preserved as a small state park. The stone bridge was in use from 1798 to about 1968. It replaced an earlier wooden bridge, built in 1700, which was destroyed in 1777 by retreating American troops after the Battle of Princeton. The Americans had hoped to go on to raid the British depot at New Brunswick, but were too tired to continue, so they burned the bridge behind them and retreated northwest to Morristown. In the meantime, the British prepared for battle at New Brunswick. Before they discovered what had happened, Washington was far north, safely west of the Delaware.

Now, return to the parking lot and head toward the two white buildings that sit prominently on the western banks of the canal. The larger of the white buildings was formerly the lock-keeper's house. Built in 1832, it is maintained by the Kingston Historical Society and the Delaware & Raritan Canal State Park. Inside you will find a display pertaining to the lock and the canal. Outside, you can pick up a map of the D&R state Park. The smaller white building is the only surviving telegraph and toll station on the canal. The canal operators were some of the first users of Samuel Morse's telegraph system.

In front of the buildings you see the first of seven locks that let barges down to sea level in New Brunswick, which is north of here. The old lock gates have been replaced by the triple sluice gates used today to control the water level.

Continue south along the six- to eight-foot wide gravel towpath that will serve as the pathway for most of this hike toward Princeton. Soon Lake Carnegie comes into view. The path passes the eastern part of the dam. It makes a wonderful picnic spot. The lake, which is about three miles long, was created in 1906 as a gift from Andrew Carnegie to Princeton University. At the upper end, on the west side of the lake, is the university's boathouse, in which the university's crew team stores their shells. The Childs Cup Race is held on the lake in the spring.

The delightfully shaded towpath continues between the lake and the canal. At intervals you will see concrete posts that, on their north side, tell the distance to Trenton and, on their south side, the distance to New Brunswick. Up to the Millstone River, the towpath is fairly straight. It then makes a sweeping bend to the right and the canal crosses the river on an aqueduct. Here, the river flows into the lake. Just before the aqueduct, there is a footbridge across the canal to a parking lot and picnic tables. This, too, is a good spot for lunch. The aqueduct is bordered by a 75-yard-long footbridge about five feet wide. The river here is a popular fishing spot.

To continue the walk on the towpath, three miles from Kingston, you will come to Harrison Street, the first of three streets along this section of the canal. Continue another 1.0 mile along the towpath to Washington Road. At this point, you are almost at the southern end of Lake Carnegie, which you may still be able to see through the trees. Washington Road goes into the center of Princeton, past the Firestone Library, to Nassau Street. As you approach the third street you will see on the right a brook (Stony Brook) that flows into Lake Carnegie. Here the canal passes through a grove of old trees. Shortly beyond is the bridge overhead that carried the railroad into Princeton. This is a short spur from the main line at Princeton Junction. When the canal was still in operation, the bridge over the canal and towpath would swing aside to let boats pass. Today the rails are continuous and the turning mechanism is gone, but the large gearwheel can be seen atop the central stone pillar, its south side mantled in honeysuckle and poison ivy.

Milepost 28/16 is just beyond, and then you are at the third street, Alexander Road. This last section passes the remains of a canal basin. These basins gave the barges a place to tie up out of the main channel, to turn around, and to stop for the night. Little remains of what was a thriving community here to serve the boatmen. The clapboard building across the canal, now a private house, was once the Railroad Hotel. The hotel served riders on the Camden and Amboy Railroad, which ran in front of the hotel until 1864, when the tracks were removed to their present location.

On the opposite side of Alexander Road is Turning Basin Park, with a parking lot, playground, pavilions, picnic tables, and, in season, water and toilets. Turn right up Alexander Street and walk to West Drive, the first street on your left. This road leads, in 0.5 mile, to the entrance of the Princeton Wildlife Refuge. This area is worth a visit when the ground is not too wet, particularly when wildflowers are in season.

Continue to walk up Alexander Road for about 1.0 mile to University Place. Turn right and ahead of you is the Princeton railroad station, where you can get a shuttle to Princeton Junction for a train back to New York. There is a grocery store on your right. Walk along this road a short distance past the railroad station and McCarter Theatres into town (Nassau Street) and the campus of Princeton University. The campus with its many fine buildings is well worth an extended visit. The oldest building there is Nassau Hall, built in 1756. The university has a renowned fine arts museum, which puts on major exhibitions from time to time, as does the Firestone Library.

Nassau Street (Route 27) is the main street of the town. The better restaurants are off on the side streets and around Palmer Square, which fronts on Nassau Street. The bus station (for a bus back to Kingston or New York) is on Witherspoon Street next to Palmer Square.

Park and Transportation Information

The telephone numbers and web site information for the parks and public transportation systems supplement the information in individual chapters. The information is valid as of March 2002 and may have changed by the time you consult it. Before you set off to take a bus or train, or to visit a park, it's a good idea to verify as much of the information as you can.

New York-New Jersey Trail Conference

Address: 156 Ramapo Valley Road (Route 202)
              Mahwah, NJ 07430
Telephone: 201-512-9348
E-mail: info@nynjtc.org
Web sites: www.nynjtc.org
              www.nynjtc.org/trails/no-car.html

New Jersey State Parks

www.state.nj.us/dep/forestry/parks/parkindx.htm

New York State Parks

www.nysparks.state.ny.us/parks

New York City Parks

www.nyc.gov/parks

Port Authority

Port Authority Bus Terminal: (212) 564-8484
George Washington Bridge Bus Terminal: (212) 564-1114

Green Line Buses

(718) 995-4700

Short Line Buses

(800) 631-8405 Ext. 111

www.shortlinebus.com

NJ Transit (Buses and Trains)

(800) 772-2222

Train Stations with maps of surrounding areas:

www.nj.com/njtransit/stations.html

Schedule with fare information, bus options, trains, light rail

www.njtransit.state.nj.us/transit.htm

PATH (Port Authority Trans-Hudson Line)

www.nj.com/njtransit/path.html

Metro-North Railroad

www.mnr.org/mnr

(800) 638-7646 (outside NYC)

(212) 532-4900 (in NYC)

Long Island Rail Road

www.mnr.org/lirr

(718) 217-5477

Staten Island Ferry

(718) 390-5253

Index

A

Alley Pond Environmental Center (APEC), 9
Alley Pond Park, 6, 21
Alley Pond Park, the walk, 8–15
Annsville Creek, 199
Anthony's Nose, 192, 197, 201, 219
Appalachian Trail (AT),
    in Rockland County, 177, 185, 189–91
    in the Hudson Highlands, 197, 199, 202, 205
Armour-Stiner House (Octagon House), 111
Ashokan Reservoir, 214, 221

B

Back 40 Trail, 151–53
Bank of River Trail, 123–24
Bare Rock petroglyphs, 127

Bear Mountain-Harriman State Park. *See* Harriman-Bear Mountain State Park
Bear Mountain, the walk, 184–91
Bear Mountain Bridge, 185, 187, 193, 197, 201, 202, 213
Belvedere, 111
Big Tree Trail, 139
Birders, 17, 49, 149
Birding sites
    Alley Pond Park, 9
    Caumsett State Park, 79, 83
    Connetquot River State Park Preserve, 74
    Delaware and Raritan Canal, 285
    Fire Island, 67
    Jamaica Bay, 17
    Muttontown, 84
    Palisades, 279
    Pelham Bay Park, 53
    Pine Meadow Lake, 169

Riverside Park, 36
Rockefeller State Park
    Preserve, 135
Teatown Lake Reservation,
    149
Black Ash Mountain, 180–82
Blackledge-Kearney House, 239
Blauvelt Mountain, 181
Blazes
    Defined, 3
    Hints on following, 3
Bloody Pond, 187, 202
Blue Disc Trail, 183
Blue Mountain, 146–47
Blue Mountain Reservation, the
    walk, 142–49
Bobcat Trail, 228
Bombay Hook, 240
Breakneck Ridge, the walk,
    219–23
Breakneck Ridge Trail, 219,
    221–23
Briarcliff-Peekskill Trail, 118, 146
Brink of Gorge Trail, 123
Bronx River Pathway, the walk,
    96–103
Brook Scenic Gorge, 266
Brook Trail, 214, 222
Bull Hill (Mount Taurus), 228
Bull Hill and Cold Spring, the
    walk, 210–17

Butter Hill (Boter Borg), 225,
    229. *See also* Storm King
    Mountain
Bunces Bridge, 74–76
By-Pass Trail, 228

C

Camp Smith Trail, the walk,
    196–203
Canada Hill, the walk, 205–09
Cannonball Road, 245, 247–48
Cannonball Trail, 247, 248–251
Cascade of Slid, 169, 172, 174
Cathedral of St. John the Divine,
    34
Catskill Aqueduct, 214, 221
Cattail Pond Trail, 13
Caumsett State Park, the walk,
    78–83
Central New Jersey walks,
    270–289
Cheesequake State Park, the
    walk, 272–81
Chapel of Our Lady, 215
Children, hints on walking with,
    59–60
City Island, 55–57
Claudius Smith Den, the walk,
    176-83
Cold Spring, 211, 213–16, 219,
    228

Colt Gun Mill, 256

Columbia University, 34

Connetquot River State Park
    Preserve, the walk, 70–77

Constitution Island, 220, 228

Cross Country Running Course,
    45, 46

Cross Country Skiing, 165

Cross River, 127, 130

Crows Nest, 224–29

Curry Pond Trail, 207

D

Dancing Rock Trail, 127

Delaware and Raritan (D&R)
    Canal, the walk, 282–89

Delaware and Raritan (D&R)
    Canal State Park, 285

Delaware Indian Resource
    Center, 127

Diamond Mountain, 173

Doodletown, 200

Douglaston Estate Windmill, 9

Dunderberg Mountain, 155, 193,
    200–01

Dutch Reformed Church, 115,
    135

E

Eagle Hill, 138, 141

Eagle Hill Summit Trail, 138

Eagle Hill Trail, 138

East Pond, 20, 21

Edward Hopper House, 167

F

Feltville (deserted village), 268,
    269

Fire Island, the walk, 62–69

Fire Island National Seashore, 63

Fire Tower Trail, 133

Following a Trail, hints on, 3

Forest View, 240–41

Foundry Cove, 215

Foundry School Museum, 215

Fringe of Forest Trail, 123

G

Ga-Nus-Quah-Rock (Stone
    Giant), 173

Garrett Mountain, 260

Garrett Mountain Reservation,
    259–60

Gateway National Recreation
    Area, 5, 17

Giant Stairs, 241

Glenview, 114

Glenwood, 114

Glover's Rock, 52

Grant's Tomb, 4, 35

Great Falls, 252, 256–258

Green Brook, 267

Green Line Bus information, 291

Grey Crag, 239–240

H

Harriman-Bear Mountain State Park, 169, 171, 177, 179, 185, 232

Havemeyer Falls, 125

Henry Lloyd Manor House, 79, 81

Hessian Lake, 185, 187, 201

Hidden Valley Trail, 151

High Rock Park, 23,26

High Tor, 155, 161, 164

Highlands Trail, 228–229

Hillburn-Torne-Sebago Trail, 172, 174

Hobby Hill Quarry, 125

Hoeferlin Memorial Trail, 245, 249–51

Hook Mountain, 155, 158, 161

Hook Mountain, the walk, 158–67

Hook Mountain State Park, 165

Hooks Creek Lake, 273, 281

Howell Trail, 223, 225, 227–228

Hudson Highlands State Park, 193, 197, 205, 219, 221

Hudson Highlands walks, 192–229

Hudson River

Chain across during Revolutionary War, 223

Views, from

Hudson Highlands, 197, 199, 205, 207, 213, 216, 219, 223, 229

New York City, 31

Northern New Jersey, 232, 233, 235

Rockland County, 185, 190

Westchester, 105, 115, 117, 138, 147

Hudson River Museum, 114

Hudson River Valley Greenway, 33

Hunter Island, 49, 52–55

I

Ice industry, 145, 163–64

Ice skating, 143, 145

Iona Island, 158, 200, 201, 204

Iron industry, 169, 180, 194, 205, 211, 214–15, 222–23, 231, 232, 245

J

Jamaica Bay, the walk, 16–21

Jamaica Bay Wildlife Refuge, 5, 6, 19–20

Jewells Brook, 112

John Muir Trail, 46
Joseph Lloyd Manor, 81

K

Kakiat Trail, 172
Kane Mansion, 118
Kazimiroff Nature Trail, 54
Kykuit, 138

L

Lake Carnegie, 287–88
Lake Sebago, 169
Lakeside Trail, 149, 151, 153
Lambert's Castle, 259
Lenoir Preserve, 112
Little Stony Point, 211
Long Island Rail Road, information, 292
Long Island walks, 58–91
Long Path
    in Northern New Jersey, 233, 235–36, 238, 240, 242
    in Rockland County, 159, 161–63, 166, 180
Lookout Trail, 250–51
Loundsbury Pond, 143, 145
Low Tor, 164
Lyndhurst estate, 111, 112

M

MacEvoy Trail, 248–49

Major Welch Trail, 189–91
Marshall Field estate, 79
Meadow Trail, 13
Mercy College, 112–13
Metro-North Railroad information and web site, 292
Meyer Arboretum, 130
Mianus River Gorge, the walk, 120–25
Mill Pond, 287
Miller House, 99
Millstone River, 287–89
Mine Hill, 205
Moses Mountain, 27
Mountain laurel, 156, 209
Mount Taurus (Bull Hill), 210–17, 228
Mt. Spitzenberg, 147
Muttontown Preserve, the walk, 84–91

N

Nevis, 112
New Jersey Transit buses and trains, web site and information, 292
New Jersey State Parks, web site, 291
New York City walks, 4–61
New York City Parks, web site, 291

New York-New Jersey Trail
    Conference, 2
    Telephone and web site, 291
New York State Parks, web site,
    291
Northern New Jersey walks,
    230–269
Notch Trail, 213–215, 222–
    224
Nyack, 159, 166–167

O

Octagon House (Armour-Stiner
    House), 111
Old Croton Aqueduct, the
    engineering project, 108–09
Old Croton Aqueduct, the walk,
    104–19
Old Croton Aqueduct State
    Historic Park, 105, 112–13
Old Sleepy Hollow Road Trail,
    138, 141
Orchard Beach, 49, 54, 55
Osborn Loop, 207
Overlook Trail, 137, 151

P

Palisades, the walk, 234–243
Palisades, the cliffs
    geology and history of, 235,
        263, 155

views from or of, 105, 112,
    147, 159, 164
Parker Cabin Mountain, 181
Paterson and Garrett Mountain,
    the walk, 252–261
Paterson Museum, 258–59
PATH web site, 292
Paw Trail, 23
Peanut Leap Falls, 241
Peekskill Hollow Creek, 199
Peggenegheck (Cross River), 127,
    130
Pelham Bay Park, the walk,
    48–57
Phillipsburg Manor, 115
Phragmites, 5, 8, 14, 19, 52, 275
Pine barrens,
    Long Island, 68
    New Jersey, 277
Pine Meadow Brook, 172
Pine Meadow Lake, 169, 172
Pine Meadow Lake, the walk,
    168-75
Pine Meadow Trail, 169, 171–74
Pitobek Trail, 13
Pocantico River, 140–41
Pocantico River Trail, 136,
    138–41
Pollepel Island, 220–21
Popolopen Creek, 187–88, 189,
    191, 194

Popolopen Gorge Trail, 185, 187, 191

Popolopen Torne, 221

Port Authority, information, 291

Port Authority Trans-Hudson Line (PATH), web site, 292

Princeton, exploring town of, 289

Princeton Wildlife Refuge, 289

Q

Quarrying, 159, 164

Queensboro Brook, 188

R

Ramapo Lake, 248, 250

Ramapo Mountain State Forest, the walk, 244–251

Ramapo River, 169, 179

Ramapo-Dunderberg Trail, 179–80, 181, 183

Rhododendron, 156

Richmondtown Restoration, 27–28

Riverside Church, 34, 35

Riverside Park, the walk, 30–39

Robert Moses State Park, 66

Rockefeller State Park Preserve, the walk, 134–41

Rockland County walks, 154–91

Rockland Lake, 161, 163

Rockland Lake State Park, 163

Rockwood Hall, 116

Rogers Locomotive complex, 258–59

S

Sailors Haven, 63, 67

Sayville, 63

Seven Hills Trail, 171, 172, 174

Seven Lakes Drive, 169, 171, 188–89, 191

1777W Trail, 189, 191

79th Street Boat Basin, 38–39

Shore Trail, 235–42

Short Line Bus information, 292

Sierra Trail, 266–69

Sing Sing, 118

Skunk Hollow, 242

Smith Point County Park, 66

Smith, Claudius, Revolutionary War bandit, 177, 182

Society for the Establishment of Useful Manufactures (S.U.M.), 257

Spook Rock legend, 139

Spy Rock Trail, 132

Staten Island Ferry, 23 Information, 292

Staten Island Greenbelt, the walk, 22–29

Stillman Spring Trail, 227–29

Stillman Trail, 225, 228–229

Stone Giant (Gus-Na-Quah Rock), 173
Stony Brook Trail, 172, 174
Storm King Mountain, 225–26, 229
Storm King Mountain, the walk, 224–29
Sugarloaf Hill, 205, 207,
Sugarloaf Mountain, 223, 228
Sunken Forest on Fire Island, 63, 66–67
Sunnyside, 111
Surprise Lake, 265, 266, 268
Swan Lake Trail, 137

T

Target Rock National Refuge, 79
Teatown Lake Reservation, the walk, 148–53
13-Bridges Trail, 132, 136–139
Timp-Torne Trail, 188–89
Tonetti estate, 242
Tower Trail, 132, 173
Transportation information, 291–92
Triangle Trail, 179–81
Turtle Cove, 49, 52
Turtle Pond, 14
Turtle Pond Trail, 14
Tuxedo-Mt. Ivy (T-MI) Trail, 181–183

Tuxedo Park, 179, 182, 183
Twin Island, 49, 54, 55
Two Pines, 200
Two Trees Island, 55

U

Undercliff Trail, 213, 214, 222
Union Church, Chagall and Matisse stained glass windows at, 135
Untermyer estate, 113

V

Van Cortlandt House Museum, 41, 47
Van Cortlandt Park, the walk, 40–47
Victory Trail, 181
Villa Leward, 11

W

Walker Pond, 26
Ward Pound Ridge Reservation, the walk, 126–33
Washburn Trail, 211, 213–14
Watchung Mountains, 155, 263
Watchung Reservation, the walk, 262–69
Westchester walks, 92–153
West Point, 188, 208, 213, 222–23, 228

West Pond, 17, 20, 21

Wetlands, 5–6, 8–15, 153

White Bar Trail, 180–81

Wilkinson Trail, 222–23

Witch's Spring Trail, 139

Woodlawn Cemetery, 6, 43–44

Membership Information

If you enjoy this book, we invite you to join the organization of hikers and environmentalists that published it—the New York-New Jersey Trail Conference. Since our founding in 1920, Trail Conference volunteers have built and presently maintain 1,500 miles of publicly accessible hiking trails in New York and New Jersey, from the Delaware Water Gap to the Catskills and the Taconics.

As a Trail Conference member, you will receive the Trail Walker, a bimonthly source of news, information, and events concerning trails and hiking. The Trail Walker lists hikes throughout the NY-NJ region by many of our 75 member hiking clubs.

Members are entitled to purchase our authoritative maps and guides at significant discounts (see the following page). Our highly accurate trail maps printed on durable Tyvek® enable you to hike with assurance in northern New Jersey, the Catskills, Harriman State Park, the Shawangunks, the Kittatinnies, Sterling Forest, and the East and West Hudson Highlands.

Trail Conference members are also entitled to discounts of 10% (and sometimes more!) at most outdoor stores and many mountain inns and lodges.

Your membership helps to give us the clout to protect and maintain more trails. If you want to experience pristine nature in the broader metropolitan New York area, you will most likely use a Trail Conference trail. As a member of the New York-New Jersey Trail Conference, you will be ensuring that public access to nature will continue to expand. So please join by contacting us now.

MEMBERSHIP CATEGORIES

	Individual	Joint
Regular	$ 25	$ 31
Sponsor	$ 50	$ 60
Benefactor	$100	$120
Student/Senior	$ 18	$ 24
Life	$500	$750*

*two adults at same address

Check out these other publications available from the New York-New Jersey Trail Conference:

	Retail	Members
Sterling Forest Trails	$7.95	$5.95
Harriman-Bear Mountain Trails	$8.95	$6.75
East Hudson Trails	$8.95	$6.75
West Hudson Trails	$7.95	$5.95
Catskill Trails	$13.95	$10.45
Kittatinny Trails	$12.95	$9.75
Shawangunk Trails	$9.95	$7.75
South Taconic Trails	$4.95	$3.75
North Jersey Trails	$7.95	$5.95
Hudson Palisades Trails	$5.95	$4.75
Hiking Long Island	$19.95	$15.95
New York Walk Book	$19.95	$15.95
Circuit Hikes in Northern New Jersey	$14.95	$11.95
Scenes & Walks in the No. Shawangunks	$10.95	$8.75
New Jersey Walk Book	$15.95	$12.75
Iron Mine Trails: NY-NJ Highlands	$8.95	$7.15
Harriman Trails: A Guide and History	$16.95	$13.55
Long Path Guide	$9.95	$7.95
A.T. Guide for NY & NJ w/6 maps	$19.95	$15.95

NEW YORK-NEW JERSEY TRAIL CONFERENCE
156 Ramapo Valley Road • Mahwah, NJ 07430 • (201) 512-9348
www.nynjtc.org